'This book is a powerful and vibrant study of the complex realities of class in modern Australia. It brings to light the intersection of class with gender, race, and the ongoing dispossession of First Nations peoples, and dispels the myth that class division is not relevant to the contemporary age.'

Sally McManus
ACTU Secretary

Class in Australia *is a timely provocation to social scientists to rethink class, offering a series of deep reflections on the complexities and opportunities of class-based analysis. An inspiring collection of authors brings new questions, conceptual frameworks and methodologies to class analysis. Acknowledging that the dynamics of settler colonialism are central, this collection is positioned to invigorate familiar approaches focusing on education, migration, and labour, gender, sexuality, and cultural representations. The new class analysis starts here.*

Johanna Wyn
*Redmond Barry Distinguished Professor,
The University of Melbourne*

'From colonial inequality to Upper Middle Bogan, *this captivating volume dives deep into how class has shaped our nation. Through studies of the unemployed, warehouse workers, unions and school students, this book presents the finest analysis of class that Australian sociology has to offer. Read it to get a richer understanding of poverty, a stronger sense of social status, and a nuanced analysis of how gender, race and sexuality intersect with class.*'

Hon Dr Andrew Leigh MP

'Class is central to Australians' lives but it is rarely analysed or even talked about. In this book Threadgold and Gerrard have pulled together the foremost thinkers on class, intersectionality and prejudice in Australia.'
Hon Dr Meredith Burgmann AM

'This is a must-read collection for anyone interested in the topic of class in Australia. This collection digs deeps and engages with relevant and timely discussions about class using both an historical and contemporary lens. For anyone who is teaching, studying, or writing about class as theory or method, this book will open up rich and productive conversations. Class is an enduring problematic, both as a descriptor, heuristic device or theoretical framework. This collection aptly responds to this problematic, engaging with class across multiple intersections including gender, race and space. It taps into class as symbolic and ephemeral whilst also highlighting the material, tangible divisions that it produces.'
Dr. Emma Rowe
Senior Lecturer in Education, Deakin University

Class in Australia

CLASS IN AUSTRALIA

Edited by
Steven Threadgold and Jessica Gerrard

MONASH
UNIVERSITY
PUBLISHING

Class in Australia

© Copyright 2022

Copyright of this collection in its entirety is held by the editors, Steven Threadgold and Jessica Gerrard. Copyright of the chapters is held by the respective author/s.

All rights reserved. Apart from any uses permitted by Australia's Copyright Act 1968, no part of this book may be reproduced by any process without prior written permission from the copyright owners. Enquiries should be directed to the publisher.

Monash University Publishing
Matheson Library Annexe
40 Exhibition Walk
Monash University
Clayton, Victoria 3800, Australia
publishing.monash.edu/

Monash University Publishing brings to the world publications which advance the best traditions of humane and enlightened thought.

This book has been peer reviewed.

ISBN: 9781922464897 (paperback)
ISBN: 9781922464903 (pdf)
ISBN: 9781922464910 (epub)

Design: Les Thomas
Typesetting: Jo Mullins

A catalogue record for this book is available from the National Library of Australia.

CONTENTS

Part 1: Situating Class Analysis in Australia 1

1. Class in Australia: Public Debates and Research Directions in a Settler Colony 3
   Jessica Gerrard and Steven Threadgold

2. Contradictory Locations of Class 23
   Greg Noble

3. The Great Divide: Property Relations and the Foundational Dynamics of Settler-Colonial Society 40
   Barry Morris

4. Some Comments on Class Analysis 58
   Mark Western

Part 2: Class, Labour and Employment 75

5. Rethinking Class through the History of Professions 77
   Hannah Forsyth

6. Advancing Debate on Precarious Workers and Class Interests: Evidence from Warehouse Workers in Australia 93
   Tom Barnes and Jasmine Ali

7. Workers in Waiting? Work Ethic, Productive Intensities, Class and Unemployment 109
   Jessica Gerrard and David Farrugia

Part 3: Cultural Formations of Class............... 125

8   Bogan Talk: What It Says (and Can't Say) about Class in Australia... 127
    Deborah Warr, Keith Jacobs and Henry Paternoster

9   Struggle Street: Poverty Porn?....................... 143
    Penny Rossiter

10 Whiteness, Neoliberal Feminism and Social Class in Australian Ru-Rom: Bridie's Choice................. 161
    Barbara Pini and Laura Rodriguez Castro

Part 4: Class and Education..................... 177

11 Schooling and Class as a Longitudinal and Psychosocial Process: Revisiting the 12 to 18 Project................. 179
    Julie McLeod and Lyn Yates

12 The Transforming Middle: Schooling Markets, Morality and Racialisation within Australia's Middle Class......... 195
    Rose Butler, Christina Ho and Eve Vincent

Part 5: Interviews.......................... 213

13 An Interview with Larissa Behrendt: Reflections on Class in Australia... 215
    Larissa Behrendt, Jessica Gerrard and Steven Threadgold

14 An Interview with Raewyn Connell: Reflections on Class in Australia... 236
    Raewyn Connell, Steven Threadgold and Jessica Gerrard

About the Contributors................................. 259

Index... 265

Part 1

Situating Class Analysis in Australia

CHAPTER 1

CLASS IN AUSTRALIA

Public Debates and Research Directions in a Settler Colony

Jessica Gerrard and Steven Threadgold

The Public Life of Class in Australia

On the night of the conservative Coalition electoral victory in 2019, Prime Minister Scott Morrison declared, 'These are the quiet Australians who have won a great victory tonight' (ABC, 2019; McKenna, 2019). Combined with the mantra of 'jobs and growth', Morrison's reference to 'quiet Australians' follows a long lineage of rhetorical terms used to evoke a majoritarian politics. You may recall John Howard's 'battlers' (McAllister, 2017) as well as populist appeals to 'ordinary Australians', 'working families' and 'middle Australia'. The rhetorical appeal and power of these figurations is that they encapsulate everything and nothing, while being easy to identify with. For both sides of politics, to be 'ordinary', 'quiet', or a 'battler', at the very least denotes being a worker. The cultural importance of work in Australian contemporary politics cannot be understated. Yet, beyond this, particularly from the political right, such terms are used to rhetorically signal a dominant Anglo, English-speaking family with a mortgage, despite the fact that this imagined figure is a distortion. The Australian population is far more diverse than such rhetoric suggests (Ting, 2017). Politically driven figures such as the battler and the quiet Australian connect with broader cultural signifiers of 'the Australian people'. They have strong repercussions for class, race, colonialist and gender relations.

In parallel, longstanding anti-elite discourses are being articulated anew in contemporary populism, ironically invoked routinely by some of Australia's most privileged and powerful. In this usage, anti-elitism, and its bedfellow anti-intellectualism, is deployed to stereotype and denigrate apparent inner-city latte sippers, who, with their education and 'progressive' political values, fail to grasp 'ordinary' people or the true national interest (see Sawer and Hindess, 2004). Simultaneously, whenever arguments about income or economic redistribution arise, we hear instant invocations of a 'class war'. The wealthy and multinational corporations position raising the minimum wage, or having a more progressive tax system, as endangering the fragile economic ecosystem of Australia's 'quiet' 'battlers'. For instance, arguing in favour of lowering the minimum wage, infamous Australian mining magnate Gina Rinehart implored Australians to 'get through the class warfare smokescreen … if you're jealous of those with more money, don't just sit there and complain; do something to make more money yourself – spend less time drinking, or smoking and socialising, and more time working' (cited in Bourke, 2012). It seems that in Australia as elsewhere, as oft-quoted US-based billionaire investor Warren Buffett quipped: 'There's class warfare all right, but it's my class, the rich class, that's making war, and we're winning'.

This is a class oriented public rhetoric that often elides the specific use of the language of class. It codifies having a solid work ethic and presents distinctions between the undeserving versus deserving poor. The domination of middle-class morals, values and tastes is normalised as the 'way things are'. However, such discourses ignore or mask the material and economic aspects of class inequality. Like most advanced capitalist countries, Australia has now reached a point where current generations inherit a lower standard of living than their parents, in relative terms. According to measures of inequality, the rich/poor gap is widening, returning to the heights of the

1920s (Leigh, 2013). Education is getting more expensive, while social welfare is increasingly difficult to access, and is punitively administrated. While political slogans about a 'fair go' and egalitarianism still abound, the reality for anyone who is not from a privileged, well-connected background is exclusion from the housing market, and the prospect of insecure work in a labour market that demands 'flexibility', 'employability', 'creativity' and 'innovation'. These neoliberal buzzwords are really ciphers for upper-middle-class qualifications and dispositions. For the majority of working people in Australia, experience of economic precarity and livelihood anxiety had become the norm even before the COVID-19 pandemic.

To be sure, class has a unique place in Australian public life. At times it looms large, acting as an organising frame to declare interests and political sentiments. When 'class' is used rather than (in)equality or (dis)advantage it denotes relationally understanding the rapidly widening gap in wealth and prosperity experienced in Australia and globally. 'Class' also has a cultural historical genealogy with deep connections to unionism and the struggle for workers' rights, including, for instance, the campaign for the eight-hour day. In other words, class is a powerful political signifier and still resonates as a form of political consciousness. While still often ignored in political and economic discourse, the topic of class has made a re-emergence in recent times. For example, ABC radio aired a multi-part series on class in 2018, including an Australia-wide survey that allowed people to find out their apparent class position. In 2014, *The Conversation* started a 'Class in Australia' series. Literary figures such as Tim Winton (2013) and Christos Tsiolkas (2014) have written prominent opinion pieces and made media appearances discussing class. In Australian news, opinion and pop culture, the figures of the hipster and the bogan, which act as proxies for cultural, consumption and moral aspects of class, are everywhere (Threadgold, 2018).

And yet, most often class is eclipsed; markedly absent from public and political debates on poverty, inequality, disadvantage and wealth. These other terms appear to roll off the political tongue with ease. They lend themselves well to policy discourse and political rhetoric where structural inequalities are broken down into a series of 'risk factors' attributed to individuals. Educational attainment, mental and physical health, marital status, ethnicity, gender, age, geographical location, parenting styles and – particularly problematically – Indigeneity (as if this can be understood as a 'factor') have become familiar descriptive markers to measure inequality, disadvantage and poverty. These markers create individualised figures of deficit for scapegoating purposes. It is made to seem as though inequality can be summed up by a series of personal characteristics or 'failings'. These individualised, over-stereotyped figurations dominate public discussion about inequality in Australia and have become embedded within the political and policy articulation of disadvantage and marginalisation (see Threadgold, 2020; 2018, for more on the political use of figures). It is evident there is a significant and increasing discrepancy between political rhetoric and the reality of inequality and disadvantage. This is an important time for scholarly considerations of class in Australia today.

Of course, not all distinctive experiences of disadvantage and inequality – gender, race, Indigeneity, sexuality, ability, age for instance – represent equivalences that can be subsumed into class. Yet a richly informed understanding of class can play a powerful role in grasping how unequal social and economic experiences are articulated through relations of property, labour, capital and value in capitalist societies. Using the term 'class' makes inequality a public issue anchored in economic structures and social/cultural institutions. We argue that class is necessary for understanding how Australian society functions, how the powerful maintain their interests, and how social and cultural institutions work to reproduce inequalities.

This book brings together current research on class as a means to open – rather than settle – questions in scholarly and public debate on the meaning, significance, constitution and role of class analysis in Australia today. To be sure, in the context of broader public reckonings with sexism, transphobia and homophobia, colonialism, and racism, there is a pressing need to renew and rethink what class does as an analytic tool. We need to ask what work is done in evoking the framing of class; and how class interconnects, and is articulated through, other modalities of difference and inequality. Thus, our aim in this edited collection is to assemble contributions that invite further public and academic debate on what it means to name and map class in Australia. In what follows, we discuss key recent trends and texts in class scholarship in Australia, *not* to provide a complete introductory review of the field, but to think through the need for further analytic attention in class-based research that centres Australia as a settler colony. We conclude by introducing the chapters in this collection and provide some brief reflections on researching class.

Class Analysis in the Settler Colony of Australia

In a recent virtual special issue of the *Journal of Sociology*, Raewyn Connell (2019) compiled a series of articles tracing what she identifies as the first two phases of sociological class analysis in Australia (and New Zealand). First were analyses of the 'how' of class, describing the local reality of class, including aspects of children's perception (Davies, 1965); classed and gendered kinship relations (Martin, 1967); and socio-economic ranking of suburbs (Lancaster Jones, 1967). Second were analyses of the 'why' of class, emphasising the relational aspects of class pertaining to political economy and power. In New Zealand, Bedggood (1974) showed how public institutions that were thought to be alleviating inequalities were actually sustaining them. Sandercock (1974) analysed the power of property developers and owners, and the State in the era of 'green bans'. Sharp (1974) offered a study of the social construction of poverty and how the distortion of the lived reality of poverty affected public discussion.

As Connell reflects in her interview in this collection, early contributions such as those were part of a 'new wave' of class scholarship in Australia. They were connected to a new experimentalism of sociology, attempting (with varying depth and breadth) to reckon with class inequality in the specific context of Australia. Of course, Connell's own work is now canonical in the study of class in Australia. First published in 1977, Connell's *Ruling Class Ruling Culture: Studies of Conflict, Power and Hegemony in Australian Life* was voted the most influential book in Australian sociology in The

Australian Sociological Association's (TASA) poll in 2003, and *Making the difference: Schools, Families and Social Division* (1982) was sixth. In *Ruling Class Ruling Culture*, Connell sketched out the connections between the leading political groups, companies and the relations, shared interests and conflicts among them. A few years later, Connell and Irving's (1980) *Class Structure in Australian History* analysed the genesis of class relations in Australia through then prominent theories of class, but more importantly, traced class developments and relations from colonial settlement in 1788. That book outlined the rise of the mercantile bourgeoisie, the working class, the industrial ruling class, and the way that class in Australia restructured following globalisation developments from 1975 onward.

Throughout the 1970s and into the 1980s class began to settle as a scholarly concern, particularly as something to be counted, and accounted for. The ongoing salience of class emerged in part from the Australian 'New Left' (Irving & Connell, 2016; see also Paternoster 2017). For instance, Sol Encel's (1970) *Equality and Authority* studied relationships between class, status and power in Australia. Drawing upon his experience as a junior clerk in Canberra, Encel was motivated to conduct a statistically and historically informed examination of the cultural, educational, political, economic and nationalist aspects of class in Australia. In 1972, Bryson and Thompson's *An Australian Newtown* vividly depicted class relations in a working-class suburb. In 1977, the edited collection by Playford and Kirsner on *Australian Capitalism* outlined class stratification at the time in some detail. In the same year, Jock Collins drew attention to the complexity of class and ethnic relations in 'A divided working class' (1977) and later, 'Immigration and class: The Australian experience' (1984). The 1978 book by Markus and Curthoys asked: *Who Are Our Enemies? Racism and the Australian Working Class*. Hillier's (1981) edited collection on class brought together prominent Australian social scientists, covering topics such as ideology, policy, law, marriage, gender, discrimination, poverty, education, and everyday attitudes and perceptions about class. Chamberlain (1983) also sought to understand class consciousness, identifying three different levels of ideological commitment to capitalism. Later, Andrew

Metcalf (1990) wrote about the 'demonology' of class in the iconography of the Australian coalminer.

Into the 1990s and 2000s, there was a research focus on the rise of a new and influential middle class (see Pusey, 2003). That body of work addressed the shifting roles and responsibilities of the state and the private sector, the shift to the right of the Australian Labor Party and globalisation, whilst maintaining a view on the relationships between class, labour, family, gender, migration, race, politics and identity from varying class analytic positions (Jamrozik, 1991; Baxter et al., 1991; Kuhn & O'Lincoln, 1996; McGregor, 2001; Catley, 1996). This was a decade of culminating activism and intellectual work on Indigenous rights, feminism, gay and lesbian liberation, race and racism, and environmentalism, both deepening and challenging class analysis. The importance of these contributions cannot be overstated. Questions that had been surfacing for some time in Australian scholarship became central to the ways in which class was understood to have (or not have) analytic power. Such questions included the role of gender in understandings of labour, the state and social power (Watson, 1990; Shaver, 1989). The context and Indigenous experience of settler colonialism was another important focus (Moreton-Robinson, 2000; Nakata, 1997; Stasiulis & Yuval-Davis, 1995; Curthoys & Moore, 1995; Wolfe, 1997). There were also significant questions raised about the relationship of racism to class and Australian nationhood (Hage, 1998), as well as the place of sexuality and sexual politics in contouring Australian culture and class politics (Altman, 1996; Dowsett et al., 1992).

In the 1990s Pakulski and Waters (1996) argued for the 'death of class'. They proposed that social changes arising from globalisation and postmodernisation had made class less tenable, less vital, as a form of analysis. The claim provoked much debate (for example, Blackmore, Thomson and Beckett, 2000). The idea of the 'death of class' coincided with new reflexive modernity theories which argued that as material 'need' in Western society diminishes, traditional forms of class become a 'zombie category', pointing particularly to the apparent decline in traditional forms of 'class consciousness' (Beck & Beck-Gernsheim, 2002; Beck & Willms,

2004, pp. 20–24). Yet, at the same time economic inequality was increasing (which Beck acknowledged) and measures of happiness and satisfaction fell or remain stagnant at best (Pusey, 2003; Hamilton & Denniss, 2005). Moreover, growing insecurity and uncertainty affected those lower on the social scale more intensely (Pusey, 2003). In that context, whilst the language of 'class' receded somewhat from scholarly and public view, notions of socio-economic status, inequality, stratification and poverty became more and more prominent.

It is perhaps unsurprising, therefore, that many Australian scholars turned to the work of French sociologist Pierre Bourdieu as a means to account for class in ways that focused on culture and the symbolic, and so did not attach class to class consciousness in the same way as traditional Marxism. For instance, the study by Bennett, Emmison and Frow (1999), *Accounting for Tastes*, drew on Bourdieu's *Distinction* (1984). It combined a neo-Marxist framework of job classification – retaining the relationship of paid work to the means of production – with a Weberian foundational precept that paid close attention to shared work and market situations as determinants of social class. The importance of culture to Australian class analysis is foregrounded in more contemporary studies of youth; a sub-field grappling with fundamentally different conditions of employment, cultures of identification and belonging, and new media representations of class – that signpost the affective economies of class (see France & Roberts, 2017; Threadgold, 2018; Idriss, 2017). More recently, the Australian Cultural Fields project has sought to renew and enrich the earlier take-up of Bourdieu for understanding class culture, creating more focus on Australia as a multicultural settler-colonial society (Bennett 2016; Bennett et al., 2020a, 2020b).

Indeed, the importance of culture and institutions remains central to Australian class scholarship. Research on education has retained a strong focus on class (see Barnes & Cahill, 2012), with particular focus on the middle classes (Campbell, Proctor & Sherington, 2009; Rowe, 2016; Stacey, 2016) and gender, youth, identity and 'transitions' (McLeod & Yates, 2006; Teese & Polesel, 2003). Bourdieusian ideas in particular have proved productive as a means to account for the cultural codes of class, and the ways in which class is not only reflected, but produced, in the cultural realm. For example, Butler's (2019) research on school and home draws upon feminist developments of Bourdieu (see Adkins and Skeggs, 2005) to understand how class mediates the way rural youth negotiate economic insecurity, deal with difference and struggle to belong.

Scholarship on class since 2000 has sketched out new class formations and categories to resonate with the socio-economic changes of recent decades. For instance, Donaldson and Poynting (2007) excavated the lives of 'ruling class men', showing how their peculiar upbringings prepared them for wielding their power in the hypercompetitive and misogynist business world of the ruling class. The survey-based research by Sheppard and Biddle (2017) found that Australians are very aware of their class identity. They formulated six contemporary classes in Australia: 'precariat', 'ageing workers', 'new workers', 'mobile middle', 'emerging affluent' and 'established affluent'. Adkins, Cooper and Konings (2019) identified property ownership as a central organising principle of class relations in contemporary Australia, as housing appreciation can now accrue more income per year than the average wage. Their five-level asset-based class scheme comprises Investors, Outright Home Owners, Home Owners with Mortgages, Renters and Homeless.

Taking all that recent work into account, the apparent decline of class consciousness and collectivity outlined by those writing some decades ago about 'reflexive modernity' was not an early indicator of the sociological decline of class as a valuable form of analysis. Rather, it reflected the recent history of a radically transformed global context within which workers must sell their labour for wages; a context characterised by increasing insecurity and new growth areas of work. Nevertheless, as a concept class is not a mirror reflection of 'reality'. As E.P. Thompson (1963, p. 9) wrote in his famous book *The Making of the English Working Class*, 'I do not see class as a "structure", nor even as a "category", but as something which in fact happens (and can be shown to have happened) in human relationships'. This quote from Thompson points to some of the continuing tensions, ambiguities and deficiencies in class theorising and the use of class as an analytical category in Australia. At base, any interactional focus on class cannot afford to leave out the increasingly polarised economic dimension – the highly inequitable distribution of wealth. Moreover, both in Australia and overseas, class scholarship has had to reckon with acknowledgement of the need to attend more closely to the ways in which class interfaces with exploitative relations of gender, colonialism, race, ability and heterosexuality. To talk about class today immediately brings those dimensions into any discussion about inequality under capitalism.

The recent developments outlined above reflect the changing uses and understandings of class, particularly in relation to how class can be meaningfully mobilised in relation to gender, sexuality, race and ethnicity, and – having particular import in the context of Australia – settler colonialism and its attendant logic of elimination surrounding Aboriginal and Torres Strait Islander people (Wolfe, 2001). Reflecting on their own early work more recently, Irving and Connell (2016) note that its treatment of race, gender and coloniality was somewhat inadequate, shaped by the tendency to draw on scholarship from 'white male theorists' from Europe and the USA. Indeed, as Connell's work on masculinity (2005) and Southern theory (2007) attests, attention to coloniality and gender – to name just two examples – is not antithetical to class analysis. Nevertheless, it does often require different ways of seeing, and different analytical resources. There is contemporary need for an approach that can 'build on the idea of mutually constituting, interacting social dynamics' of inequality, disadvantage and lack of representation (Irving & Connell, 2016, p. 12). In Australia, the foundational importance of settler colonialism and migration must be central to the ways in which class can be thought of – and worked with – anew for better understanding class formation and experience in the context of the particular Australian development of capitalism. Put simply, settler colonialism is the enabler – and contouring structure – of capitalism and the relations of class in Australia.

This in part reflects how class has always been expressed in ever shifting racialised terms, connected to a kind of 'white paranoia' articulated through Australian settler colonialism (Hage, 2002). We must look to the interlinking of capitalism and colonialism for the ways that the refused recognition and attempted erasure of Indigenous peoples has defined the meaning and practice of class. Those denials and abuses were articulated through what Moreton-Robinson describes as a 'white possessive' (2015). As Behrendt reflects in this collection, historically speaking, to be a 'worker' in Australia was an economic and social category not afforded to Indigenous Australians, despite the intensely exploitative forced work of Indigenous peoples across Australia (see also Curthoys & Moore, 1995). Indeed, in the lead-up to the publishing of this book, a class action launched against the West Australian government for wage theft brought media attention to the tens of thousands of Indigenous workers whose earnings were sent to governmental authorities rather than paid to individuals (Collard, 2020). Too often the experience of Indigenous Australians is aligned to poverty and too easily individualised and separated from broader Australian social, cultural, economic and labour and classed relations under capitalism.

The complex articulation of class in settler colonialism has led to recent debate surrounding the emergence, significance and experience of an 'Aboriginal middle class' and Indigenous professionals (see Bargallie, 2020; Lahn, 2012). Wiradjuri/Kamilaroi journalist and scholar Stan Grant, for instance, has reflected on the growing numbers of Indigenous professionals, declaring, 'the new black middle class is developing its own consciousness' (2016, n.p.). And yet, this is not straightforward social mobility as Behrendt reflects later in this collection. As Ballardong Noongar writer and urban planner Timmah Ball (2016) notes:

> More than ever the socio-economic status of Aboriginals is shifting, with many of us becoming middle class. But as levels of education and professional status rise, misconceptions continue to mark us and new tensions emerge. Aboriginal people have worked tirelessly to overcome injustice and dispossession. While this fight has improved the lives of many, poor health outcomes, deaths in custody and racism remain at appallingly high levels.

In other words, even when some social mobility takes place, the experience of Indigenous Australians still calls attention to the complex modalities of class and race in the context of settler colonialism.

There is evident need for in-depth research that can address the question of how largely international theories of class can be understood and used in the Australian context. Class scholarship in Australia has tended to use international theoretical tools that do not set settler colonialism at the centre of their analyses and have yet to truly reckon with these complex dynamics. Settler colonialism is of course connected to the global imperialist project. It connects Australia not only to England, but also to intertwining transnational practices of capitalism and colonialism. It also, therefore, assists to draw attention to the position of Australia in contemporary flows of labour, capital and production. For instance, Australia, so often aligned culturally and politically with the geographically distant US and UK, is deeply threaded into local economies and flows of capital and labour in the Pacific and South-East Asia. Indeed, the crisis in 'fruit pickers' due to the border closures surrounding COVID-19 in Australia highlights the national reliance on poorly paid, precarious work carried out by international workers sourced from the local region (see Stead, 2020). Thus, whilst on the one hand the settler colonialism context demands a rethinking of the social, economic and cultural formations of class in Australia, it also gestures towards the complex global flows of capital, class and exploitation.

Researching Class: This Book

Research on class, as Greg Noble reflects in this collection, must reckon with the complexity of everyday life in which class is both contradictory and ambiguous. Indeed, Noble argues that there is often 'an enigmatic quality to class given this lived complexity; there is something always not open to explanation' (p. 36). Whilst it is undeniable that the concept of 'class' remains an enduring presence in Australian scholarship, it does often take on an enigmatic character. Arguably, it is frequently used lightly within scholarship as a means to indicate a kind of politics of the author/s, rather than a clear analytic framing and conceptual explanation. In contrast, the chapters in this book each take class as their analytic focus, bringing empirical and conceptual light to the ways in which class offers a relational and structural understanding of inequality, social and cultural relations, and affective modalities.

The collection begins with a group of chapters that all in some way reflect on what it means to deploy a class analysis in the Australian context. Greg Noble reflects on his own trajectory into 'class studies', and explores methodological tensions between quantitative and qualitative perspectives by reporting on the theoretical basis and empirical findings of the recent Australian Cultural Fields project. Examining the question, 'if class is the answer, what is the question?', Noble suggests the need to embrace, rather than turn away from, complexity and ambiguity in class analysis. Barry Morris traces the genesis of Australia's class system in the context of settler colonialism after the declaration of *terra nullius*. He focuses on the translation, and new expression, of class in the Australian colony in relation to male convict labour and the emergence of a male and white elite capitalist class. Mark Western then reflects on class analysis through the lens of his own long standing and influential work, tracing the key conceptual considerations he has relied upon while critically engaging with some new conceptions of Australia's class system.

In the second section of the book on class, labour and employment, Hannah Forsyth charts the growth of middle-class professions throughout the 20th century. Forsyth argues that the historical shifts and contestations surrounding the moral order and occupational structure of the professional class has significant implications for understanding class in the present. Tom Barnes and Jasmine Ali draw upon the influential work of Eric Olin Wright to critically engage with another influential concept, the 'precariat' (see Standing, 2011). Through a case study of warehouse logistics, they argue that the debate needs to shift beyond a simplistic duality in which precarious workers are either an undifferentiated part of a working class with common interests, or a separate class with conflicting interests. Finally in this section, Jessica Gerrard and David Farrugia examine the contemporary conditions of unemployment, arguing that unemployment is characterised by what they term 'productive intensities', which bring the subjective formation of class into unemployment.

Section three of the book then looks at cultural formations of class relations. Deborah Warr, Keith Jacobs and Henry Paternoster analyse that icon of the working class, the 'bogan'. Presenting a genealogy of the bogan, Warr, Jacobs and Paternoster demonstrate how 'the bogan' is culturally represented to be tacitly working class and socially regressive, with bad taste and poor behaviour. Penny Rossiter then discusses the SBS TV series *Struggle Street*, situating it between 'compelling viewing' and 'poverty porn' in an affective economy that is likely to provoke ambivalent responses in viewers. Next, Barbara Pini and Laura Rodriguez Castro put the recent rise of rural romance (RuRom) novels under the spotlight. They take up critiques of the white moral imaginary of farmers and farming in Australia, focusing on the genre's intersections with class, gender and sexuality, where class is not named but morally coded.

Section four moves to the field of education. Julie McLeod and Lyn Yates return to their influential Making Modern Lives project, reflecting on their own theoretical and empirical interests surrounding class, their methodological decisions, the importance and role of gender, and their focus on those 'in the middle' rather than at the extremes. Rose Butler, Christina Ho and Eve Vincent then draw upon their work in two different projects in Sydney schools to show how ethnicity complicates straightforward understandings of class hierarchies in education. The emergence of a 'new' global middle class with diverging sensibilities challenges the moral conceptualisation of good citizenship and the 'correct' way to learn and reproduce social status.

The book concludes with interviews with two prominent thinkers and scholars who each reflect on the role and place of class in Australian society and research. First, Eualeyai/Kamilaroi scholar Larissa Behrendt considers class in relation to settler colonialism, and the ways in which Indigenous peoples have been subject to foundational exclusions, whilst also heavily governed and surveilled. In doing so Behrendt highlights the challenges that Indigenous sovereignty, history and culture brings for understanding class in Australia. Reflecting on her own career, Behrendt highlights the ways in which Indigenous trajectories, social status, careers and activism must be understood on its own terms and as constitutively framed by race and racism. Second, Raewyn Connell reflects on the establishment of sociological class studies in Australia and her own class trajectory. Situating her own research on class in the context of broader conceptual debates surrounding class analysis, and in relation to her scholarship on gender and Southern theory, Connell points to the need for analyses of gender, race, sexuality and settler colonialism.

Collectively, this set of interdisciplinary chapters represent significant contemporary thinking about the theorisation, practices, experiences and cultures of class in Australia. Each – in different ways – opens up new questions about class analysis. Of course, no collection can be a full representation of the scholarship of the day, and gaps are inevitable. Yet, if class analysis is to have an ongoing role in scholarly and public debates about Australian life, then the important considerations raised in this book – race and whiteness; work, labour, education and unemployment; research practices and theoretical resources; gender and sexuality; and cultural representations – offer productive starting points. Each chapter contributes an important perspective for understanding class in Australia and each addresses key questions that face class-based research. What is the role of class analysis in Australia? What work is done when class is mobilised in the Australian context? And, the perennial question: how can we engage, represent, and address interrelationships of class, gender, sexuality, race, ethnicity and coloniality? We hope that this collection contributes to a renewed and enlivened field of research characterised by deep engagement with – and questioning of – the theoretical and methodological approaches, and research foci, of class.

References

ABC (2019, November 14). Who are Scott Morrison's quiet Australians? [Television broadcast]. In *7.30 Report*. Retrieved from https://www.abc.net.au/7.30/who-are-scott-morrisons-quiet-australians/11706370

Adkins, L. & Cooper, M. & Konings, M. (2019). Class in the 21st century: Asset inflation and the new logic of inequality. *Environment and Planning A: Economy and Space, 53*(3), 1–25.

Adkins, L. & Skeggs, B. (Eds.). (2005). *Feminism after Bourdieu*. Oxford: Blackwell.

Altman, D. (1996). On global queering. *Australian Humanities Review, 2*(2), 1–8.

Ball, T. (2016). Who's Afraid of the Black middle class?, *Meanjin*, Spring 2016. Retrieved from https://meanjin.com.au/essays/whos-afraid-of-the-black-middle-class/

Bargallie, D. (2020). *Unmasking the racial contract: Indigenous voices on racism in the Australian Public Service*. Canberra: Aboriginal Studies Press.

Barnes, T. & Cahill, D. (2012). Marxist class analysis: A living tradition in Australian scholarship. *Journal of Australian Political Economy* (70), 47–69.

Baxter, J., Emmison, M., Western, J., & Western, M. (Eds.). (1991). *Class analysis and contemporary Australia*. Crow's Nest: Macmillan.

Beck, U. & Beck-Gernsheim, E. (2002). *Individualization: Institutionalized individualism and its social and political consequences*. London: Sage.

Beck, U. & Willms, J. (2004). *Conversations with Ulrich Beck*. Cambridge: Polity Press.

Bedggood, D. (1974). Power and welfare in New Zealand: Notes on the political economy of the welfare state. *The Australian and New Zealand Journal of Sociology, 10*(2), 104–111.

Bennett, T. (2016). Adjusting field theory: the dynamics of settler-colonial art fields. In L. Hanquinet & M. Savage (Eds.), *Routledge International Handbook of the Sociology of Art and Culture* (pp. 247–261). Abingdon: Routledge.

Bennett, T., Carter, D., Gayo, M., Kelly, M., & Noble, G. (Eds.). (2020a). *Fields, Capitals, Habitus Australian Culture, Inequalities and Social Divisions*. London: Routledge.

Bennett, T., Emmison, M., & Frow, J. (1999). *Accounting for tastes: Australian everyday cultures*. Cambridge: Cambridge University Press.

Bennett, T., Stevenson, D., Myers, F., & Winikoff, T. (2020b). *The Australian art field practices, policies, institutions*. London: Routledge.

Blackmore, J., Thomson, P., & Beckett, L. (2000). Editorial: What's happened to social justice lately? *Australian Educational Researcher, 27*(3), i–iv.

Bourdieu, P. (1984). *Distinction*. Cambridge, MA: Harvard University Press.

Bourke, E. (2012, August 30). More work, less play: Rinehart sets out road to riches. [Television broadcast]. In *ABC News*. Retrieved from https://www.abc.net.au/news/2012-08-30/rinehart-sets-out-road-to-riches/4232326?nw=0

Bryson, L., & Thompson, F. (1972). *An Australian Newtown*. Melbourne: Penguin Books.

Butler, R. (2019). *Class, culture and belonging in rural childhoods*. Singapore: Springer.

Campbell, C., Proctor, H., & Sherington, G. (2009). *School choice: How parents negotiate the new school market in Australia*. Crows Nest: Allen & Unwin.

Catley, B. (1996). *Globalising Australian Capitalism*. Cambridge: Cambridge University Press.

Chamberlain, C. (1983). *Class Consciousness in Australia*. Sydney: Allen & Unwin.

Collard, S. (2020, October 19). Class action launched against West Australian Government over Indigenous stolen wages. [Television broadcast]. In *ABC News*. Retrieved from https://www.abc.net.au/news/2020-10-19/wa-government-faces-class-action-over-stolen-wages/12737046

Collins, J. (1977). A divided working class. *Intervention*, *8*, 64–78.

Collins, J. (1984). Immigration and class: The Australian experience. In G. Bottomley & M. DeLepervanche (Eds.), *Ethnicity, class and gender in Australia* (pp. 10–31). Sydney: Allen and Unwin.

Connell, R. (1977). *Ruling class, ruling culture: Studies of conflict, power and hegemony in Australian life*. Cambridge: Cambridge University Press.

Connell, R. (2005). *Masculinities*. Cambridge: Polity Press.

Connell, R. (2007). *Southern theory: The global dynamics of knowledge in social science*. Cambridge: Polity Press.

Connell, R. (2019). Sociology and the mystery of class: Highlights from the first ten years of the Journal. *Journal of Sociology*, Virtual Special Issue, 1–4. Retrieved from https://journals.sagepub.com/page/jos/class

Connell, R., Ashenden, D., Dowsett, G. & Kessler, S. (1982). Making the difference: Schools, families and social division. Abingdon: Routledge.

Connell, R., & Irving, T.H. (1980). *Class structure in Australian history* (2nd ed., revised 1992). Melbourne: Longman Cheshire.

Curthoys, A., & Moore, C. (1995). Working for the white people: An historiographic essay on Aboriginal and Torres Strait Islander Labour, *Labour History*, *69*, 1–29.

Davies A.F. (1965). The child's discovery of social class. *The Australian and New Zealand Journal of Sociology*, *1*(1), 21–37.

Donaldson, M. & Poynting, S. (2007). *Ruling class men: Money, sex, power*. Bern: Peter Lang.

Dowsett, G.W., Davis, M.D., & Connell, R.W. (1992). Working class homosexuality and HIV/AIDS prevention some recent research from Sydney, Australia. *Psychology and Health*, *6*(4), 313–324.

Encels, S. (1970). *Equality and authority: A study of class, status and power in Australia*. Melbourne: Cheshire.

France, A., & Roberts, S. (2017). *Youth and social class enduring inequality in the United Kingdom, Australia and New Zealand*. London: Palgrave.

Grant, S. (2016). New Indigenous middle class finds place in modern economy. Retrieved from https://pursuit.unimelb.edu.au/articles/new-indigenous-middle-class-finds-place-in-modern-economy

Hage, G. (1998). *White nation: Fantasies of white supremacy in a multicultural society*. Annandale: Pluto Press.

Hage, G. (2002). Multiculturalism and white paranoia in Australia, *Journal of International Migration and Integration, 3*(3&4), 417–437.

Hamilton, C., & Denniss, R. (2005). *Affluenza: When too much is never enough.* Crows Nest: Allen & Unwin.

Hillier, P. (Ed.). (1981). *Class and inequality in Australia: Sociological perspectives and research.* Sydney: Harcourt Brace Javanovich Group.

Idriss, S. (2017). *Young migrant identities: Creativity and masculinity.* London: Routledge.

Irving, T.H., & Connell, R. (2016). Scholars and radicals: writing and re-thinking class structure in Australian history. *Journal of Australian Studies, 40*(1), 3–15.

Jamrozik, A. (1991). *Class, inequality and the state: Social change, social policy and the new middle class.* South Melbourne: MacMillan.

Kuhn, R., & O'Lincoln, T. (Eds.). (1996). *Class and class conflict in Australia.* Melbourne: Longman.

Lahn, J. (2012). Aboriginal Urban Professionals and 'Middle Classness'. In D. Howard-Wagner, D. Habibis, & T. Petray (Eds.), *Theorising Indigenous sociology: Australian perspectives workshop proceedings* (https://ses.library.usyd.edu.au/handle/2123/8630) (pp 1–11), Sydney: University of Sydney.

Lancaster Jones F. (1967). A social ranking of Melbourne suburbs. *The Australian and New Zealand Journal of Sociology, 3*(2), 93–110.

Leigh, A. (2013). *Billionaires and battlers: The story of inequality in Australia.* Collingwood: Redback.

Markus, A.B., & Curthoys, A. (1978). *Who are our enemies? Racism and the Australian working class.* Sydney: Hale and Iremonger.

Martin J.I. (1967). Extended kinship ties: An Adelaide study. *The Australian and New Zealand Journal of Sociology, 3*(1), 44–63.

McAllister, I. (2017). Howard's battlers and the 1996 election, in T. Frame (Ed.), *The ascent to power, 1996: The Howard government*, Volume 1 (pp. 80–95). Sydney: NewSouth Publishing (an imprint of University of New South Wales Press).

McGregor, C. (2001) *Class in Australia: Who says Australia has no class system?* (2nd ed.). Ringwood: Penguin.

McKenna, M. (2019, July). Scott Morrison's quiet Australians. *The Monthly.* Retrieved from https://www.themonthly.com.au/issue/2019/july/1561989600/mark-mckenna/scott-morrison-s-quiet-australians#mtr

McLeod, J., & Yates, L. (2006). *Making modern lives: Subjectivity, schooling, and social change.* Albany: Suny Press.

Metcalfe, A.W. (1990). The demonology of class: The iconography of the coalminer and the symbolic construction of political boundaries. *Critique of Anthropology, 10*(1), 39–63.

Moreton-Robinson, A. (2000). *Talkin' up to the white woman: Aboriginal women and feminism.* St Lucia: University of Queensland Press.

Moreton-Robinson, A. (2015). *The white possessive: Property, power, and indigenous sovereignty.* Minneapolis: University of Minnesota Press.

Nakata, M. (1997). *The cultural interface: An exploration of the intersection of Western knowledge systems and Torres Strait Islanders positions and experiences* (Doctoral dissertation). James Cook University, Brisbane.

Pakulski, J., & Waters, M. (1996). *The death of class*. London: Sage.

Paternoster, H. (2017). *Reimagining class in Australia: Marxism, populism and social science*. Cham: Springer.

Playford, J., & Kirsner, D. (Eds.). (1977). *Australian capitalism: Towards a socialist critique*. Melbourne: Penguin.

Pusey, M. (2003). *The experience of middle Australia*. Cambridge: Cambridge University Press.

Rowe, E. (2016). *Middle-class school choice in urban spaces: The economics of public schooling and globalized education reform*. Abingdon: Routledge.

Sandercock L. (1974). Reform, property and power in the cities. *The Australian and New Zealand Journal of Sociology, 10*(2), 120–128.

Sawer, M., & Hindess, B. (2004). *Us and them: Anti-elitism in Australia*. Perth: API Network.

Sharp G. (1974). Interpretations of poverty. *The Australian and New Zealand Journal of Sociology, 10*(3), 194–199.

Shaver, S. (1989). Gender, class and the welfare state: The case of income security in Australia, *Feminist Review, 32*(1), 90–110.

Sheppard, J., & Biddle, N. (2017). Class, capital, and identity in Australian society. *Australian Journal of Political Science, 52*(4), 500–516.

Stacey, M. (2016). Middle-class parents' educational work in an academically selective public high school. *Critical Studies in Education, 57*(2), 209–223.

Standing, G. (2011). *The precariat*. London: Bloomsbury.

Stasiulis, D., & Yuval-Davis, N. (Eds.). (1995). *Unsettling settler societies: Articulations of gender, race, ethnicity and class*. Thousand Oaks: Sage.

Stead, V. (2020, March 24). Australia's food supply relies on migrant workers who are facing coronavirus limbo, *The Guardian*, Retrieved from https://www.theguardian.com/world/commentisfree/2020/mar/24/australias-food-supply-relies-on-migrant-workers-who-are-facing-coronavirus-limbo

Teese, R., & Polesel, J. (2003). *Undemocratic schooling: Equity and quality in mass secondary education in Australia*. Melbourne: Melbourne University Publishing.

Thompson, E.P. (1963). *The making of the English working class*. London: Victor Gallancz.

Threadgold, S. (2018). *Youth, class and everyday struggles*. London: Routledge.

Threadgold S. (2020). Figures of youth: on the very object of Youth Studies. *Journal of Youth Studies, 23*(6), 686–701.

Ting, I. (2017, August 3). 'Ordinary' Australia probably isn't where you think it is, [Television broadcast]. In *ABC News*. Retrieved from https://www.abc.net.au/news/2017-08-03/census-2016-ordinary-australia-probably-isnt-where-you-think/8680052?nw=0

Tsiolkas, C. (2014, May). Whatever happened to the working class? *The Monthly*. Retrieved from https://www.themonthly.com.au/issue/2014/may/1398866400/christos-tsiolkas/whatever-happened-working-class

Watson, S. (Ed.). (1990). *Playing the state: Australian feminist interventions.* London: Verso.

Winton, T. (2013, December – January 2014). The C word. *The Monthly*. Retrieved from https://www.themonthly.com.au/issue/2013/december/1385816400/tim-winton/c-word

Wolfe, P. (1997). History and imperialism: a century of theory, from Marx to postcolonialism. *The American Historical Review, 102*(2), 388–420.

Wolfe, P. (2001). Land, labor, and difference: Elementary structures of race. *The American Historical Review, 106*(3), 866–905.

CHAPTER 2

CONTRADICTORY LOCATIONS OF CLASS

Greg Noble

Introduction: Locating Class?

As a young PhD student enamoured of Marxist theory, I enthusiastically worked my way through the class debates of the 1970s and 1980s, and furiously debated with my peers[1] the pros and cons of various approaches: whether they were 'true' to Marxist theory in their structuralist or culturalist inclinations, where they fell in the prioritising of the relations or means of production, and whether European theory was relevant to an Australian context. I treasure that training in theoretical debate because what I got out of it ultimately was a scepticism towards the easy, rhetorical flourishes of the language of class found all too often in academic discourse. This scepticism was grounded in the habits of critical and engaged thought: thinking in complexity, thinking empirically and thinking sociologically. I don't want to revisit those debates here – enough ink has been spilt on this over the decades – but I do want to situate my discussion of class in Australian cultural fields by a sense of the 'lessons learnt' from these debates.

I found discussions of class in Australia unsatisfying, with the exception of the work of Connell and colleagues, and journals like *Arena*. Connell, in an account of class in the social sciences in Australia, documented the preoccupation with 'description and measurement, not analysis and synthesis', even in the new field of sociology (1977, p. 23). In a rich body of work through the 1970s and 1980s, Connell began to develop theoretically informed and empirically focused accounts of class that rejected 'categorical' approaches for more 'generative' ones and which acknowledged complexity (1977, pp. 3–4). Moreover, *Class Structure in Australian History* promised a distinctively Australian focus, arguing that the British state could not simply be transplanted into Australia (1980, p. 32). Yet, while the content of this was historically rich, the presence of Indigenous and migrant populations in the narrative was minimal. Moreover, this work avoided 'definitions' (1983, p. 83) or a 'comprehensive account' of class (1977, p. ix) – what I was looking for. Connell's theory, moreover, was largely a series of engagements with European scholars, such as Poulantzas, rather than an elaborated framework, to which I then turned.

Through the work of Poulantzas (1978) I began to think more about the multiple dimensions through which class relations are made – what he characterised as the domains of the economic, the political and the ideological. What I gleaned from the writing of scholars such as E.P. Thompson (1963) and Raymond Williams (1958) – both of whom became lifelong influences – was a strong sense of the historical contexts of class experience and relations. But it was Erik Olin Wright who perhaps gave me the strongest sense of the tools I needed to think about class while I researched the sociology of intellectuals and the middle classes. While others had acknowledged the multiplicities and the internal complexities of class formation, Wright elevated these to a key principle through his conceptualisation of *contradictory class locations*. Wright (1985) argued that we need to take into account the diverse relations of exploitation and axes of differentiation (1997), around ownership and expertise, which revealed a number of intermediate positions within the class structure. These were not epiphenomena, but central to class structures in contemporary societies. Central to this was his claim that they are only identifiable in terms of contradiction because they inhabited positions which represented competing modes of constitution.

Wright's model provided several things that shaped my thinking about class. First, the foregrounding of multiplicity and contradiction interested me, rather than the identification of particular classes. This emphasis pointed to the multiple logics shaping class position, and it also suggested that contradiction could be central to human sociality. Against stratification approaches, such as the work of Goldthorpe, this complexity was 'deep' and not simply a proliferation of positions on the ladder of social hierarchy. This pointed to the fact that class structure as an abstraction did not account for class formation or, more to the point for me, the experience of class. Wright insists that the typology he develops out of this approach does not represent classes as such, but 'maps of class locations', that is, 'locations within class relations' rather than classes-as-groups (1997, p. 23). Wright embraces the empirical and conceptual constraints posed by class analysis and, importantly, stresses in his work on the middle classes that class is an empirical problem not simply a theoretical one (1985, pp. 24–6).

I never became a 'Wrightian', but these ideas freed up my use of class and pointed, unexpectedly, to a later interest in Bourdieu. In my PhD research I was unenthused by Bourdieu – I found his concepts hard to pin down and at odds with my desire for clear sociological definitions of class and intellectuals.[2] 'Field', as vague as it is, became a useful idea because it pointed to the 'sectoral' contexts of intellectual practice in a way that Marxism (and other approaches) didn't, and his characterisation of intellectuals as 'paradoxical beings' (1989a) pointed again to the centrality of contradiction or the tensions between the multiple logics that constitute their practice. Bourdieu famously outlined the necessity of the 'break' with 'substantialism', economism and objectivism in class analysis, which he saw manifest in Marxism (1985, p. 723).[3] Importantly, though sometimes forgotten, he also insisted on the break with 'subjectivism' (1989b, p. 21), central to his project of moving beyond the impasse of structure and agency, objective and subjective, the structural and the generative. He opposed theory which produced abstract 'classes on paper'; he proposed instead a relational approach which foregrounded one's objective location in the 'space of relationships' based on principles of differentiation (1985, pp. 724–5):

> The social world can be conceived as a multi-dimensional space that can be constructed empirically by discovering the main factors of differentiation which account for the differences observed in a given social universe, or, in other words, by discovering the powers or forms of capital which are or can become efficient, like aces in a game of cards, in this particular universe, that is, in the struggle (or competition) for the appropriation of scarce goods of which this universe is the site (1987, pp. 3–4).

The significant consequences of this are the emphases on maintaining the sense of the objective dimensions of class without succumbing to the abstractions of the 'theoreticist illusion' (Bourdieu, 1987, p. 7) and foregrounding class as an empirical project. Moreover, Bourdieu extended the recognition of the multiple dimensions of class to an argument about the economic, social and cultural as different forms of capital which not only contributed centrally to the formation of class positions, but constituted different modes of class formation: most evident in his insights into how people can be rich in cultural capital but relatively poor in economic capital. As Bourdieu (1984, pp. 437–8) observed: 'it would be a mistake to seek the explanatory principles of the responses in one factor or in a set of factors combined by addition'. Moreover, Bourdieu's approach, not without its flaws, allows one to hold onto a conceptually nuanced understanding of class whilst insisting upon a careful and critical reflection upon terms to avoid theoretical reification. As Wacquant (2013, p. 282) eloquently puts it: 'Bourdieu reformulated the classic problem of domination and inequality by *questioning the ontological status of groups* and by forging tools for disclosing how these come to be practically made and unmade in social life'. In a country such as Australia, with arguably a 'looser' class structure than Britain but certainly less of a tradition of class discourse, this complexity and caution seemed apposite to the analysis of the role of class in cultural consumption through the Australian Cultural Fields project.

Corresponding to Class

The Australian Cultural Fields project examined patterns of taste, knowledge and participation in six cultural fields in Australia – art, literature, media, sport, music and heritage – especially in terms of relations of inequality around class, gender, age, race/ethnicity. It investigated the forms of cultural capital and habitus associated within and across these fields. The research drew directly on the model developed by Bourdieu in *Distinction* (1984), but did not do this uncritically. As in previous work (Bennett et al., 1999; 2009), it was more about challenging and refining Bourdieu's approach than 'applying' it – and, in this case, in relation to the specific contexts of Australia, a settler-colonial society in which both Indigenous and migrant populations were key aspects of social and cultural formation. So the project was interested in how cultural fields were being reshaped through a changing national and transnational environment. The research involved a national survey consisting of a main sample of 1202 and a further 259 participants recruited as 'boost samples' of about 50 each for people of Indigenous, Chinese, Indian, Italian and Lebanese background. This was followed by household interviews with 42 of the survey respondents (again with some representation of the 'boost samples') and 22 interviews with 'experts' from each of the cultural fields (Bennett et al., 2021).

The issue of class was, then, always central to the project, but it involved questions, acts of interpretation, and choices of data. As Atkinson (2015, p. 3) argues, how you *study* class (and not just theorise it) is not a simple issue: 'how do we convert a theoretical concept into a tool of research? … Is it best mobilised as a variable in large-scale statistical research looking at national patterns or treated as an element of experience in in-depth qualitative research?' Or both? Moreover, is class the thing we are examining or is it something we construct as a thing to examine something else? These questions are pertinent for any project, but especially so in one using multiple methods. We must always be wary, following Bourdieu's cautions, of the researcher's sleight of hand: we construct a category to enable research, then present it as though we are examining that thing. For example, in survey research on taste, we invent a way to measure class, then say, 'how does taste reflect class?' These processes are often hidden in the process of publication, as boring or unimportant, so we must always be alive to the processes of construction we as researchers undertake. In this section I will focus on the role of the survey in thinking about class and in the next, the household interviews.

In the survey we aimed to collect as much data as we could that was relevant to questions of class as well as other socio-demographic characteristics: we asked people about occupation, employment, family assets, household value, home tenure, household income, postcode and education (including which university, if attended), but also partner's job and education, parents' education, and we used the occupation data to classify them into first an eight-class typology, then reduced this to four classes then three classes, to gauge what provided the sharpest analytical contrasts while acknowledging complexity. But we also asked how they would *classify themselves* in terms of class, and also what class they would *prefer* to be in. In the end, we had probably too much data or, rather, we had to make decisions about what was salient and what could be simplified.[4] But collecting 'too much' data was necessary to the task of working out what we could do with class.

In meetings we discussed the value of different models in operationalising class in statistical research: here, 'ruling', 'middle' and 'working' mean little without detailed content. So there is a necessary logic in falling back on the occupational categories used by researchers such as Goldthorpe as a starting point. The Great British Class Survey (GBCS) developed a much-debated seven-class model: elite, established middle class, technical middle class, new affluent workers, traditional working class, emergent service workers, precariat (Savage et al., 2015). An ANU study, influenced by the GBCS, presented an equally contentious six-class model (Sheppard & Biddle, 2017): precariat, ageing workers, new workers, established middle, emerging affluent and established affluent. I do not want to engage with those attempts here, though our book, *Fields, Capitals, Habitus*, does: the point here is that these studies similarly attempt to devise models drawing on multiple sources of criteria, acknowledging that they aren't finding the ultimate, 'real' classes but deploying data to create categories which are empirically useful. An appendix in *Fields, Capitals and Habitus* explains something of the long discussions we had about this and the process of distillation we undertook. The first development of the data resulted in an eight-class model (Bennett et al., 2021, pp. 349–51):

1. Large owners/high managers
2. High professional
3. Lower managers/professionals
4. Intermediate occupations
5. Small employers/own account workers
6. Lower supervisory/technical occupations
7. Semi-routine occupations
8. Routine occupations

This was derived from existing international classification systems but involved 'conversion procedures' to articulate these categories with Australian standards. This was then used to develop a four-class model (1+2; 3; 4+5; 6+7+8), and then a three-class model (1+2+3; 4+5; 6+7+8), in a similar way to Bennett et al. (2009). There were two key reasons for this: first, different cuts of the occupational data were useful for doing different things and, second, preliminary analyses showed that the finer distinctions were not all relevant to the arguments being made. We could also add that moving from occupational categories (often called 'classes', but problematically so) to the simpler grouping returns to a more conventional and recognisable model of a three-class structure presented in class theory, though this is of course not uncontroversial.

So what did the various configurations of class tell us? Most obviously, the research showed that class continues to play a central role in the formation of taste, the distribution of cultural capital and the overall reproduction of inequalities in Australia. But it did so with a degree of complexity and nuance not always present in such studies. It showed, for example, that the experience of class in Australia was woven intimately with the experience of ethnicity and race, as well as gender, both for Aboriginal Australians and those of diverse ethnic ancestries. It explored the emergence of Indigenous cultural capital as a distinct phenomenon, both amongst Indigenous and non-Indigenous Australians, and particularly the formation of an Indigenous middle class (Bennett, Dibley & Kelly, 2021). It showed that the broader significance of class is hard to disentangle from the multivalences of migrancy, ethnicity and generation, especially in transnationalised fields of consumption (Noble, 2021).

But it is the methodological and analytical complexities of class itself that I want to reflect upon here. A key point to make is about the function of multiple correspondence analysis (MCA) and cluster analysis (Bennett et al., 2021, pp. 347–8).[5] The MCAs 'map' the extent to which items are related to each other. Moreover, MCAs work to identify the key axes of differentiation in these patterns. So rather than start with variables like class as given, it starts with patterns of similarities and differences in the distribution of cultural resources, and locates things like class in relation to those patterns. We then used cluster analysis to foreground more clearly how tastes are 'clustered' into identifiable groups. So the point of these techniques is to avoid a method which mechanically assumes the significance of class, then unsurprisingly finds it. It maps class onto the complexity of cultural consumption to leave the complexities visible.

The research showed that class, organised around occupational categories, was a crucial factor in all six cultural fields, but unevenly so. Class was only a relatively independent axis of differentiation in sport – it usually acts in tandem with education, for example. Significantly, as per Bourdieu's arguments, while class and education are interwoven, the latter is not reducible to class – the acquisition of cultural capital, especially among professionals, operates in almost parallel fashion with the possession of economic capital, not as a consequence of it. The other axis of differentiation would typically be age (art, literature, heritage, music) or gender (sport, television) (Bennett, Gayo & Pertierra, 2021,

p. 121). Even with class and education combined, it was only the major axis of differentiation in four of the fields.

Further, while cultural hierarchies continue to exist, they appear more strongly in some fields than others (art vs television), and even in the fields where there have been the strongest divisions between 'legitimate' and 'popular' taste, these hierarchies are not as powerful as they once were: partly because of the changing composition of cultural capital, including, for example, the historically recent valorisation of Indigenous items. The cluster analysis, which more explicitly brought to the fore the groupings of taste patterns, demonstrated the mix of socio-demographic factors involved in defining clusters. These clusters (which, admittedly, are artefacts of analytical procedures around distinctions between notions of high, middle and popular tastes, and around distinctions between established/traditional and alternative/contemporary forms) affirm the role of class, but do not represent classed-defined 'taste cultures' (Bennett, Gayo & Pertierra, 2021, p. 144). When you look within clusters, the relationship between these things changes: in some fields it may be that class, age, education or gender – or some combination – dominates more in some clusters than in others. Shifting from an eight-class model to a three-class model brings the class dimensions of cultural practices and their relations to social inequalities into sharper relief – but it also brings into sharper relief a set of issues that need consideration, such as the temporal and social *trajectories* of capital accumulation, which are partly hidden by differentials in age, and so on. Looking at parents' education in relation to the clusters shows that while there are articulations between class and cultural capital, these are uneven, reflecting the fact that class positions are the result of distinct family histories of accumulation and transmission (or not) (Gayo & Bennett, 2021, p. 161).

The overarching lesson from the statistical analysis is that while class continues to be a significant feature of cultural practices, it is not simple nor direct, but marked by complexity, contradiction and ambiguity. Moreover, as Gayo and Bennett spell out, we must be super aware that the methodological decisions we make affect the categories we employ and how we interpret the data (2021, pp. 164–5). Sadly, statistical analysis – whether conventional or via MCAs and clusters – doesn't explain everything. It provides correspondence between social phenomena and factors, but causality is not always clear. We either leave it as is, or we have to engage in the work of interpretation.

'I Must Be the Contradiction to the Rule': A Classed Life

The emphasis on individuals' positions and trajectories above takes us to the role of class in the consideration of interviewees' accounts of their cultural practices. Robert was a 66-year-old man who had left school early and trained as a fitter and turner, then worked on the docks, before retraining as a graphic designer. He is now retired but works casually in the local tourist industry. He had a raft of handyman projects, and had been a keen photographer for many years. He lives with his wife in a large house in a comfortable part of a coastal area whose socio-economic profile is slightly higher than national averages. He identified as working class in the survey, and confirmed this 'very much so' in the interview, linking it to being 'a pinko'. Is it analytically adequate to take his self-identification as 'working class'? When we quote him in the book, we describe him as 'a 66-year-old retired graphic designer'. Is this adequate? The standard move in interview-based research is to bracket key demographic variables, but such forms of compression do not do justice to the life of the person. In the occupational class categories, we located him as lower management/professional, but this designation never seemed accurate given his only training was vocational, he was 'self-taught' as a designer and had not had tertiary education.

Robert's tastes do not conform to a simple pattern either. He spoke, for example, about his love of music – particularly ABC classic FM and older rock such as Van Morrison. He listened constantly to music while he worked in his shed. He also talked about his interest in art – he loves *Blue Poles* but has little artwork in his house, and doesn't even display his own photographs. But the most interesting thing about Robert is his longstanding passion for history, particularly in military and maritime history. He only seemed to read history books – things that were pragmatically related to what he was interested in at the time: he joked that he'd only ever read three novels in his lifetime. He also loves history and nature documentaries on TV, and lists *Lawrence of Arabia* as his favourite movie of all time. He is an avid ABC fan, but he also loves Australian Rules football. Yet he cited his favourite players for very distinct, non-sporting reasons: Brett Kirk, because he was Buddhist, and Adam Goodes, because of his stand on Indigenous issues and racism.

Robert's mix of middle-class and working-class tastes is not entirely unusual – many of our interviewees expressed similar combinations and the statistical analysis showed this as well. But his tastes were complex, and they plot oddly in the visualisations of taste patterns afforded by MCAs. In the 'cloud of individuals' Bennett and Gayo (2020, p. 106) developed based on survey results, Robert was often at some distance from the positions of the likes and dislikes he indicates in the survey and the interview. Of course, this could be the discrepancy in the representation of his survey responses (where people have to respond to items we have chosen) compared to an interview (where they can roam more widely), which is a reminder again of how positions are always an artefact of the methodologies employed to elicit and map them. But, as Bennett and Gayo (2020, p. 110) argue in discussing similarly discordant profiles, we have to guard against the tendency in some Bourdieusian research work to see taste preferences as representing a unified habitus determined by class location; we need, rather, to acknowledge the sometimes 'contradictory influences exerted by different aspects of individuals' social positioning'. Contradiction can be at the heart of people's tastes, and not just a curious anomaly. Being 'in the middle' is often seen as lacking distinctiveness, but in Robert's case it is probably because he had wide and divergent tastes, overlapping 'high-', 'middle-' and 'lowbrow', and he had a high degree of involvement in cultural pursuits.

These discordances in people's tastes might reflect the point Bourdieu makes about the different social trajectories that individuals (and social groups) experience over time. Bennett and Gayo (2020, p. 105) see this in class terms, but when asked about whether his tastes were typical for someone of his class background, Robert was perplexed: 'I don't really know to tell you the truth. I don't think I can really answer that. I don't know. I don't know'. Pressed on whether his interest in the art of Turner and Monet was typical amongst people of working-class origins he said, 'probably not ... I don't know where it comes from, you know. I sometimes wonder what makes a person, you know, like they are. I don't know'. And pressed on how he went from being a fitter and turner to becoming a graphic designer, he was similarly unsure:

> I don't know where it comes from. I think, you know, probably my mother, at an early age fostered my interest in drawing I suppose. So therefore, you know, you get an interest in art. So therefore you get an, you know, in doing your own art. Then an interest in other people's art.

Robert could see the issue was interesting but he couldn't explain it apart from a vague sense of family – but his mother was a seamstress and his father a sheet metal worker with no particular interests in art. Similarly with his obsession with history:

> I sometimes wonder what, you know, what creates it; what sets people to have these interests. As I say, you know, why at seven years old, you know, I was just fascinated, well, my – some of my older cousins had a history book and whenever we'd go to visit them the first thing I'd do was grab the history book and read it. So, you know, there was a natural progression then when, you know, Christmas rolled around I wanted a history book of my own. But then why did I, you know, go to ... the history book ...? I mean, dad used to also play cricket in the backyard. I was never really interested in playing cricket. We also, you know, played touch footy and all that sort of stuff and I was never interested in any of that.

Asked if attending a Catholic school had an effect in shaping that childhood interest in history, he said no, and added:

> In those days the catholic church had a lot of trouble coming to terms with a lot of its past history. I was reading history independently and being taught the Catholic version of history at school and it did get me into a little bit of confrontation with some of the … Brothers … because I would sort of say, 'Well, hang on a sec, that doesn't seem to, you know, be quite right'.

So, it did not come from his parents or his educators and yet seems to be central to his particular configuration of cultivated tastes. It also does not coincide with interests in other forms of reading, such as fiction. As Robert reflects, 'is it Jesuits who say, you know, "give me the child until they're seven and" …? Well, I guess, you know, I must be the contradiction to the rule'.

Here we have a further methodological and analytical problem: to capture these changes over time, we often have to rely on people's accounts of their classed (and otherwise) histories. And they do not remember. Class mobilities may be somewhat enigmatic, then, because they cannot be traced back to 'the moment'. There are some trajectories which Robert can explain. While he had played Rugby League as a young man, when his son wanted to play he said as a parent he found it too dangerous. So he switched his son to Aussie Rules under the influence of some 'ex-pat Victorians' 'down the road'. He became very involved in the club as parents often do, 'and I got to understand the game and got to, you know, see how it was played. It's that Australian element too that I really like'. And then he took on increasingly senior roles in the local club: 'So I was really actively involved in that and I just, I just loved it'. But this is more about life course than class – becoming a parent, looking after your children and then finding in it an enthusiasm. Or perhaps it is that the classed trajectory of his life is entangled with other forms of personal and social trajectory.

Conclusion: If Class Is the Answer, What's the Question?

Robert's account and the statistical analysis of class and taste both point out several issues around class. The former gives us a sense of the lived complexity of class lives, the second gives us a socially comparative perspective on the role of cultural practices in class positioning, and how this relates to the reproduction of inequalities. Neither conforms to a clear sense of a class theory, but they both, in particular ways, point towards elements of what I referred to in the opening sections as the contradictory and ambivalent nature of class. I have suggested, drawing on class theory, that this contradictoriness is a key aspect of an individual's social position and their life, so it needs to be central to class analysis, but also certain aporia, contingencies and ambiguities. I would go so far as to argue that there is often an enigmatic quality to class given this lived complexity; there is something always not open to explanation. The problem, however, is that class analysis often aims for a form of purification; a desire to reduce complexities to comprehensible and simple models of class and power. I understand this desire, but as scholars, we need to maintain that complexity in our analyses of social phenomena. Reduce complexity, by all means, when it is a useful function for public debate or classroom pedagogy, but only ever as a starting point, not an end in itself. Foregrounding this complexity is especially important if we are to fully understand the intersectional logics of a settler-colonial society such as Australia, immersed in a world transformed by transnationalism.

This returns us to the issue of what class models are 'for', and Wright, who asked, 'if class is the answer, what's the question?': 'specific definitions and elaborations of the concept of class … are shaped by the diverse kinds of question class is thought to answer' (Wright, 2005, p. 180). He identifies six such foci, but notes these are endless depending on empirical focus: distributional location, subjective salience, life chances, conflicts, historical change and emancipation. I would go further and argue that we have to constantly ask ourselves a series of questions:

- Are we interested in examining class or are we interested in using class to examine something else?
- Does class explain things, or is it the thing to be explained?
- What assumptions are built into our models of class, and what bits are left out?
- How does our methodology shape our findings?
- Are we 'measuring' class or using it heuristically?
- Are we trying to demonstrate class reproduction, or are we trying to situate the lived experiences of actors?
- Are we trying to capture class synchronically or diachronically?
- How do we build into our analyses the temporal and socio-spatial dimensions of class?
- Do we see class as destiny or as resource for living?
- How are (classed) trajectories affected by contingencies versus larger socio-structural factors?
- And, of course, how does the intersection with gender, race/ethnicity and so on reshape the classed nature of these trajectories?

Arguably, a productive and reflexive use of class asks more questions than produces answers. A Bourdieusian approach is attractive to me not because of the measurable and comparable quality of his statistical methods, but because he attempts to move away from a narrow 'group' sense of class to the idea of social space in which simple boundaries cannot exist; moreover, he develops a strong temporal sense of class in terms of trajectory and accumulation. But, most importantly, he argues that 'concepts have no definition other than systemic ones, and are designed to be *put to work empirically in systematic fashion*' (Bourdieu & Wacquant, 1992, p. 96). Often, however, the work they are put to do is to confirm our belief in the existence of the category as a thing. I am suggesting that it is important to mine the contradictory nature of class, and to reflect upon the stability of our categories. As Skeggs (2004, p. 5) argues, class analysis should 'aim to capture the ambiguity produced through struggle and fuzzy boundaries; rather than to fix it in place ... To ignore this is to work uncritically with the categories produced through this struggle'.

Endnotes

1 Especially the 'Friday group', to whom I am forever grateful.
2 My engagement with feminism and critical race theory was regrettably limited at the time for the same reason.
3 Bourdieu characterises this as a break with Marxism, but I believe it is possible to articulate the theoretical qualifications of Wright and others with the Bourdieusian project.
4 Where relevant, this data was used in conjunction with gender, but the complexities of the boost samples, where ethnicity, language, faith, generation and time since arrival intersected, made cross-tabs difficult (Noble, 2021).
5 The expertise of Modesto Gayo was invaluable in making sense of MCAs and cluster analysis.

References

Atkinson, W. (2015). *Class*. Cambridge: Polity.
Bennett, T., Carter, D., Gayo, M., Kelly, M., & Noble, G. (Eds.). (2021). *Fields, capitals, habitus: Australian culture, inequalities and social divisions*. London: Routledge.
Bennett, T., Dibley, B., & Kelly, M. (2021). Indigenous cultural tastes and capitals. In T. Bennett et al. (Eds.). *Fields, capitals, habitus: Australian culture, inequalities and social divisions* (pp. 224–246). London: Routledge.
Bennett, T., Emmison, M., & Frow, J. (1999). *Accounting for tastes: Australian everyday cultures*. Melbourne: Cambridge University Press.
Bennett, T., & Gayo, M. (2020). Liking Australian art, liking Australian culture. In T. Bennett, D. Stevenson, F. Myers, & T. Winikoff (Eds.), *The Australian art field: Practices, policies, institutions* (pp. 98–113). London: Routledge.
Bennett, T., Gayo, M., & Pertierra, A. (2021). The Australian space of lifestyles. In T. Bennett et al. (Eds.). *Fields, capitals, habitus: Australian culture, inequalities and social divisions* (pp. 119–146). London: Routledge.
Bennett, T., Savage, M., Silva, E., Warde, A., Gayo-Cal, M., & Wright D. (2009). *Culture, class, distinction*. London: Routledge.
Bourdieu P. (1984). *Distinction*. London: Routledge.
Bourdieu, P. (1985). Social space and the genesis of groups. *Theory and Society, 14*(6), 723–44.
Bourdieu, P. (1987). What makes a social class? On the theoretical and practical existence of groups. *Berkeley Journal of Sociology, 32*, 1–17.
Bourdieu, P. (1989a). The corporatism of the universal: The role of intellectuals in the modern world. *Telos, 81*, 99–110.
Bourdieu, P. (1989b). Social space and symbolic power. *Sociological Theory, 7*(1), 14–25.
Bourdieu, P. & Wacquant, L. (1992). *An invitation to reflexive sociology*. Chicago: The University of Chicago Press.
Connell, R.W. (1977). *Ruling class, ruling culture*. Cambridge: Cambridge University Press.

Connell, R.W. (1983). *Which way is up? Essays on sex, class and culture.* Sydney: Allen & Unwin.
Connell, R.W., & Irving, T. (1980). *Class structure in Australian history.* Melbourne: Longman Cheshire.
Gayo, M. and Bennett, T. (2021). Class and cultural capital in Australia. In T. Bennett et al. (Eds.) *Fields, capitals, habitus: Australian culture, inequalities and social divisions* (pp. 147–168). London: Routledge.
Noble, G. (2021). Cultural diversity and the ethnoscapes of taste in Australia. In T. Bennett et al. (Eds.). *Fields, capitals, habitus: Australian culture, inequalities and social divisions* (pp. 247–264). London: Routledge.
Poulantzas, N. (1978). *Classes in contemporary capitalism.* London: Verso.
Savage, M., Cunningham, N., Devine, F., Friedman, S., Laurison, D., McKenzie, L., Miles, A., Snee, H., & Wakeling, P. (2015). *Social class in the 21st century.* London: Pelican.
Sheppard, J., & Biddle, N. (2017). Class, capital, and identity in Australian society. *Australian Journal of Political Science, 52*(4), 500–516.
Skeggs, B. (2004). *Class, self, culture.* Routledge: London.
Thompson, E. P. (1963). *The making of the English working class.* London: Victor Gollancz.
Wacquant L. (2013). Symbolic power and group-making: On Pierre Bourdieu's reframing of class, *Journal of Classical Sociology, 13*(2), 274–291.
Williams, R. (1958). *Culture and society.* London: Chatto and Windus.
Wright, E.O. (1985). *Classes.* London: Verso.
Wright, E.O. (1997). *Class counts.* Cambridge: Cambridge University Press.
Wright, E.O. (2005). If 'class' is the answer, what is the question? In E.O. Wright (Ed.). *Approaches to class analysis* (pp. 180–192). Cambridge: Cambridge University Press.

CHAPTER 3

THE GREAT DIVIDE

Property Relations and the Foundational Dynamics of Settler-Colonial Society

Barry Morris

Introduction

The political foundations of Australia were of a totalising character. The early settler-colonial states took an extreme form as a penal colony, occupying territory under the doctrine of *terra nullius*, land owned by no-one. Political and economic power emerged from a colonial exploitation that took the form of dispossession through the wholesale expropriation of Indigenous lands. This chapter examines the emergence of colonial class dynamics in this context, focusing in particular on the emergence of a male and white elite capitalist class in relation to male convict labour. Rather than just focus upon pastoral expansion as a largely economic imperative, this chapter also brings attention to the moral and ethical mores of emergent social class relations. The penal colony existed as a hierarchical, disciplinary society, whereby governance was able to determine, effectively unchallenged, the social and legal conditions of the existence of all inhabitants. Privilege and power became concentrated in the patronage networks of a colonial governor, who oversaw appointment to official positions and land grants.

The colonial beneficiaries were propertied men engaging capitalist methods of land-extensive pastoral production. The pastoralists became the most powerful socio-political and economic social class in Australia seeking to imitate the British upper classes.

The Original Disciplinary Society

The Australian colonies formed a system of punishment that, concurrent with the subjugation and subordination of Indigenous peoples, was cemented with convicts' banishment through transportation and continued with a system of work as punishment. Convicts' treatment as a 'criminal class' to be reformed of their indolence and proclivity for crime assumed a more homogenous assemblage than actually existed. The penal colony's distinctive feature was the State's central role directly intervening and shaping the most intimate aspects of life of the criminal population. The State's role involved the inculcation of the habits of labour and the facilitation of marriage in the family, which reflected its totalising character from its inception. The reform of the convicts constituted the administrative and institutional conditions of the colony for as long as the shiploads of convicts arrived (Davidson, 1991). They were transported to the colony of New South Wales as punishment, but also as an experiment in redemption. What developed was a relationship between domestic governance 'exercised by the male head of the household and the government of the state that ... institutionalised male political rule' (Grimshaw et al., 1994, p. 4). The experiment for the colonial administration required detailed knowledge of the convicts, their names, origins, criminal records, age, size, weight height and the lashes inflicted (see Davidson, 1991, pp. 33–4). Daily life calibrated the moral retraining of this criminal class in the habits of reflection and industrious labour. As Reverend Samuel Smith stated in 1821, 'There must be a great deal of solitude, coarse food, a dress of shame, hard incessant, irksome, eternal labour, a planned and unrelenting exclusion of happiness and comfort' (cited Smith, 2002, p. 30). The penal colony provided the circumstance where this subordinate group's subjectivities were to be reconstituted.

Convict reform was constituted in gendered terms. Conformity to the institution of marriage and the family was of utmost concern to the colonial administrators. Gendered roles were assigned, as ex-convict Margaret Catchpole stated of herself and her female friends, 'we are free of all hard work' (Grimshaw et al., 1994, p. 50). The demands to reform intimate relations and familial ties fell on all convicts. However, for the reformers, family within marriage provided women their highest moral state of order in their domestic responsibility for socialising and civilising future generations. The penal colony's official returns constantly showed an 'illegitimacy problem' and low rates of female marriage amongst the convicts. Governor King (1806) reported that two-thirds of the births were illegitimate and only 395 of the 1430 female convicts were married (see Davidson, 1991, pp. 32–3). Illegitimacy rates were understood to reflect the sexual mores of the convicts and the depth of their immorality. The imperative for reform would determine not only its moral character, but also the productive future of the colony. The Reverend Marsden found 'damning evidence' of many convict women as 'concubines' (Grimshaw et al., 1994, pp. 51–2, 55–61). For Marsden, matrimony was the means to establishing domestic order in the colony between men and women, parents and their children (Grimshaw et al., 1994, p. 56). In his rendering of gender relations, women *naturally* control matters to do with the family and domestic life. The male convict's immorality was idleness that must be converted into productive industry. Through labour discipline responsibility could be inculcated. Such cultural beliefs and practices also underpinned the governance of Indigenous labour, familial ties and intimacies implemented later on segregated government reserves.

The penal colony's administration used whatever force, regulation and control to reform those under their control. In Australia, the concept of biopower could be said to be there from its inception (Foucault, 1981). However, power was repressive and negative – control over life achieved in public spectacles of executions and whippings. The flogging of convicts was an institutionalised practice of punishment and a public spectacle, staged, for instance, outside Hyde Park Barracks, the public centre of

Sydney Town (Smith, 2002, p. 32). Between 1830 and 1837, the number of floggings ordered by magistrates rose each year from 2985 to 5916 and the number of lashes rose from 12,433 to 268,013 (Smith, 2002, p. 32). Kociumbas estimates that in New South Wales between 1833 and 1837 some 25 per cent of the male convict population were 'flogged at least once a year, and that of these, most received close to fifty lashes' (2001, p. 158). Reform existed side by side with regimes of punishment inscribed on the body. Work remained central to reform the male convicts and punishment through floggings to maintain discipline and control of the convict system.

Convicted by the English and Irish courts, the transported population was more a loose-knit assemblage, a heterogeneous collection of diverse persons, occupations and origins. Transportation as individual offenders effectively stripped the convicts of their social ties. The policy occurred as Britain was undergoing economic and social change in the form of the industrial revolution. Sent to participate in what was seen to be a largely agricultural enterprise, surprisingly only 400 were farm labourers (Nicholas & Shergold, 1988, p. 68). When one includes 'ploughman, cowkeeper, dairyhand, herdsman, horsebreaker, reaper and shearer – the number approaches 2000 or just 12 per cent of the total male workers' (Nicholas & Shergold, 1988, p. 69). The survey conducted by Nicholas and Shergold (1988, p. 68) showed the working skills of the convicts, and the single largest group of men, some 4000, consisted of labourers, road, factory and farm labourers. The vast majority of convicts had urban-based skills. They were better educated than the 'average' English worker as 'three-quarters of the English convicts could read or read and write: the convicts' literacy was significantly higher than the average for all English counties (58 per cent)' (Nicholas & Shergold, 1988, p. 75). Paradoxically, while their skills related specifically to social conditions befitting urban-based society, convicts were ultimately deployed to serve the emerging pastoral economy and England's industrial manufacturing needs.

Commissioner Bigge's report into the penal colony sought to transform the direction of labour resources. He arrived in Sydney in 1819 to find convict men worked on the docks, the lumber yards and in the stone cutting gangs and brickyards building Sydney and its roads (Kociumbas, 2001, p. 150). Others worked labouring on government farms at Grose Farm, clearing and grubbing the land, erecting farmhouses and cultivating vegetables; at Longbottom, cutting and sawing timber; and one-third on government farms preparing maize and wheat crops (Kociumbas, 2001, pp. 150–1). Employers were heavily reliant on convict and ex-convict labour (94 per cent men and 69 per cent women) (Kociumbas, 2001, p. 155). The commissioner's report initiated a greater emphasis on pastoral endeavours. Bigge argued that the convict work system was failing because too many men were in government service, leaving too few to meet the labouring needs of the pastoral economy, to meet the increasing demand for wool by English manufacturers (Kociumbas, 2001, p. 151). Convicts in demand, such as carpenters and ploughmen, avoided reconsignment to 'up country', while those without useful skills found themselves dispatched to penal stations 'up country' or in chain gangs used for building roads (2001, p. 159). Bigge's report was pivotal in shifting State policies to those that gave impetus to reshaping the foundation of the colonies from a penal colony to a settler colony.

The redemptive experiment emerged in the flux of major social change where European forms of servitude were transforming themselves in England and in the Americas. In England the most servile condition, villeinage, which had bound men through heredity and custom transmitted from father to son, had almost ceased in England by the 18th century (Handlin, 1957, pp. 4–5). For those convicted of crimes or through poverty, the danger in England and in the colonies was of being sold off to the highest bidder and their labour sold over for a term (Handlin, 1957, p. 5). This involuntary servitude for the majority ultimately ended. The condition of the convicts in the Australian colonies was one of a range of forms of servitude practised in England and the colonies. For Handlin, in the United States of America, the transformation from forms of servitude to free labour contributed to the consolidation and intensification of slavery as conditioning the Black American experience, solidifying the racial divide between white and Black Americans (1957, pp. 21–2). The transition from servitude to free labour was neither unique to the Australian colonies, nor were the state-sanctioned predatory practices, the expropriation of Indigenous lands, that fed both settler-colonial and British-capital expansion.

Class in Emergent Settler-colonial Elites

When the British invaded Australia, the land was declared *terra nullius*, land owned by no-one, and, hence, the British government dispensed the land at its own convenience, dismissing the existence and rights of Indigenous peoples. The right to occupy land came through grants purchased or bestowed by the British government's representative. The annexing and occupation of new territories provided for the implementation of land-extensive capitalist production of commodities through expanded access to new resources, raw materials, labour markets and consumption needs. Unlike other colonial formations, settler colonialism is defined as a territorial undertaking in which imperialist possession of Indigenous lands operates as the 'proprietary anchor' of white supremacy and acquisitive capital expansion (Moreton-Robinson, 2015, p. 16). As Wolfe (2006) has asserted, existing Indigenous connection to such desired territories was an obstacle to be 'eliminated'. Land as property formed the basis for the emergence of a landowning capitalist class, which is crucial to understanding the histories of race/class formation. The accumulation of property followed violent dispossession. As Niel Black, western districts squatter and Victorian Legislative Council member, recalled:

> The best way [to procure a run] is to go outside and take up a new run, provided the conscience of the party is sufficiently seared to enable him without remorse to slaughter natives right and left. It is universally and distinctly understood that the chances are very small indeed of a person taking up a new run being able to maintain possession of his place and property without having recourse to such means – sometimes by whole sale … (9 December 1839) (MacKellar, 2008, pp. 107–8).

Where title through Indigenous systems of law, custom and original occupation pre-existed, as in Australia, access to land required the rule of force and not the rule of law. For the men of substantial landed property, the land provided the means not only for newly created wealth, but also the means to improve one's social ranking. The carnage of occupation was erased in the scramble for land and elevated social status from Britain.

The colonies provide a rare entrée into the creation of a colonial elite in which the status of birth, blood and rank could be reinvented. In the colonies, it was most commonly achieved by those of 'lower class and yeomanry origins' (Bolton, 1968, p. 326). This aspirational propertied class attached its cultural and moral moorings to Britain's aristocratic elite. Yet, their title to land was not by birth, but by purchase. Lacking aristocratic status, the colonial gentry was elevated, Denholm argues, to positions in an aristocratic form of governance:

> ... the early colonial governors selected particular settlers to fill the functions performed in England by the titled aristocracy and landed gentry. These expectations reflected several facts of English life: that the economy was basically landed: that much of the everyday functioning of power was kept tightly in the hands of the upper landed classes ... that education was the possession of the few... (1979, p. 164).

A diverse assemblage of squatters and professionals emerged broadly as a propertied class in the early colony through the autocratic exercise of the colonial governor's patronage, bestowing official positions and land grants. The 'effective measure of power was the amount of patronage that a man could dispense' (Denholm, 1979, p. 166). Power and influence were enmeshed in webs of patronage that radiated from the titular head of the colony.

This propertied class in Victoria involved 'a small group of land owners, officials, bankers and merchants whose interests relied in large measure on their relations with the government ... convict labour, government office and, above all, land leases and title were in the power of the government to regulate and bestow' (Boyce, 2012, p. 205). Economic power and wealth emerged out of land-extensive pastoral production of sheep, particularly wool, the colony's major export. Leisure and education were effectively dependent on wealth to provide access to civil service and administration. A fundamental step to colonial gentry status was for the colonial governor 'to bestow upon the settler the status of Esquire, honorary Justice of the Peace' (Denholm, 1979, p. 166). As magistrates, many squatters exercised considerable local authority to participate in colonial politics and serve their own economic interests. Power was both seen and exercised autocratically. As Denholm stresses, power and authority was visible, whether in the exalted title of esquire, a voting qualification based upon property, educational access to civil service; that is 'a particular historical manner in which that power was projected upon society' (1979, pp. 174, 176). This way of life stood in significant contrast to the movement to representative democracy and the more meritocratic impulses that supported political processes in which the ideology of power and privilege shifted from social origins to individual merit.

Blood ties of race and class were amplified in this antipodean colony. Social distinction took a 'sharper edge' because of the 'levelling principles which might be found among shopkeepers and proletarians of convict origin' (Bolton, 1968, p. 319). The emerging colonial gentry's status was compromised further by their subordinate relationship with England. The power and status of the titled aristocracy of Britain was based upon the agriculture-based manorial system that vested legal and economic power in the Lord of the Manor. The British manorial system was the organising principle of rural life, where land was divided between the demesne lands for the Lord's personal use and the land worked by his tenant farmers. Privileged status and wealth were connected with agriculture rather than pastoralism. Pastoral stations in the colonies held only derivative status and power. The landed gentry in the colonies held only leasehold land subject to renewal every eight to fourteen years (O'Malley, 1979, p. 275). Despite selected colonisers' performing roles reserved for hereditary titled nobles, aspirations for status and respectability were limited by the subordinate connection to Britain, which saw colonial status as second best. As Denholm emphasises:

While society remained colonial, the best that the emerging elite could be was an interesting appendage to the titled aristocracy and landed gentry of Great Britain and Ireland … it naturally suffered by comparison with its prestigious parent. It could even look ridiculous (1979, p. 171).

Status and power exercised for the emerging gentry was limited to local agency through its control of the Bench, military forces and civil service appointments. Derivative and, perennially, second best, imitation here subverts the identity of what is being represented, which is met not so much as a threat, but as a source of derision.

The issue for the colonial elite was to consolidate power. In the newly established colony of Victoria, patronage, as suggested earlier, secured influential positions in civil service, the legislative council and the magistrates' Bench, which required not only wealth, but also the leisure and educational requirement to fulfil honorary roles. The propagation of such status and control involved not simply economic and political dominance, but the social and cultural reproduction of the British class structure. Privilege and exclusivity were premised upon the traditions of the English landed gentry and its fee-paying Public School model. The property class, squatters and professionals, increasingly sent their sons to receive this same educational outcome as in Britain. Education was a mechanism to perpetuate rather than ameliorate the reproduction of class inequalities. The colonial elite 'distinguished themselves largely by the nature of education. In Melbourne, Adelaide and Sydney the 19th century saw the growth of great public schools on a pattern which, if derived from the British Public School tradition, was tailored effectively to meet the needs of boys designed for leadership in Australia' (Bolton, 1968, pp. 325–6). Exclusive religious schools offered a privileged education to the emerging social elite – King's School for Boys (1831), Sydney Grammar (1857), Newington College (1863). In Victoria these included Scotch College (1851), Geelong Grammar (1855), Melbourne Grammar (1855), Wesley College (1866) and Xavier College (1872). The Church of

England's King's School, Parramatta, Australia's oldest elite school, was founded by command of King William IV of England, to give the colony its next generation of leaders. The class status of the colonial gentry denoted men of 'good family'. Exclusive schools created a privileged social class that took on the visible signs of the English upper classes.

The establishment of the Melbourne Club (27 October 1838), strengthened and entrenched the exclusivity of the propertied classes. The founding members were squatters, civil servants, judges, professional men, merchants, military officers and police commissioners (McNicoll, 1988). The Melbourne Club created both a formal meeting place for the colony's male elite and a place to establish personal social networks and webs of mutual associations where the stratagems of patronage played out (see McNicoll, 1988). The colonial hierarchy involved the institutional advancement of an elite group based upon class privilege and wealth. The adoption of exclusive private institutions provided the infrastructure for the social reproduction of intergenerational family-based privilege. Educational institutions and private clubs were essential to create exclusivity. Such institutions instil the cultural practices and symbolic behaviour that involve codes of honour, manners of speech, accent, etiquette, leisure and organised styles of sport that set the colony's gentlemen apart. In the new colonies, the exclusivity of class was affirmed through fraternity and filiation. 'Titles, the veneration of landed estates, the hierarchical attitudes, the myth of gracious living' (Bolton, 1968, pp. 326–7) mimicked the British upper classes.

The Convict Taint

The economic and socio-political power of the squatters was grounded in pastoral expansion, reliant upon the convict system for labour. Convicts and ex-convicts, referred to as 'servants', provided the labour on the early pastoral frontiers in the eastern states. On this side of the social class divide, the convicts and the 'free' immigrant labourers were essentially controlled by a number of repressive acts of legislation. Such legislation mirrors the more intensive regimes of intervention imposed upon Indigenous communities through various state policies across Australia. State controls on physical movement, on work, on marriage existed alongside pedagogic 'retraining' programs implemented in segregated and supervised Aboriginal reserves and the specialised institutions created for the removal and control of Aboriginal children (Rowley, 1973; Morris, 1989; Haebich, 2000). To maintain control, the ruling elite adjusted their common political interests through legislation rather than direct force. In the case of convicts, even as they ended their sentences, under the *Sydney Police Act* (1833) convicts had to register with the courts if they moved from outside the colony to New South Wales (Davidson, 1991, p. 104). Such legislation worked in tandem with the *Masters and Servants Act* (1828), to enforce service and punished breaches in employment by employees, such as the servant leaving his employment before the agreed-upon time. The breaches were treated as criminal offences, which included hard labour and solitary confinement. In effect, the legislation governing the 'dangerous classes' was more repressive than in Britain. While this legislation was directed at the convict population, free immigrant labour was little better off (Davidson, 1991, p. 104). The legislation operated in the interests of the employer as the servant's freedom of movement relied on their relations with the employer and, cumulatively enforced, the legislation could keep them in perpetual servitude.

The subordinate status of the convicts, emancipists and ticket of leave convicts was exacerbated in the 1850s by the strident attempts by colonists to end the transportation of convicts from Britain. The strength of the anti-transportation movement highlighted the stigma that convicts and former convicts carried collectively. The continuing transportation of convicts was deemed to effectively condemn the colonists to ongoing disrepute and degradation. The leaders of the anti-transportation movement, the Australasian League, queried the British secretary of state, Earl Grey, in 1851:

> How is a great and enlightened nation to stand justified before God and man for rearing a second Sodom in the Southern Hemisphere (cited Serle, 1977, p. 126).

In this world, sin and evil provides a cultural logic for classifying, separating and ranking behaviours of both individuals and groups. Purity and impurity unify and divide social classes. The foundational presence of convicts is given an equivalence accorded the legendary 'wickedness' of the Old Testament's Sodom, which so offended God that its evil was purged by God's righteous violence. The convict's condemnation moved beyond their individual failure to live up to social laws and moral codes to be perceived to have had a collective effect on all colonists. Deputations to England followed and convict transportation to Van Diemen's Land ended in 1852 (Serle, 1977, p. 126). The situation was heightened as a consequence of gold being discovered in Victoria. The immediate danger of ex-convicts moving to Victoria was dealt with through the enactment of the *Convicts Prevention Act* (1852) (Serle, 1977, pp. 126–7). Such was the mobilisation and strength of feeling in the colony that Britain's opposition to the bill's draconian measures failed. Justice Redman Barry acknowledged the bill was full of 'harshness, injustice and severity', but if ex-convicts flocked to the Victorian goldfields, he added it 'would become the plague spot of the Globe' (Serle, 1977, p. 129). Convict status was 'regarded with revulsion, as polluted persons whom no respectable colonist ought to have in touching distance' (de Serville, 1991, p. 16). Bodily boundaries become extensions of social boundaries against contagion. The convicts and ex-convicts' caste-like status relegated them to the lowest rungs of white colonial society and repositioned them as not only impeding, but also contaminating the settler colonists and the colony's future.

A Laboratory of Democracy?

With the gold rushes came more meritocratic impulses that opposed such political processes and supported social democracy in which power and privilege sought to be established in terms of individual merit and not social origins. The meritocratic pursuit of policies through politics sought more egalitarian outcomes in the economy and education. This historical period marked major innovative changes to public politics, most importantly, the beginning of a socio-political transition from the politics of the sovereign to the politics of society (see Foucault, 1981, p. 137). The colony of Victoria separated from New South Wales in 1851 installing its own governor and Legislative Council. Simultaneously, political change accelerated demands for parliamentary forms of representative democracy, which were introduced into the new colony by 1855. Parliament now contained a Legislative Assembly, responsible to its citizens. State government involved two houses, the Legislative Assembly, which was designated as the seat of government and the Legislative Council, designated as a 'House of Review'. These reforms followed after the British parliament passed the *Australian Colonies Government Act* (1850), whereby the colonies became self-governing and moved towards representative government. In both New South Wales (NSW) (1853) and Victoria (1854), the formulation of constitutions framed the basis for parliamentary government. The reforms included the establishment of a bicameral system of parliament with an elected Legislative Assembly in both NSW and Victoria. Major innovations such as the secret ballot (1856) and manhood suffrage (1857) for the Legislative Assembly, were passed. (Members possessed freehold property worth £2000 (Serle, 1977, p. 148).) Australia 'was conceived as the most advanced laboratory for the democratic experiment in the English-speaking world' (Thompson, 1994, p. 11). These political and institutional reforms were drawn from the Chartists agenda, which had been too threatening and was rejected in England (Thompson, 1994, p. 11). Progressively, an assemblage of constitutional elements gradually crafted a representative democracy.

Nevertheless, the movement to representative democracy did not erase the pre-existing structures of socio-political and economic advantage of the squatter class. The initial benefactors were those people who were in parliament, the landed propertied classes. Direct political influence exercised through the Legislative Council, as a house of review, fortified the dominance of the propertied classes. (Members possessed freehold property worth £5000 and voters freehold property worth £1000 (Serle, 1977, p. 148).) Until the remuneration of parliamentary members (1870 in Victoria and 1889 in NSW), the parliament remained controlled by the wealthy propertied classes. Despite manhood suffrage, executive power in the colony remained in the house of review (see Thompson, 1994). In effect, the squatters continued to exercise significant influence on legislation and the parliamentary process in general. The politically powerful elite exercised considerable influence throughout the 19th century. They defended the foundations of their power and, in particular, sustained their opposition to measures directed at achieving greater egalitarian access to parliament. The ambiguous status of land tenure became a major political issue in the decades following parliamentary government. For the pastoralists, the parliament, particularly their hold on the Legislative Council, provided a forum to protect their land and convert from leasehold to freehold title (see McQuilton, 1979; O'Malley, 1979). In the newly established colony of Victoria, these political struggles rigidified class divisions involving agricultural smallholders and the squatters' land dominance.

Opposition to the squatters' continued dominance came from ex-gold diggers, urban land reformers and farmers, who established the Victoria Land League, demanding the new parliament bring in land reform (McQuilton, 1979, p. 25). The vision of the land reform involved the 'Chartist ideal of the yeoman farmer or small independent agriculturalist' and sought policies that directly threatened squatter interests, principally, the abolition of pastoral occupancy and free commonage on the runs (McQuilton, 1979, p. 25). Nevertheless, with access to capital, political influence and intimate knowledge and experience of the land, the squatters retained their dominant position. The *Nicholson Land Act* (1860) provided a boon for the squatters. As McQuilton stated:

> Over 80 per cent of them [squatters] had obstructed selection in a variety of ways ranging from purchase at auction, personal selection and the use of legal loopholes, to dummying and the corruption of local officials. Armed with detailed knowledge of the quality of land on their runs, occupying positions of power and influence at a local

level, and with ready access to capital, the squatters were willing and able to use all three to protect property they believed was rightfully their own (1979, pp. 27–8).

Land reform became the major political struggle between the two houses of parliament. Dramatic confrontations occurred with the formation of Victoria's second parliament. By 1864, of the estimated 1,833,000 acres of alienated land, the squatters secured 1,600,000 acres (McQuilton, 1979, pp. 27–8). The squatters' success was achieved not only by economic power, but by 'illegal' land activities such as 'dummying', making agreements with individuals to buy land that they would sell back to the squatters, and 'peacocking', buying all waterfront land and hence denying others access to rivers or lakes. This parliamentary fight was over the spoils of violently expropriated Indigenous lands. The squatters' and the selectors' competing interests to control Victoria's rural land resources ended in a one-sided victory for the former.

The pastoralists' successful move to convert leasehold to freehold title secured their economic power and affirmed their position of socio-political dominance in the colonies. This was not a colony that asserted a moral and ethical superiority to the Old World. The cultural anxieties and aspirations of displacement for this landed gentry resulted in an ambivalent relationship to Australia, because of their desire to conform to British upper-class customs and manners. For de Serville:

> Property was after all the economic prop of gentility. For gentlemen to have no title, no legal right, to the land they occupied was an intolerable ambiguity and the gentlemen squatters were prominent in the fight for security of tenure (1980, p. 43).

Cultural imperatives underpinned the securing of full title as well as economic and socio-political factors. The orientation of this colonial elite was of deference to Britain, not of breaking away.

Conclusion

So fundamental was securing land as property to embedding settler-colonial economic and social order that for pastoralists the pitiless destruction of pre-existing Indigenous peoples was a normative agenda. White possession required the dispossession of Indigenous peoples of their land (Moreton-Robinson, 2015). The legal fiction of *terra nullius* – land owned by no-one – rendered Indigenous peoples' 'propertyless'. It was not labour, but a violent expropriation of collectively inhabited Indigenous territories that settler-colonial regimes sought. For the squatter class, land-extensive production engaging commodity production for profit was crucial to their emergence as an economic and socio-political force. Yet, the capitalist development of pastoralism, the dominant economic export, intensified conformity to traditional norms and values transplanted from Britain's upper classes. Penal colony reforms were facilitated within a masculine economy of meaning that prescribed gender roles and hardened the separation between social classes into the propertied and propertyless. The fledgling pastoral economy was absolutely dependent on non-market forms of labour coordinated and supplied by the State. The distinction between free settlers, convicts and their descendants remained a critical part of the settler colony. Convict descent signified the lowest (non-Indigenous) rungs of the colonist's social order well after the end of transportation. The conservative socio-political structures continued the dominance of social and cultural processes aligned with appointments to administrative and legal structures of the colony that perpetuated an elite, male, white group whose progress was based on class privilege and landed wealth. The substantial landowners were essentially a capitalist class, which sought to change the *personnel* rather than the *functions* of the ruling class. In the early colonies, status was explicitly linked to socially ranked patronage networks that shaped the hierarchically ordered society. While the distribution may have been contingent, the norms about entitlements, rights and appropriate behaviours sought conformity with the British upper classes. The colonies provided a place to do well, a position of new status and power, but also a place of exile from Britain – the centre of culture and civilisation. The deracination the free settler colonists endured was compensated, at best, by the grafting of British culture and its institutions onto the Australian colonies.

References

Boyce, J. (2012). *1835: The founding of Melbourne and the conquest of Australia*. Collingwood: Black Inc.
Bolton, G. (1968). The idea of a colonial gentry. *Australian Historical Studies, 13* (51), 307–328.
Davidson, A. (1991). *The invisible state: The formation of the Australian State, 1788–1901*. Cambridge: Cambridge University Press.
de Serville, P. (1980). *Port Phillip gentlemen*. Melbourne: Oxford University Press.
de Serville, P. (1991). *Pounds and pedigrees: The upper class in Victoria, 1859–80*. Melbourne: Oxford University Press.
Denholm, D. (1979). *The colonial Australians*. Harmondsworth: Penguin Books.
Foucault, M. (1981). *The history of sexuality*, Volume One. Harmondsworth: Penguin Books.
Grimshaw, P., Lake, M., McGrath, A., Quartly, M. (1994). *Creating a nation 1788–1990*. Ringwood: McPhee Gribble.
Haebich, A. (2000). *Broken circles: Fragmenting Indigenous families, 1800–2000*. Fremantle: Fremantle Press.
Handlin, O. (1957). *Race and nationality in American life*. Boston: Doubleday Anchor Books.
Kociumbas, J. (2001). *The Oxford history of Australia, Possessions, 1770–1860*. Oxford: Oxford University Press.
MacKellar, M. (2008). *Strangers in a foreign land: The journal of Niel Black and other voices from the Western Districts*. Melbourne: the Miegunyah Press.
McNicoll, R. (1988). *Number 36 Collins Street: Melbourne clubs 1838–1988*. North Sydney: Allen & Unwin/Haynes book.
McQuilton, J. (1979). *The Kelly outbreak 1878–1880*. Melbourne: Melbourne University Press.
Moreton-Robinson, A. (2015). *The white possessive: Property, power and Indigenous sovereignty. Minneapolis:* Minnesota University Press.
Morris, B. (1989). *Domesticating resistance: the Dhan-Gadi Aborigines and the Australian state*. London: Berg.
Nicholas, S., & Shergold, P. (1988). Transportation as global migration. In S. Nicholas & P. Shergold (Eds.), *Convict workers: Reinterpreting Australia's past* (pp.28–39). Cambridge: Cambridge University Press.
O'Malley, P. (1979). Class conflict, land and social banditry, *Social Problems, 26* (3), 271–283.
Rowley, C.D. (1973). *Outcasts in white Australia*. Harmondsworth: Pelican Book.

Serle, G. (1977). *The golden age: a history of the colony of Victoria 1851–1861*, Melbourne: Melbourne University Press.

Smith, T. (2002). *Transformations in Australian art: The nineteenth century – landscape, colony and nation.* St Leonards: Craftsmen House.

Thompson, E. (1994). *Fair enough: Egalitarianism in Australia.* Sydney: University of New South Wales Press.

Wolfe, P. (2006). Settler colonialism and the elimination of the native, *Journal of Genocide Research*, 8(4), 387–409.

CHAPTER 4

SOME COMMENTS ON CLASS ANALYSIS

Mark Western

In this chapter,[1] I address three questions: What is class analysis? What are some important developments in recent class analysis? What are some ways forward? I will argue that class analysis explains who gets what and how, and thus helps understand social and economic inequality. Class powers come from the capacities individuals, groups and organisations have to mobilise different kinds of resources to secure advantages and maintain or usurp relations of power and inequality. Asset-based accounts are the key building blocks for analytically useful class concepts.

What is Class Analysis?

Class analysis attempts to explain inequality, who gets what, and how. Marx's (1948; Marx & Engels, 1952) political, historical and analytic writings focused on this question, as did Weber's (2020) short essays and more extensive analyses. Current class conceptions, especially those that define it in terms of assets or forms of capital (Adkins, Cooper, & Konings, 2019; Savage et al., 2015; Savage et al., 2013) frequently motivate their analyses this way. Even research that principally examines topics like class identity, attitudes, political behaviour, or day-to-day interactional practices that make class 'happen' in people's lives (Bottero, 2004; Devine, 1992; Devine, 2004; Emmison & Western, 1991; Emmison & Western, 1990;

Lareau, 2011; Phillips & Western, 2005), does so because these identities, politics and practices may help link class to inequality.

My approach has been heavily influenced by US sociologist Erik Olin Wright but also departs in some key respects. The elements of the framework that informs my class research are as follows:

1. The three most important concepts in class analysis are class structure, class formation and class inequality. Class structure is the foundational concept.
2. We can think about class analysis at micro- and macrolevels. Microlevel class analysis is about understanding how class structures position individuals and potentially create differences in attitudes, behaviours and distributional outcomes for them. Macrolevel class analysis examines how societal level institutions or attributes, like welfare state policy configurations or the distribution of national income, embody 'class content' or equivalently, reflect class processes. Most of my research has been microlevel but some has also combined levels to show how macrolevel factors influence microprocesses. One example is my research on comparative social mobility, which attempts to explain class mobility in different countries by a microlevel mobility theory 'refracted through' societal (macro) variations in welfare states and trajectories of capitalist development (Western, 1994; Western & Wright, 1994).
3. Class structures are structures of social positions, defined via relations of ownership and control of resources or assets that yield social advantages. These positions create potentials for attitudes, behaviours and unequal outcomes in relation to socially valued rewards like income, consumption, health and personal efficacy. The way I think about class structure draws on Wright (1985; Wright, 1997) but is also influenced by Savage (2015) and some readings of Bourdieu (1984; 1985; Weininger, 2005). By focusing on social relations in production and paid work it also shares a fundamental similarity with other 'employment-related' class

schemes such as those of John Goldthorpe (Erikson & Goldthorpe, 1992; Erikson, Goldthorpe, & Portocarero, 1979; Goldthorpe, Llewellyn, & Payne, 1980).

4. Class formation is the empirical realisation of class structures in social groupings and organised forms of class representation. However, while class structures may give rise to attitudinal, behavioural and organisational class formations, these are empirically contingent. Trade unions, political parties, forms of workplace organisation, and class communities have all contributed to organisationally represented and explicitly articulated class formations of this type (Eidlin, 2014). These class formations were not only class-structured (linked to different classes) but discursively framed in class terms. Recently the decline of trade unions and class-based parties (Weakliem & Western, 1999), new forms of work, such as temporary and gig work, and cultural and ideological narratives about individual identity have arguably undermined class formations (Eidlin, 2014)[2] and worsened macrolevel class inequality (Stansbury & Summers, 2020).[3]

5. The two primary causal mechanisms associated with class relations are exploitation and opportunity hoarding or its converse, social closure/or exclusion. Exploitation occurs when one class derives its economic welfare from the activities of another class (Roemer, 1982; Wright, 1998). Opportunity hoarding occurs when one class derives welfare by monopolising ownership or control of resources. Opportunity hoarding by one group typically implies social closure and exclusion against another and hence these mechanisms are two sides of the one coin (Massey, 2007; Tilly, 1998). I find opportunity hoarding and social closure most useful for class analysis. I do not find exploitation generally necessary or useful for developing class explanations.

6. Class relations do not comprehensively explain social variations in attitudes, behaviours and inequalities, which also reflect other enduring social relations, especially gender, race, ethnicity and

First People's status. Attitudes, behaviours and distributional inequalities also reflect life-course and longitudinal processes where individuals' lives are organised according to socially significant sequences such as infancy, early childhood, adolescence, and older adulthood in social environments like families, schools, workplaces and communities. Such arrangements are historically and politically formed (Baxter & Western, 2001) and help explain why class formation and class inequality differ in settings (countries or time periods) with similar class structures.

I next expand some of these ideas.

Class Structure in Class Analysis

My research usually starts with the concept of class structure often drawing on the work of Erik Wright (1985; 1997). Wright defined classes variably, but I have emphasised his definition in terms of assets that contribute to producing goods and services and yield income to asset holders. The three types of productive income-generating assets in capitalist societies are productive property, which is owned by the self-employed classes, and organisational resources, and occupational skills, which are controlled and mobilised by employees. Class positions are defined by ownership or lack of ownership/control of these assets. Employers own their own businesses and employ others, and the petty bourgeoisie own and work their own small businesses. Expert employees use and mobilise specific skills and bodies of knowledge. The professions, which regulate entry through credentialing, registration and certification are archetypal expert occupations, but so are technical occupations requiring advanced training and education. Managerial employees hold organisational positions that enable them to make organisational decisions, supervise others and exercise delegated authority on behalf of employers and business owners. Workers do not exercise managerial authority or use knowledge and skills that are tightly formally regulated and socially and symbolically rewarded.

Relationships of ownership and control of these assets define class locations which researchers measure at different levels of granularity (for instance by distinguishing large and small business owners or upper and lower managers). The number of class locations depends on how many distinctions researchers introduce but these decisions are somewhat arbitrary and I am not aware of analyses where the level of asset ownership as opposed to its presence or absence matters.

Wright's conception (1985; 1997) involves a hierarchy of assets. The primary class distinction under capitalism is between owners and non-owners of productive property, which in empirical work, usually operationalises as the distinction between self-employed business owners and employees. Secondary distinctions follow for the self-employed around the number of employees (which proxies the size or scale of property ownership). Among employees the secondary distinctions relate to control of occupational skills and managerial authority rights.

Wright emphasises productive property before occupational skills and managerial authority as the pre-eminent capitalist class relation because capitalism is defined by private ownership and control of economic assets and the sale and purchase of labour. The gains from private capital ownership go to capital owners (capitalists), the gains from the sale of labour to employees. Linking class relations to the economic logic behind the production of goods and services is a core element of classically informed class analysis from Marx and Weber, through contemporary accounts like Wright (2009) and Goldthorpe (Erikson et al., 1979; Erikson, Goldthorpe, & Portocarero, 2010; Goldthorpe, 1981, 1982, 2016). From this perspective, economic relationships enabling production define classes and the logical analytic connections between class, class formation and inequality come from empirical connections between productive activity, paid employment and income generation (Breen, 2005; Goldthorpe, 2000a, 2000b). Developments in production, the division of labour and relevant institutions also explain changing processes and patterns of class inequality. This focus on economic relations and employment distinguishes classical class analysis from other contemporary resource and asset-based accounts, for example, Adkins et al. (2019) and Butler and Savage (2013).

Actually-existing capitalism is, of course, more complex. Hall & Soskice (2001) for example, distinguished liberal market economies (e.g., US, UK, Australia, New Zealand) from coordinated market economies (Germany, Sweden, Japan) by centralisation or decentralisation of industrial relations, the extent to which vocational training and education systems are coupled to jobs and industries, and variations in corporate governance and interfirm relations. From my perspective, these differences, differences in welfare state regimes (Deeming, 2017; Esping-Andersen, 1990) and other macroinstitutional variations are contingent features which shape empirical variations in class structures, class formation and class inequality.

Using national surveys of the adult population from 1986 to 2014, I show the Australian class structure according to Wright's conceptualisation (Table 1). These distributions are for individuals who receive an income from paid work. I could include others such as retirees and the unemployed, or present the class structure of households rather than working individuals. I could also look longitudinally at the different class locations individuals occupy over the life course.

Table 1. Class Distributions for Women and Men, Australia, 1986–2014
(column percentages)

Class	1986 Women (n=526)	1986 Men (n=669)	1995 Women (n=529)	1995 Men (n=733)	2005 Women (n=502)	2005 Men (n=474)	2014 Women (n=656)	2014 Men (n=640)
Employers	4	6	5	9	6	10	9	11
Petty Bourgeoisie	6	11	6	12	6	16	3	8
Expert Managers	15	20	22	26	20	17	13	15
Managers	19	17	9	14	10	13	18	15
Experts	11	7	23	16	16	11	16	13
Workers	45	39	36	24	41	33	41	39

Source: Western, J.S. et al., 2018; Kelley et al., 2019; Western, M.C. et al., 2018; Western et al. 2016

Between 1986 and 2014 about 10 to 12 per cent of women have been self-employed (employers or petty bourgeoisie), while the number of self-employed men has varied between about 17 and 20 per cent, apart from in 2005, where it is 26 per cent (Table 1). Between about 40 and 45 per cent of men are in 'middle class' locations (expert managers, managers and experts), apart from 1995, where the survey report is higher. Between 45 and 49 per cent of women are in these locations, apart from 1995. Working-class men are about 33 to 39 per cent of the male workforce, and working-class women are about 40 to 45 per cent of the female workforce. Again the 1995 figures are discrepant.[4]

These figures suggest reasonable stability in class distributions over time. The index of dissimilarity comparing the 1986 distribution to the 2014 distribution is 0.1 (or ten per cent) for women and men. This means that 10 per cent of women would need to be in a different class location in either 1986 or 2014 for the two distributions to be identical. The same is true for men. This simple analysis ignores other compositional issues within and between classes, such as the occupation, industry or public/private sector spread, unionisation, or the nature of employment contracts, but the initial impression is of reasonable stability of the overall class structure. The table also ignores occupational, industry and organisational sex-segregation (Workplace Gender Equality Agency, 2019) which further structure the class experiences of women and men.

I have previously used Wright's concept to develop a theory of income inequality between classes based on economic rents (Western, 1991). Economic rents are disproportionate income returns that exceed the cost of producing or bringing about the labour of individuals (Sørensen, 2000). The mechanisms linking class membership to income vary. Employers set their own income levels as one of the property rights of capital ownership. Managers occupy decision-making positions and employers need to promote managers' loyalty and discourage managerial turnover. Their positional power enables managers' income claims. Top managers in large organisations also derive capitalist-like income, such as bonuses and stock options, in addition to salary. Expert rents occur because entry to expert jobs is restricted by formal educational requirements that drive up the costs of expert labour (Western, 1991). Managers' rents describe similar mechanisms as efficiency wages (Katz, 1986) while expert rents are a form of monopoly rent. My early work used the idea of economic rents to explain point-in-time income differences between individuals in different classes (Western, 1991; see also Morgan & McKerrow, 2004; Morgan & Tang, 2007). I have also developed a theory of class-segmented labour markets to show how expertise and managerial authority enable different earnings trajectories and profiles over a working life (Western, 2020).

One difficulty with the concept of a 'rent' is that it implies a counterfactual 'true value' – what someone would earn without the rent. For economists this is typically a market-clearing wage for employees in a perfectly competitive labour market. This is difficult to determine theoretically and empirically so the rent is also difficult to determine. Rather than employment rents I now prefer to talk about class-based earnings capacities to realise income based on positional advantages associated with property ownership, managerial authority and expert skills. These positional advantages are different forms of opportunity hoarding and closure (Western, 2020).

Newer Asset-based Class Models

Wright's concept of class structure hinges on productive assets. Productive property (and property in general) is also a source of wealth. In more recent accounts, privately owned property assets, especially houses, define classes (Adkins et al., 2019; Woodman, 2020). The authors motivate their approach by noting that while house prices have consistently increased over time, employment incomes have stagnated, resulting in a new logic of inequality. In particular, 30 years of rising house prices supported by financial deregulation, the liberalisation of housing credit, negative gearing and reductions on capital gains tax have built 'upward momentum' (Adkins et al., 2019, p. 6) into the housing market. In contrast employment earnings have stayed flat, locking many out of home ownership and forcing younger home buyers to rely on parental financial support rather than employment savings. Economic inequality is driven by asset ownership rather than production and employment resulting in a new class scheme with major classes – investors, outright home owners, home owners with mortgages, renters, and the homeless (Adkins et al., 2019), subdivided by whether they also receive employment income, have investment properties, and receive social welfare payments.

This work potentially identifies a new important basis of life-course inequality. Wealth is more unequally distributed than income and the family home is most people's largest asset. However, from the conventional view, it is not clear why home ownership and associated inequality entails a new class logic rather than a separate inequality process. Housing and productive property are part of the stock of wealth and subject to capital gains and losses but residential housing (rather than investment housing) does not generate an income stream over the life course as productive assets do. It is possible to talk about imputed rent – the rent a homeowner would pay to live in their house – as an income return to a residential property but this does not necessarily translate into differences in realisable income for home owners. Investment property ownership generates income (rent) but housing property investors who live on investment income are analogous to other property owners, such as shareholders or employers who live off property incomes.

The empirical argument that housing has become the primary financial asset driving economic inequality among individuals and households (Adkins et al., 2019) also appears unfounded. Employee income is the main source of income for nearly 80 per cent of individuals, and is also the highest median source of income (Australian Bureau of Statistics, 2020) while median investment income for individuals (which includes rent) is less than $200 per year (Australian Bureau of Statistics, 2020, Graph 1).

Investment property generates income and is arguably a stronger basis for defining class than residential housing. However, more than 80 per cent of investment properties are owned by home owners who are predominantly self-employed, professionals, managers and skilled trade workers (Yanotti, 2017) looking for a secondary income source. And while new home buyers increasingly rely on financial assistance from parents, parent's employment class is a major determinant of intergenerational financial transfers to children (Huang, Perales, & Western, 2021). Buying a house is therefore a process that class enables rather than a new class logic. That said, housing inequality is worsening and linking these processes to class and other (for example, gender and life-course stage) inequality dynamics is an important research area (Christophers, 2021).

Other asset-based approaches are associated with Pierre Bourdieu. In his early work Bourdieu (1985) defined class locations in terms of amounts and types of economic (productive property), cultural (competence with cultural goods and resources) and social (social connections and networks) capital. Building on these ideas Savage et al. (2013; 2015) proposed a multidimensional class scheme from individuals' economic, social and cultural resources. Savage et al. (2013) justify these resources by saying that class schemes like those of Wright (1997) and Erikson and Goldthorpe (1992) do not incorporate social differentiation associated with identities, cultural behaviours and social activities, which also matter for inequality.

To measure class multidimensionally Savage et al. (2013) use survey questions assessing social connections, cultural behaviours (leisure, music, eating and holiday preferences) and economic resources (household income, savings and house price). This gives measures of economic, social and cultural capital which the researchers use to classify people into classes. The approach yields different class schemes (i.e., sets of classes) because different statistical solutions are possible. Researchers choose among these. Savage et al. (2015, 2013) select a seven-class solution: an elite, established middle class, technical middle class, new affluent workers, traditional working class, emergent service workers and precariat. Each class has different economic, social and cultural capital.

Sheppard and Biddle (2017) have similarly identify six classes in Australia: established affluent, emerging affluent, established middle, new workers, ageing workers and precariat. To interpret their classes Biddle and Sheppard examine not only their average economic, social and cultural resources but characteristics such as age, gender, education, household income, occupation and parents' employment and occupation.

This approach differs from mine in several respects. First the authors combine social and cultural characteristics into the class definition because class is supposed to explain identity, lifestyle, and social interaction. By design this combines in one concept what I refer to as class structure and class formation (Savage et al., 2015). Second this approach gives rise to classes that are not theoretically defined in advance but inductively derived from the sample, data and algorithm. These classes are always 'formed'; they combine structural or objective characteristics with behavioural and attitudinal phenomena. This assumes away questions about contingent relationships between class structure and class formation. The approach also produces class models which depend entirely on the data, method and researchers' choices about input variables and the preferred solution. In this context it is not clear what comparative analysis means. Sheppard and Biddle (2017, p. 5) acknowledge this point themselves. If two analyses give different class models, how do we compare them or their relationships to other phenomena, and what does this tell us about class in the world beyond our data?

The method also imposes practical and analytic difficulties. If for instance we want to examine social mobility, a central topic in class analysis (Breen, 2004), by relating the class of parents to those of their offspring, we need detailed economic, social and cultural information about parents and their adult children to derive class schemes for each and examine their relationships. This is extremely data demanding. It also introduces new complications because there is no guarantee that parent and offspring class schemes will be the same.[5] A bedrock assumption of social mobility research is that the categories for parents and children are the same (Hout, 1983), otherwise concepts like changing classes, staying in the same class, moving up, down or sideways, make no sense.[6]

Sheppard and Biddle (2017) recognise some of these issues and address them by looking at the occupational composition of their classes, saying this allows them to validate their classes through post-hoc comparisons with employment-related variables. However, this validation only makes sense if the occupation and employment variables are validation benchmarks. If they are, much of the theoretical argument for the new approach, that it captures a new class logic that has superseded the old, falls away.

Future Directions

My primary objections to these new approaches relate to calling them class processes, the conflation of class structure and formation, the inductive empirical methods, and the overemphasis on housing assets. But there are also many valuable ideas. Social and cultural resources are real sources of advantage alongside economic assets. Cultural capital allows people to define situations, and provides signals that others interpret and evaluate. Some signals attract esteem, opportunities and rewards, while others invite disparagement (Vassenden & Jonvik, 2019). Perceptions, performances and evaluations of cultural competence and 'suitability' matter significantly in interactions and settings where economic and social advantages are secured or lost. Social capital likewise allows individuals to access resources through their networks and connections and is directly linked to processes of inequality and social and economic attainment (Huang & Western, 2011; Lin, 2001). We can endorse the idea of multidimensional capitals as further supplementing the study of inequality, while also objecting to the methods used to obtain classes (Savage et al., 2015).

The newer approaches also identify one form of exclusion that classical class analysis largely ignores, complete exclusion from the labour market or at best, very marginal, insecure and poorly rewarded paid employment. For Sheppard and Biddle (2017) drawing on Standing (2016), this is likely to be the precariat. I also believe that individuals and households who experience medium to long-term labour market exclusion occupy a distinct social group that is potentially class-like. Long-term labour market exclusion whether from repeated spells of unemployment, one or more spells of long-term unemployment, or persistent very low-paid, insecure employment, is exclusion from the fundamental productive asset in capitalism, a decent paying job. It needs to be incorporated in class analysis. The difference between this group and other classes is the temporal requirement. Labour market exclusion needs to be relatively long-lasting to be a class phenomenon. Many individuals experience a period of low pay, or short-term unemployment, often as the result of life-course processes, without enduring consequences for their life chances or inequality. To say that anyone experiencing unemployment or low pay, no matter how fleeting, is part of the precariat, or some other term connoting the most excluded dilutes the core insight about the severity of labour market exclusion in capitalism.

The most important issue is not whether new asset approaches are 'class analysis'. They identify potential mechanisms and processes of inequality that complement classical class analysis and focus attention on processes that may be supplanting or transforming class processes. New forms of asset-based inequality invite questions like the following: How are classical classes related to social formations built around other assets? How do class and other asset relationships matter for social and economic inequality? How are people's life chances influenced by these processes? Are classical assets-based mechanisms weakening while new asset-based processes are becoming more significant? These questions define an important agenda for inequality studies regardless of whether we use the word 'class' to describe this agenda.

Endnotes

1. I thank Sonia Pervin for her research assistance.
2. Attitudinal, behavioural and organisational class formations can exist even if 'class' is not a salient cultural or discursive category, if members of different classes have distinctive ways of thinking about themselves and others.
3. Stansbury and Summers (2020) do not use this terminology but argue that income has been redistributed from workers to capital owners because of similar processes.
4. There are small measurement differences across surveys which introduce some non-comparability and may account for some of this variability.
5. A researcher can force the algorithm to extract the same number of classes for parents and their offspring, if they have comparable variables for each, but this is not required.

6   Such an approach could radically transform mobility studies. Rather than modelling over time movement between classes with the same sets of categories, we could potentially investigate over time movement between two different class schemes, in which categories themselves vary. While novel, it is hard to see how this could yield a coherent research foundation.

References

Adkins, L., Cooper, M., & Konings, M. (2019). Class in the 21st century: Asset inflation and the new logic of inequality. *Environment and Planning A: Economy and Space, 53*(3), 1–25.

Australian Bureau of Statistics. (2020). Personal income in Australia. Retrieved from https://www.abs.gov.au/statistics/labour/earnings-and-work-hours/personal-income-australia/latest-release

Baxter, J., & Western, M.C. (Eds.). (2001). *Reconfigurations of class and gender*. Stanford: Stanford University Press.

Bottero, W. (2004). Class identities and the identity of class. *Sociology, 38*(5), 985–1003.

Bourdieu, P. (1984). *Distinction: A social critique of the judgement of taste*. Cambridge, Massachusetts: Harvard University Press.

Bourdieu, P. (1985). The social space and the genesis of groups. *Theory and Society, 14*(6), 723–744. doi:10.1007/BF00174048

Breen, R. (2004). *Social mobility in Europe*. New York: Oxford University Press.

Breen, R. (2005). Foundations of a neo-Weberian class analysis. In E.O. Wright (Ed.), *Approaches to class analysis* (pp. 31–50). New York: Cambridge University Press.

Butler, T., & Savage, M. (Eds.). (2013). *Social change and the middle classes*. London and New York: Routledge.

Christophers, B. (2021). Class, assets and work in rentier capitalism. *Historical Materialism, 29*(2), 3–28. doi: https://doi.org/10.1163/1569206X-29021234

Deeming, C. (2017). The lost and the new 'liberal world' of welfare capitalism: A critical assessment of Gøsta Esping-Andersen's *The Three Worlds of Welfare Capitalism* a quarter century later. *Social Policy and Society, 16*(3), 405–422.

Devine, F. (1992). Social identities, class identity and political perspectives. *The Sociological Review, 40*(2), 229–252.

Devine, F. (2004). *Class practices: How parents help their children get good jobs*. Cambridge, New York: Cambridge University Press.

Eidlin, B. (2014). Class formation and class identity: Birth, death, and possibilities for renewal. *Sociology Compass, 8*(8), 1045–1062.

Emmison, M., & Western, M.C. (1990). Social class and social identity: A comment on Marshall et al. *Sociology, 24*(2), 241–253.

Emmison, M., & Western, M. (1991). The structure of social identities. In J.H. Baxter, J.M. Emmison, J.S. Western, & M.C. Western (Eds.), *Class analysis and contemporary Australia* (pp. 279–305). Melbourne: Macmillan.

Erikson, R., & Goldthorpe, J.H. (1992). *The constant flux: A study of class mobility in industrial societies*. New York: Clarendon Press.
Erikson, R., Goldthorpe, J.H., & Portocarero, L. (1979). Intergenerational class mobility in three western European societies: England, France and Sweden. *The British Journal of Sociology, 30*(4), 415–441.
Erikson, R., Goldthorpe, J.H., & Portocarero, L. (2010). Intergenerational class mobility and the convergence thesis: England, France and Sweden. *The British Journal of Sociology, 61*, 185–219.
Esping-Andersen, G. (1990). *The three worlds of welfare capitalism*. Princeton: Princeton University Press.
Goldthorpe, J.H. (1981). The class schema of social mobility and class structure in modern Britain: A reply to Penn. *Sociology, 15*(2), 272–280.
Goldthorpe, J.H. (1982). On the service class, its formation and future. In A. Giddens & G. Mackenzie (Eds.), *Social class and the division of labour* (pp. 162–185). Cambridge: Cambridge University Press.
Goldthorpe, J.H. (2000a). *On sociology: Numbers, narratives, and the integration of research and theory*. Oxford, UK: Oxford University Press.
Goldthorpe, J.H. (2000b). Rent, class conflict, and class structure: A commentary on Sørensen. *American Journal of Sociology, 105*(6), 1572–1582.
Goldthorpe, J.H. (2016). Social class mobility in modern Britain: changing structure, constant process. *Journal of the British Academy, 4*, 89–111.
Goldthorpe, J.H., Llewellyn, C., & Payne, C. (1980). *Social mobility and class structure in modern Britain*. New York: Oxford University Press.
Hall, P.A., & Soskice, D.W. (2001). *Varieties of capitalism: The institutional foundations of comparative advantage*. Oxford: Oxford University Press.
Hout, M. (1983). *Mobility tables*. Beverly Hills, Newbury Park, California and London: Sage Publications.
Huang, X., & Western, M. (2011). Social Networks and occupational attainment in Australia. *Sociology, 45*(2), 269–286.
Huang, Y., Perales, F., & Western, M. (2021). The long arm of parental advantage: Socio-economic background and parental financial transfers over adult children's life courses. *Research in Social Stratification and Mobility, 71*, 100582.
Katz, L.F. (1986). Efficiency wage theories: a partial evaluation. *NBER Macroeconomics Annual, 1*, 235–276.
Kelley, J., Bean, C., & Evans, M.D.R. (2019). National social science survey, 1995/96. ADA Dataverse, V1. doi:10.26193/R70QJY
Lareau, A. (2011). *Unequal childhoods class, race, and family life* (2nd ed.). Berkeley: University of California Press.
Lin, N. (2001). *Social capital: A theory of social structure and action*. Cambridge, UK: Cambridge University Press.
Marx, K. (1948). *The eighteenth Brumaire of Louis Bonaparte*. Moscow: Foreign Languages Publishing House.
Marx, K., & Engels, F. (1952). *Manifesto of the Communist party*. Moscow: Foreign Languages Publishing House.

Massey, D.S., & Russell Sage Foundation. (2007). *Categorically unequal: The American stratification system*. New York: Russell Sage Foundation.

Morgan, S.L., & McKerrow, M.W. (2004). Social class, rent destruction and the earnings of Black and White men, 1982–2000. *Research in Social Stratification and Mobility, 21*, 215–251.

Morgan, S.L., & Tang, Z. (2007). Social class and workers' rent, 1983–2001. *Research in Social Stratification and Mobility, 25*(4), 273–293.

Phillips, T., & Western, M. (2005). Social change and social identity: Postmodernity, reflexive modernisation and the transformation of social identities in Australia. In F. Devine, M. Savage, J. Scott, & R. Crompton (Eds.), *Rethinking class: Culture identities and lifestyles* (pp. 163–185). Basingstoke: Palgrave Macmillan.

Roemer, J.E. (1982). *A general theory of exploitation and class*. Cambridge: Harvard University Press.

Savage, M. (2015). *Social class in the 21st century*. London: Pelican.

Savage, M., Devine, F., Cunningham, N., Friedman, S., Laurison, D., Miles, A., Snee, H., & Taylor, M. (2015). On social class, Anno 2014. *Sociology, 49*(6), 1011–1030.

Savage, M., Devine, F., Cunningham, N., Taylor, M., Li, Y., Hjellbrekke, J., Le Roux, B., Friedman, S. & Miles, A. (2013). A new model of social class? Findings from the BBC's Great British Class Survey experiment. *Sociology, 47*(2), 219–250.

Sheppard, J., & Biddle, N. (2017). Class, capital, and identity in Australian society. *Australian Journal of Political Science, 52*(4), 500–516.

Sørensen, A.B. (2000). Toward a sounder basis for class analysis. *The American Journal of Sociology, 105*(6), 1523–1558.

Standing, G. (2016). *The precariat: the new dangerous class* (revised ed.). Bloomsbury Academic.

Stansbury, A., & Summers, L.H. (2020). *The declining worker power hypothesis: An explanation for the recent evolution of the American economy* (27193). Retrieved from https://www.nber.org/system/files/working_papers/w27193/w27193.pdf

Tilly, C. (1998). *Durable inequality*. Berkeley: University of California Press.

Vassenden, A., & Jonvik, M. (2019). Cultural capital as a hidden asset: Culture, egalitarianism and inter-class social encounters in Stavanger, Norway. *Cultural Sociology, 13*(1), 37–56.

Weakliem, D.L., & Western, M. (1999). Class voting, social change, and the left in Australia, 1943–1961. *The British Journal of Sociology, 50*(4), 609–630.

Weber, M. (2020). Class, status and party. In R. Swedberg (Ed.), *Essays in economic sociology* (pp. 83–95). Princeton: Princeton University Press.

Weininger, E. (2005). Foundations of Pierre Bourdieu's class analysis. In E.O. Wright (Ed.), *Approaches to class analysis*. Cambridge: Cambridge University Press.

Western, J.S., Boreham, P., Emmison, M., & Marks, G.N. (2018). Social structure of Australia project, 1986. ADA Dataverse, V1. doi:10.26193/EB4KZQ

Western, M.C. (1991). The process of income determination. In J. Baxter, M. Emmison, J. Western, & M. Western (Eds.), *Class structure in contemporary Australia*. Melbourne: Macmillan.

Western, M.C. (1994). Intergenerational class mobility among women and men. *The Australian and New Zealand Journal of Sociology, 30*(3), 303–321.

Western, M.C. (2020). *Class segmented labour markets in Australia.* Unpublished paper.

Western, M.C., Baxter, J.H., Pakulski, J., Tranter, B., & Western, J.S. (2018). Neoliberalism, inequality and politics: Public policy and the transformation of Australian society, 2005. ADA Dataverse, V1. Doi:10.26193/RSVYVG.

Western, M.C, Huang, X., Bian Y. Li, Y., & Huang, Y. (2016). National survey on social networks and subjective wellbeing in Australia (AuSNet Survey), 2014. Computer file, Institute for Social Science Research, The University of Queensland.

Western, M.C., & Wright, E.O. (1994). The permeability of class boundaries to intergenerational mobility among men in the United States, Canada, Norway and Sweden. *American Sociological Review, 59,* 606–629.

Woodman, D. (2020). Generational change and intergenerational relationships in the context of the asset economy. *Distinktion: Journal of Social Theory,* 1–15.

Workplace Gender Equality Agency. (2019). *Gender Segregation in Australia's Workforce.* Canberra: Australian Government.

Wright, E.O. (1985). *Classes.* London: Verso.

Wright, E.O. (1997). *Class counts: Comparative studies in class analysis.* Cambridge: Cambridge University Press.

Wright, E.O. (1998). Exploitation, identity, and class structure: A reply to my critics. In E.O. Wright (Ed.), *The debate on classes.* London, UK: Verso.

Wright, E.O. (2009). Understanding class: Towards an integrated analytical approach. *New Left Review, 60*(1), 101–116.

Yanotti, M. (2017). Three charts on: who is the typical investor in the Australian property market? *The Conversation.* Retrieved from https://theconversation.com/three-charts-on-who-is-the-typical-investor-in-the-australian-property-market-81319

Part 2

Class, Labour and Employment

CHAPTER 5

RETHINKING CLASS THROUGH THE HISTORY OF PROFESSIONS

Hannah Forsyth

In recent times, class behaviour in Australian politics, as elsewhere, has seemed confused. In the face of neoliberal economic reforms, the 'moral middle class', as political historian Judith Brett saw them originally underpinning the conservative Liberal Party, transferred their moral fervour to issues supported by Labor or the Greens. The working class, by contrast, transferred some allegiance to climate-change-denying capitalists (Brett, 1993; McDougall, 2019). These developments had melodramatic parallels internationally. After the 2015 Brexit vote in the UK and the 2016 election of Donald Trump in the USA, Terry Irving (2017), co-author of *Class Structure in Australian History* (1980), expressed a certain bitterness over what was now a four-decades long debate:

> So class is part of the zeitgeist again, as it was in the 1970s … [before] the twin 'turns' were foisted upon us all – the neo-liberal turn of Thatcher and Reagan … and the cultural turn … which saw a generation of liberal scholars burbling on about the terrible injustice of failing to recognise minority identities.

I was taught by the 'burbling' scholars of the cultural turn, who sought something new, in contrast to the radical nationalist tradition that once dominated Australian historiography. Materialist historians such as Brian Fitzpatrick, Geoffrey Serle and Russel Ward had situated working-class life at the centre of Australia's historical development. After the cultural turn, class was still important, though for new generations of Australian historians like Marilyn Lake, Richard White, Greg Dening and Tom Griffiths there were new questions to ask about oppression, marginalisation, cross-cultural encounters, environmental degradation and inequality. As well as understanding the ways particular actors deployed discursive forms of power, these historians also explored the ways that groups and individuals resisted economic and social structures. This required, many historians often implicitly believed, a softening of their commitment to historical materialism as the key driver of historical change. Categories like meaning, agency and performance offered a kind of political hopefulness and intersectional inclusiveness that a generation of scholars felt *labour versus capital* did not.

Frustrated by the ways cultural history allowed us to see why things mattered but not the material forces that brought them into being, as graduate students, fellow historian Sophie Loy-Wilson and I began talking about combining economics with cultural history. Inspired by the post-Marxist structural analysis that underpinned settler-colonial studies on one hand and Indigenous place-based history on the other, we sought a new approach to history that connected a materialist framework in a Marxist sense to the agentive, discursive politics of the cultural turn (Forsyth & Loy-Wilson, 2017).

In pursuing this, I hypothesised that to understand the strange class behaviour transforming Australian political life in the early 21st century, we would need to consider the historical structure of the Australian labour force. Over the 20th century, white-collar professional work increased from approximately 3 per cent of the Australian labour force in 1901 to 18 per cent in 2001 – more than 50 per cent using a wider white-collar definition. The effect of white-collar expansion on class structure had been the subject of re-examination by British scholars Giddens (1980) and Perkin (1989), but merely pointed to the questions raised by 'third way' politics in the period in which they wrote, it did not explain more recent class allegiances.

Changes in occupation structure, however, need not by themselves represent transformations in the nature of class and class conflict. Professionals, I will argue in this chapter, nevertheless constituted a class in and for themselves from the late 19th century to the present. Through three distinct phases of change in the history of professions, white-collar experts exhibited a consciousness of their middle-class status that went beyond what some dogmatic Marxists called 'false consciousness' to restructure capitalism in their own moral image. They did so via the key logic of capitalism: return on investment, or what Marx (1867) summarised as 'M-C-M', where money invested in commodities produces more money, with profit.

Settler-colonial Australia and the Rise of the Professional Class

In the 19th century, a global middle class spread throughout the world to help administer empire (Manjapra, 2019). On the Australian continent, these British members of what was becoming a global class surveyed settler colonies, designed roads and bridges, drafted and implement laws, ministered to parish communities, treated and nursed illnesses and injuries, taught children and facilitated communication across regions, especially via newspapers. Their work in the Australian settler colonies was infused by transformations in the British middle class in the mid-19th century, which drew on the likes of poor law reform to combine the kind of economic expansion that characterised settler colonisation, with a kind of moral investment in societies, with a view to personal and social returns (Harris, 1992; Lake, 2019).

As white-collar occupations formed professional associations – usually in Britain first and extending across empire – they began to formalise moral norms into professional standards. Values like duty, charity, probity, thrift, hygiene, conscientiousness and truth became intrinsic to the professions. Each profession had its own unique set of virtues but they were interrelated.

Together these professional moral assemblages formed a moral-economic system. This was what Judith Brett (1993) defined as the moral middle class, but it went much further than a set of values that the middle class tended to hold. Instead, these values were built into the work that people actually did. And in so doing, those moral values also became intrinsic to the economy.

Contrary to the stance of theorists like Poulantzas (1979), the kind of morality that the professional class espoused was not just ideological. Rather, morality was integrated into the performance of work and was central to its efficacy. Cleanliness actually made for good nursing, probity made for good accounting, truth made for good journalism and mathematical conscientiousness ensured bridges stayed up. Middle-class people in every Australian town and city did not just bring moral ideas with them, they performed those ideas every day in their work. This real, embodied work made morality material and virtue economic.

This enables us to see that the kind of materialism that Marx described – capitalist value, produced by the logic of return on investment – applied to professional virtue too. In material terms, this constituted investment in their own 'human capital', investment in social goods like healthcare and education, investment in 'civilising' both Indigenous and convict society. They invested both money and their work, producing a combination of social and economic profit. The fact that most of this profit went to professionals is no coincidence. Profit for them looked like good jobs, growing incomes, high social standing, profound political influence and a role in systems of social engineering. Such profit was evidence, taking an expansive reading of Weber's (1905) account of the protestant ethic, of the virtue of their work. It is also evidence that the professionals were not just an occupation category, they were a class.

Individual professionals performed this morality in their work, but they did not do it alone. Like all class behaviour it was collective. As colonial institutions bureaucratised, professional virtue was increasingly systematised (see Weber, 1952). Government departments and regulations, professional associations, educational institutions and regulatory bodies multiplied.

The real, embodied activity of the professional class spread through the settler colonies and became materially embedded in the global economy.

The professions expanded from the 1870s onwards, when the global economy entered a financialising phase (Arrighi, 1994). This initial growth was driven largely by massive expansions in nursing and teaching, both professions dominated by women. All other major professional occupations also grew at a rate well above population growth and labour force expansion (Forsyth, 2019). Professional associations developed, regulating each profession. From the 1890s into the 1920s they began the process of enclosing access to each occupation via examination and claiming jurisdiction over particular realms of expertise (see Abbott, 1988). Discursive ideals like education, hygiene, health, social cohesion, probity and lawfulness became moral values shaping the lives of those who went to school, needed medical treatment, relied on assistance from a social worker or religious organisation, ran a business or bought property. Which is to say, pretty much everyone. Financial investment and professional work together produced a material, moral economy.

Although the professional class benefited from their morality, both materially and in gaining authority, this need not suggest their morality was contrived. Indeed, the polarity between 'real' and 'manufactured' ethics seems a false, or at least overstated, distinction. Hypocrisy was central to many 1970s critiques of the professions, though these were, as I will show, themselves part of a shift in the moral foundations of the professional class then underway. It may also be a response to our understandable suspiciousness when we see the fruits of class power. Think of our feelings as we pass the surgeon's Ferrari in the carpark, for example. However, while there are certainly badly-behaved doctors, we have every reason to believe that on the whole medical practitioners are in fact animated by moral codes. We might wish their morality invited a little less swagger and fewer expensive cars, but this need not lead us to believe that the moral underpinnings to professional work are not authentic. Their virtues were not always in fact moral, as we will see, but I think we can assume that for most professionals they were real.

Moral Hegemony of the Mid-century Professional Class

The 20th century soon produced the conditions that would allow the professional class to flourish. The economic shock of the Great Depression gave economists and bankers the authority to manage capitalism, intervene in markets, set trade policy and offer forms of financial relief (Millmow, 2010). The Great War had already produced a similar moral shock. It showed that 'civilisation', in Paul Valéry's words (Latour, 2007), was 'mortal' and needed expert protection. By the time the Second World War came around, expertise – particularly science – was seen to be the foundation and justification for civilised behaviour. 'Give scientists a chance', future British prime minister Winston Churchill begged the empire's enemies, contrasting science's civilising capacity to war. 'The barbaric method of forcibly imposing one population upon another and of exterminating or subjugating the vanquished is hopelessly inefficient and out of date' (Churchill, 1939). Of course, on both sides of the conflict, science then became the mechanism for efficient elimination of enemy populations. Other experts assisted by assuring morale among troops tasked with killing and among populations waiting to hear of the death of loved ones. More experts transferred their attention from poetry to censor documents.

Even before that war was over, technocratic expertise was seen by those with power as the solution to post-war reconstruction (Mitchell, 2002). As the end of the war loomed, social scientists, agricultural scientists and anthropologists planned the research that would underpin new phases of colonial rule as imperial control was reshuffled (Forsyth, 2017). Engineers designed the snowy mountains scheme and dammed the nation's rivers to promote agriculture; economists planned the post-war economy; arbitration lawyers reviewed the basic wage; and social workers were central to the new welfare state (Macintyre, 2015). Using their longstanding transnational networks, they also planned the World Trade Organization, the World Health Organization, the Food and Agriculture Organization and the World Bank. The professional class designed the mid-20th century global political economy and they organised it as a moral structure.

In terms of power and resources, they also benefited from it the most. This was because the professional class was allied with the state on one hand and managerial capitalism on the other. British social historian Harold Perkin (1989) argued that the welfare state best expressed the 'professional ideal', but the history of the professional class, even before post-war reconstruction, was inseparable from the history of the modern state. The alliance between the professional class and the state was grounded in a combination of factors. Some, like law, were the foundation of the state, writing and administering state legislation. Others, like accountancy, emerged in concert with state systems to facilitate the flow of capital, which as the end of the Melbourne land boom showed, was prone to disruption by individual interests and collective corruption. Medicine and nursing became connected to the state by administering public health and then by the expansion of public hospitals and the pharmaceutical benefits scheme. Public schooling, which spread teachers through every town and suburb, was administered by government. Most engineers, until the late 20th century, were government employees. Professionals, as Magali Sarfatti Larson (1978) argued, used their morality ideologically, to help hide the class interests of the modern state, but they also literally ran the place. Just as the global bourgeoisie administered empire, so the professional class that they became now administered the state.

Administration in 20th-century capitalism was becoming a complicated business that was not confined to the growing task of governing society and economy. The increasing size of all enterprises and institutions, including law and accountancy firms, hospitals, corporations, schools and banks, created the conditions for the rise of what Alfred Chandler and others dubbed managerial capitalism (Chandler, 1984). Whereas under 19th-century capitalism, the owners of capital also typically managed it, by the mid-20th century a new class of managers worked on their behalf. Throughout those organisations and up to board and partner level, professionals applied their expert work to the management of both government and capitalist enterprise (Wright & Forsyth, 2021). Often tempering some of the worst effects of capitalism through their influence on government regulation and, more directly, via the morality underpinning their professional work, professionals and managers together formed what Barbara Ehrenreich and John Ehrenreich (1976) called the 'professional-managerial class'.

The professional-managerial class was not only managerial in their role in public and corporate enterprise, they were also managerial in manner. Barbara Ehrenreich and John Ehrenreich pointed to their emergence in the United States during the progressive era (around the 1890s to 1920s), where middle-class reformers reshaped the political economic landscape. The application of such middle-class morality to social engineering accelerated in the mid-20th century.

Despite some tendency among scholars to idealise it (e.g., Judt, 2010), this 'rule of experts' was not that great for everyone. Considering the experience of people of different backgrounds can help. For middle-class people living in (say) the eastern suburbs of Sydney, professionals like the family doctor, accountant, colleagues and the children's teachers, constituted their habitus in Bourdieu's (1984) sense. Encounters with professionals helped confirm their shared moral stance on family, money, health and education; their social networks shaped their moral and financial prosperity. Working-class families did not typically experience it this way. To them, professionals like the town's teachers and doctors implicitly made them feel inadequate when they told them how they ought to behave, eat and raise their children. Most were still better off than women like Millicent, whose story is recounted in the *Bringing Them Home* report (Australian Human Rights Commission, 1997) on the forced separation of Aboriginal and Torres Strait Islander children from their parents. Millicent's life was ruled by professionals. They determined what she could buy, where she could live and the nature of her work. When Millicent gave birth to a daughter, professionals forcibly removed the child, just as Millicent had been stolen from her own mother, also by professionals. The professional class brought morality into their work, but this does not mean their work was always in fact moral. Indeed, in utilising the forms of morality that became embodied in their work, the professional class was responsible for some of Australian history's most shameful epochs, including the stolen generations.

Professional relations to those they imagined as 'below' them in terms of class, financial position and race remind us, as E.P. Thompson (1966) did, that class is a relationship. Relations between professionals and 'others' expose the forms of extraction by which their moral and economic profit was attained. This was not confined to the redirection of some of capital's surplus into education and healthcare, which drove the initial professionalisation of the economy (Forsyth, 2019). Moral profit, as the professional class accumulated it, was extracted from 'below'. Indeed, the fact that their sense of superiority was both moral and material also reveals just how inextricable the moral was from the economic.

Emergence of a New Class Conflict

In the 1970s, a new generation of the moral middle class began to question the extractive practices of traditional professional virtue. When the global economic order began to unravel in the late 1960s, emerging as serious economic shocks from 1973 onwards (Eich & Tooze, 2016), the moral component of the economy also destabilised. In the archives and published journals of each profession, members displayed an existential crisis that went to the heart of their claims to virtue. Teachers recognised their role in producing compliant children for the machine that was industrial capitalism; engineers reconsidered the environmental effects of the massive infrastructure for which they had been largely responsible; lawyers noticed that they primarily served the rich; journalists saw their tradition of 'straight' reporting as a form of complicity with power; and social workers realised that their work reinforced normative ideas of family. All of them began to make the dismantling of older forms of virtue a part of their new moral regime. Revised expressions of moral legitimacy emerged.

The inclusion of minority groups in recruitment to the professions came to be regarded as evidence that merit was working. This required them to reconfigure merit itself. Merit had emerged in the early 20th century as a system that selected for white, middle-class characteristics (see Jackson, 2014; Markovits, 2019). Since the 1970s, however, a new conception of merit was legitimised by the inclusion of people that 'merit' had previously excluded by their class, gender (depending on profession), race or sexuality. It also evidently gave rise to the 'burbling' scholarship of the new cultural history.

The moral order for the managerial class was also undergoing transformation, though it moved in the opposite direction. To an emerging breed of entrepreneurial managers, the kind of virtue long espoused by the professional class began to seem self-serving (which it was, as we have seen). The new moral frameworks professionals developed were even worse for capitalist interests, however, since unlike their earlier versions when they helped settler-colonial expansion, the moral priorities of the professional class no longer aligned to the key goal of managerial capitalism: profit. By the 1980s, entrepreneurial types responding to financial globalisation, revelled in rejecting virtue and embracing greed (Collins, 2007).

Professionals were not immune to the entrepreneurial transformation. Some of the coolest professionals were those who flagrantly broke the rules: being unethical and entrepreneurial became somehow correlated. Disgraced medical practitioner Geoffrey Edelsten, who died in June 2021, profited from the emergence of Medicare. His medical waiting room famously featured a white grand piano and glitzy 1980s chandeliers, while the examination rooms had mink-covered treatment tables. Edelsten was hailed as a 'prophet' for a new age of medicine that was unconstrained by older norms (Masters, 1984). Edelsten was stripped of his medical license, jailed for soliciting a hitman (a crime he admitted to in 2001, but in the same proceedings said he 'couldn't remember'). Until his death he still maintained a website espousing his academic and entrepreneurial credentials.

A much lower-profile case, *Returning to the Light: the Memoirs of Rex Johnson* is a quite touching autobiography of this otherwise unknown accountant that tells of the heady days of 1980s accountancy when the staid old rules that combined morality with professional competence were let go and drinking in the office started at about midday. His memoir, deposited in the State Library of Victoria, was an apology to his grown children for the illegal activity he participated in, in the name of entrepreneurial accountancy (Johnson, 2017).

While the press sought to redress their past failings by a massive expansion into investigative journalism, some took the entrepreneurial path in the other direction (Schultz, 1994; 1998). Ethical considerations, by contrast to their lucrative power in the mid-20th century now constrained money and power. When Sydney radio station 2GB's John Laws and Alan Jones were caught in 1999 accepting 'cash for comment' their lawyers explained that they were entertainers, not journalists, and ethical rules did not apply to them (Lumby & Probyn, 2003). The slippery slope is evident, from the Laws and Jones scandal to Fox and Sky News, whose mission evidently includes opposition to the tenets of the 'liberal elite' whose interest in race, gender and sexuality inclusion are now denigrated as 'virtue signalling' (McKnight, 2010).

As was the case earlier in the 20th century, such morality was material, as well as ideological. Global capital, newly flexible and mobile as currencies floated and governments deregulated their economies, now required many more professional administrators. Education, which also helped drive the initial professionalisation of the economy, grew spectacularly (especially at university level) as a global 'knowledge economy' underpinned profitability based on innovation (Olssen & Peters, 2005). Investment in healthcare continued, but turned from nursing (which was still important) to a wider variety of specialised professions. Accounting, finance and information technology also grew with capitalism's latest financialisation phase, which commenced in the 1970s (Arrighi, 1994).

No white-collar occupation grew, however, like management and business, the latter including marketing, public relations, business analysis and related work. In the 1980s, the interests of this ascendant managerial class diverged from that of the professionals. Just as early in the 20th century the professionals redirected surplus into the fields that made sense to them morally and benefited them financially, so now the managerial class redirected resources away from the coalface of professional work. The value produced by professionals as they nursed and treated patients, taught students, audited financial records or provided engineering or accountancy consulting services was now extracted for the benefit of a managerial, rather than professional, elite. Resources were increasingly squeezed at the point of value production and redirected outwards. The managerial logic was that, rather than assure quality professional services, enterprises should prioritise strategic development, marketing and infrastructure growth. Ever more productivity, under an increasingly audited regime, was required from professional work, especially at lower levels. Professionals, now working in much larger enterprises, became a proletarianising 'managed' class (Duménil & Lévy, 2018).

The alliance the professional and the managerial once shared collapsed on both moral and material grounds. Because of the moral, the proletarianisation of professionals was incomplete, however. Professionals continued to regulate merit through education, administer health and other forms of policy, oversee the rule of law and influence the media. The result was that the professional class's moral authority continued to threaten managerial-capitalist expectations for growth and power. Managerial control continually tightened, as the managerial class rightly saw the moral authority asserted by professionals as a form of class-based interest. Such moral power threatened managerial authority to make the increasingly autocratic decisions required to pursue capital accumulation in the era of lower growth since the end of the three decades spent rebuilding capital stock after two world wars and the Great Depression (Piketty, 2013).

Compelled by the imperative to growth, the managerial class could not allow the professional class's moral authority to accrue. The professional class in turn could not permit the managerial class to undermine the expert-based economy for moral reasons – actual moral reasons, not just class-based ones. This ensured both sides were coerced, and the cycle of conflict was perpetuated. On the basis of transformations in the legitimation of merit since the 1970s, moreover, this new intra-bourgeois conflict also focused on race, gender and sexuality. Conflict between managerial capitalists and professional technocrats grew into a profoundly harmful race and gender war, which is currently playing out in politics and workplaces in Australia and worldwide.

Conclusion: Rethinking Class in Australia

In this chapter I have promiscuously deployed a range of theories to reconsider class through the history of professions. Weber's protestant ethic helps explain the relations between the moral and the financial, and the bureaucratic mechanisms by which it spread through the Australian settler colonies and then the global economy. E.P. Thompson reminded us to watch for class *relations*. Combined with Bourdieu, Thompson helps show the ways a professional habitus helped professionals extract moral and financial value from those they imagined to be below them. A modified, Marxist-ish materialism helps us to combine the discursive power of the professional class – and in so doing we should nod to Foucault (1980) – with their embodied work. The consequences, as we have seen, are materially economic. For historians seeking to re-think class, it is inadequate, as Terry Irving evidently hoped we would, to dismiss the intersectional goals of the cultural turn – though historicising the 'turn' as part of the history of professional morality would have some value. Rather, the task at hand is to integrate the discursive into the structural and coercive forces of the Marxist tradition that informed Connell and Irving's *Class Structure*.

The rethinking required here, however, takes more than a marriage between theoretical frameworks. The history of professions in particular uncovers much more than transformations in the occupation structure of the Australian workforce since 1870. When Marx described class relations in the mid-19th century, most people's experience of class was governed by labour versus capital. By the end of the 20th century, white-collar employment dominated work in Australia. This transformation, far from undermining Marx's description of the logics of capital, utilised the key tenet of capitalism – return on investment – to constitute itself as a class for whom moral profit paralleled and justified economic gain. They were not immune from class conflict, however. Having extracted value from those they deemed below them for much of the 20th century, the professional class is recently embattled. The intra-bourgeois conflict between them and those who manage resources and set strategy, has taken on destructive qualities in the past decade, with little end in sight.

References

Abbott, A. (1988). *The system of professions: An essay on the division of expert labor.* Chicago: University of Chicago Press.

ABC News (2004, 29 January). Former doctor to remain struck off register. *ABC News*. Retrieved from https://www.abc.net.au/news/2004-01-29/former-doctor-to-remain-struck-off-medical-register/127140

Arrighi, G. (1994). *The long twentieth century.* London and New York: Verso.

Australian Bureau of Statistics. Censuses of Australian Colonies 1871, 1881, 1891, 1901, Australian Data Archive. Censuses of the Commonwealth of Australia 1911, 1927, 1933, 1947, 1957, 1961, 1971, 1981, 1991, 2001, 2006.

Australian Human Rights Commission. (1997). *Bringing them home: Report of the national inquiry into the separation of Aboriginal and Torres Strait Islander children from their families April 1997.* Retrieved from https://humanrights.gov.au/our-work/bringing-them-home-report-1997

Bourdieu, P. (1984). *Distinction: A social critique of the judgement of taste.* Cambridge, MA: Harvard University Press.

Brett, J. (1993). *Robert Menzies' forgotten people.* Sydney: Pan Macmillan Publishers Australia.

Chandler, A.D. (1984). The emergence of managerial capitalism. *The Business History Review, 58*(4), 473.

Churchill, W. (1939, July 28). The hush of Europe: Hitler's chance to ponder: July lights and shadows. *Sydney Morning Herald.*

Collins, R.M. (2007). *Transforming America: Politics and culture in the Reagan years.* New York: Columbia University Press.

Connell, R.W., & Irving, T.H. (1980). *Class structure in Australian history.* Melbourne: Longman Cheshire.

Duménil, G., & Lévy, D. (2018). *Managerial capitalism: Ownership, management and the coming new mode of production.* London: Pluto Press.

Edelsten, G. (2020). G [personal website]. Retrieved from https://www.geoffedelsten.com.au/

Edelston v MPBV [2001] VCAT 723 (31 May 2001). Retrieved from http://www.austlii.edu.au/cgi-bin/viewdoc/au/cases/vic/VCAT/2001/723.html?context=1;query=Geoffrey%20Edelsten%20Flannery%20;mask_path=

Ehrenreich, B., & Ehrenreich, J. (1976). The professional-managerial class. *Radical America, 11*(2), 7–32.

Eich, S., & Tooze, A. (2016). The great inflation. In L. Raphael, T. Dietrich, S. Back, T. Schlemmer, E. Seefried, A. Boes (Eds), *Vorgeschichte der gegenwart: Dimensionen des strukturbruchs nach dem boom.* Germany: Vandenhoeck & Ruprecht.

Forsyth, H. (2017). Post-war political economics and the growth of Australian university research, c.1945–1965. *History of Education Review, 46*(1): 15–32.

Forsyth, H. (2019). Reconsidering women's role in the professionalisation of the economy: Evidence from the Australian census 1881–1947. *Australian Economic History Review, 59*(1): 55–79.

Forsyth, H., & Loy-Wilson, S. (2017). Seeking a new materialism in Australian history. *Australian Historical Studies, 48*(2): 169–88.

Foucault, M. (1980). *Power-knowledge: Selected interviews and other writings, 1972–1977*. Brighton: Harvester Press.

Giddens, A. (1980). *The class structure of the advanced societies*. London: Hutchinson.

Harris, J. (1992). Political thought and the welfare state 1870–1940: An intellectual framework for British social policy. *Past & Present, 135*(1), 116–141.

Irving, T. (2017). History and the working class now: The collective impulse, tumult and democracy [Web blog post]. Retrieved from http://radicalsydney.blogspot.com/p/his.html

Jackson, B. (2014). *Equality and the British left: A study in progressive political thought, 1900–64*. Manchester: Manchester University Press.

Johnson, R. (2017). *Returning to the light: The memoirs of Rex Johnson*. Victoria: Rex Johnson.

Judt, T. (2010). *Ill fares the land*. New York and London: Penguin.

Lake, M. (2019). *Progressive new world: How settler colonialism and transpacific exchange shaped American Reform*. Cambridge MA: Harvard University Press.

Larson, M.S. (1978). *The rise of professionalism: A sociological analysis*. Berkeley: University of California Press.

Latour, B. (2007). War of the worlds: What about peace? In S. During (Ed.), *The cultural studies reader* (3rd ed.) (pp. 304–13). London: Routledge.

Lumby, C., & Probyn, E. (2003). Interview with Mike Carlton, money versus ethics. In C. Lumby & E. Probyn (Eds.), *Remote control: New media new ethics* (pp. 100–106). Cambridge: Cambridge University Press.

Macintyre, S. (2015). *Australia's boldest experiment: War and reconstruction in the 1940s*. Sydney: NewSouth Publishing.

Manjapra, K. (2019). The semiperipheral hand: Middle-class service professionals of Imperial capitalism. In C. Dejung, D. Motadel, & J. Osterhammel (Eds.), *The global bourgeoisie: The rise of the middle classes in the age of empire* (pp. 184–204). Princeton NJ: Princeton University Press.

Markovits, D. (2019). *The meritocracy trap*. New York and London: Penguin.

Marx, K. (1976, original 1867). *Capital a critique of political economy. Volume One*. London: Penguin.

Masters, C. (Reporter). (1984). Branded [Television broadcast]. In Jonathan Holmes (producer), *Four Corners*. Sydney: ABC. Retrieved from https://www.abc.net.au/4corners/branded---1984/2832026

McDougall, D. (2019). ScoMo's miracle: The Australian federal election of 18 May 2019. *The Round Table, 108*(5), 493–506.

McKnight, D. (2010). Rupert Murdoch's News Corporation: A media institution with a mission. *Historical Journal of Film, Radio and Television, 30*(3), 303–316.

Millmow, A. (2010). *The power of economic ideas: The origins of Keynesian macroeconomic management in interwar Australia 1929–39.* Canberra, Australian Capital Territory: Australian National University Press.

Mitchell, T. (2002). *Rule of experts Egypt, techno-politics, modernity.* Berkeley: University of California Press.

Olssen, M., & Peters, M.A. (2005). Neoliberalism, higher education and the knowledge economy: From the free market to knowledge capitalism. *Journal of Education Policy, 20*(3), 313–45.

Perkin, H. (1989). *The rise of professional society: England since 1880.* London and New York: Routledge.

Piketty, T. (2013). *Capital in the twenty-first century.* Cambridge MA: Harvard University Press.

Poulantzas, N. (1979). The New Petty Bourgeoisie. *The Insurgent Sociologist, 9*(1), 56–60.

Schultz, J. (Ed.) (1994). *Not just another business.* Sydney: Pluto Press.

Schultz, J. (1998). *Reviving the fourth estate: Democracy, accountability and the media.* Cambridge: Cambridge University Press.

Thompson, E.P. (1966). *The making of the English working class.* London: Vintage.

Weber, M. (2013, first published 1905). *Protestant ethic and the spirit of capitalism.* Hoboken, Hoboken: Taylor and Francis.

Weber, M. (1952). The essentials of bureaucratic organization. In R.K. Merton, A. Grat, B. Hockey, & H.C. Selvin (Eds.), *Reader in bureaucracy* (pp. 18–26). New York: The Free Press.

Wright, C.E., & Forsyth, H. (2021). Managerial capitalism and white-collar professions: Social mobility in Australia's corporate elite. *Labour History*, forthcoming.

Professional Journals

Accountant in Australia 1930–2000
Australian Journalist 1912–1927
Australian Nurses' Journal 1951–1993
Australian Nursing Journal 1993–2001
Australasian Accountant and Secretary 1918–33
Australasian Nurses' Journal 1903–1951
Australasian Medical Gazette 1882–1914
Commonwealth Journal of Accountancy 1921–1933
Journal of the Institution of Engineers Australia 1920–2000
Journalist 1927–2000
Law Institute Journal 1935–2000
Medical Journal of Australia 1914–2001
Professional Engineer 1956–1991
Public Accountant 1901–29
Teacher 1911–1914
Teachers Journal 1956–1989

CHAPTER 6

ADVANCING DEBATE ON PRECARIOUS WORKERS AND CLASS INTERESTS

Evidence from Warehouse Workers in Australia

Tom Barnes and Jasmine Ali

Introduction

In the decade since the publication of *The Precariat* (2011), Guy Standing's claims about the global emergence of a new class of precariously employed workers – known as the 'precariat' – have attracted widespread attention and criticism. Standing questioned the political and industrial relevance of trade unions as epitomes of outdated labourist politics. One of the underlying implications of this argument is that many unions are incapable of including or advancing the interests of precarious workers. Other scholars sharply criticized Standing's arguments on a range of grounds, including his claim that the precariat represented a class with distinctive and unified class interests which could be clearly distinguished from other classes of labour (Alberti et al., 2018).

This controversy provides the focus for this chapter. Among several critics of Standing's argument, we follow Erik Olin Wright's (2015; 2016) attempt to move beyond these class distinctions while also modifying class theory to better address the different circumstances, material conditions and experiences of workers employed under different degrees of precarity. In his later writings, Wright developed a critique of Standing in which the interests of workers employed under different conditions could be articulated on different levels of power. We argue that Wright also offers a useful framework for extending the debate about problematic relations between trade unions and precarious workers who are traditionally excluded from the collective voice in the workplace. To illustrate this argument, we deploy a case study of a trade union which intervened successfully in the allocation of workplace rights during a dispute over a major warehouse closure in Melbourne.

The chapter proceeds as follows: the second section provides an overview of criticisms of Standing's claims about precarious workers and social class. It outlines Wright's alternative and discusses how this might be operationalised empirically. The third section outlines our methodology and provides a background to our case study, including the nature of work in warehouse logistics. The chapter then provides data from our case study which grounds Wright's concepts of class and power in practice. This fourth section explores this data at what Wright called the 'institutional level' of power while the fifth section does so at the 'situational level' of power.

Through evidence from our interviews with workers, we show how different institutionally defined categories of worker were reflected in everyday experiences in the workplace. In the final summarising section, we reiterate the useful role that Wright's framework can play when analysing industries and workplaces in which precarious employees undertake similar types of work to secure employees despite their experience of inferior employment conditions and unequal treatment in the workplace.

The Articulation of Precarious Workers' Interests

Standing (2011; 2014) argues that his concept of the 'precariat' allows us to better understand the distinctive circumstances of precarious workers which, he suggests, have been overlooked due to labour politics' historical privileging of the traditional working class. He argues that trade unions will only be relevant if they reorient their activities to precarious workers as an 'emerging class'.

For Standing (2014), the precariat is constituted by three elements. The first is 'distinctive relations of production' which are indicated by the absence of 'labour-related security'. Standing lists seven forms of labour-related security: labour market security (sufficient access to paid work), employment security (protection from arbitrary dismissal or job loss), job security (opportunities for career development or status advancement), work security (protection from unsafe or hazardous working conditions, including long or unsociable working hours), skills reproduction security, income security and representation security (collective voice). The second element is what he calls 'distinctive relations of distribution', which illustrates the form in which income is acquired. Reflecting his earlier work (Standing, 1999), the precariat is characterised by reliance on money wages rather than non-wage enterprise benefits or income derived from private savings and assets, a condition that exposes workers' vulnerability to economic shocks. The third and final element of his definition concerns 'relations to the state', which are represented by growing demonisation and marginalisation by political leaders.

Standing also proposes three sub-groups within the precariat. The first group is the 'atavistic' precariat which is a generation of people from traditional working-class backgrounds, particularly in manual labour occupations, whose livelihoods have been undermined by neoliberal globalisation and economic restructuring. Second is a 'nostalgic' precariat of migrants and ethnic minorities whose precarity is co-determined by immigration controls and citizenship rules (also see Anderson, 2010); third is a 'progressive' precariat of younger, tertiary-educated workers whose long years of study do not lead to secure jobs, leading to anomie and status frustration.

While the precariat has been adopted as a label in recent studies of class stratification (Savage et al., 2015; Sheppard and Biddle, 2017), the generalisations involved in conflating individuals from these sub-groups into a single class category has contributed to an 'over-stretching' of precariousness as a concept (Alberti et al., 2018) and an exaggeration of the extent to which all individuals in these categories can be regarded as precarious (Doogan, 2009; Campbell & Price, 2016; Rubery et al., 2018). These lines of scholarship have also questioned the extent to which workers in these circumstances can be regarded as possessing a unified class interest.

Wright (2015; 2016) has arguably gone the furthest in questioning this class dimension of Standing's claim. According to Wright, any attempt to distinguish a precariat on a basis of a set of unified class interests which are different from other classes of labour is untenable. The central question he raised was not whether conditions of precarity differently affected groups within the working class – he argued they clearly do – but whether these conditions are sufficient to describe a separate and distinct social class. In contrast to Standing, Wright speculated that precarious workers may represent a distinctive stratum within the broader working class.

To substantiate this claim, Wright focused on the extent to which there is a differentiation of interests among workers employed under conditions of varying insecurity or precarity. His innovation was that the class interests of workers are not reified or static but expressed on three levels of power: at the systemic level, the institutional level or the situational level.[1] At the system level, he reiterated the classical Marxist argument that workers have similar interests in resisting the political and social domination of capital. Taken in isolation, the logic of this position represents the polar opposite of the precariat thesis; whereas Standing posits the existence of precarious workers as a separate class, this position implies that precarious workers are simply part of the working class and, therefore, have the same broad class interests.

That this logic struggles to explain why movements of precarious workers often fail to find common cause with traditional union struggles led Wright to posit the articulation of workers' class interests at two alternative levels. At the institutional level, workers have differentiated interests over formal rules, regulations and reforms, or what Wright called the 'rules of the game'. For instance, the implementation of a rule which protects a relatively secure worker's job might not be in the interests of a relatively precarious worker who is looking for more or better-paid work since it might restrict available job opportunities. At the situational level – or what we can also call the 'everyday' level – workers similarly have differentiated interests over 'moves within a fixed set of rules'. For example, conflicts emerge because precarious workers experience unequal or discriminatory treatment in the workplace.

Wright's framework enables an integration of the conditions of precarity into the analysis of social class without reducing those conditions to a preconceived concept of unitary class interest as the basis for common cause among workers. While several recent studies have shown how precarity and class overlap in dynamic ways (Millar, 2017; Paret, 2017; Barnes, 2020), Wright's deployment of different levels of power has the additional benefit of specifying how material interests differentiate *within* social classes and, therefore, helps to clarify that the interests of people who occupy a single class position are not the same in every circumstance. However, this framework has largely remained at a high level of abstraction and would benefit from testing through case study analyses to draw out the manifestations of these different levels of power in practice. Promising sites include firms that employ a combination of workers under different degrees of economic security and social protection even though they perform similar tasks in the workplace.

This chapter seeks to ground Wright's three levels of class power with a case study of workers at a single site: a wholesale warehouse which, until its closure in 2019, was the largest supermarket supplier in Melbourne. This workplace employed a combination of securely and precariously employed workers: a core on permanent contracts, a large minority of casual workers who lack employment security, and a smaller minority of agency workers – known in Australia as 'labour-hire' workers – who were hired through a third-party contractor. Almost all workers were engaged in a similar type of work, which involved the physically demanding task of moving goods between palettes and shelves for distribution to dozens of retail supermarkets across Melbourne. Tensions between workers employed in these different categories coalesced around a single issue: the company's decision to close the warehouse. As we show in the following section, this case study demonstrates how workers' class interests are articulated at the institutional and situational levels of power and, importantly, how the union at the site responded to this challenge.

Precarious Work in Warehousing: Case Study and Methodology

This chapter draws on a case study of a major wholesale distribution warehouse used to supply Woolworths retail supermarkets in Melbourne. Until its closure in 2019, the Hume Distribution Centre (hereafter 'Hume DC') was the largest wholesale supply facility in Melbourne for Woolworths, which is one of two corporations that dominate the Australian retail supermarket sector. The Hume DC was based in the Melbourne suburb of Broadmeadows, which is located about 17km north of the city centre.

The Hume DC was a major job-provider in a relatively job-poor area. In June 2015, Woolworths announced plans to gradually close the Hume DC at the cost of around 680 jobs. The company proposed to relocate its main Melbourne DC to a new, highly automated site in the south-east of Melbourne, over 50km away.[2] Data for this chapter is drawn mainly from the period between August 2015 and March 2017. We gained access to workers through the assistance of the main trade union at the site, the United Workers Union,[3] which represented over 80 per cent of the workforce. During this period of research, we conducted two sample surveys at the site – one in August 2015 with 105 workers and a follow-up survey with 140 workers 12 months later, in August 2016. We also conducted interviews with 25 workers randomly selected from the survey participants and held in two rounds – first, in March 2016 and, second, in March 2017. This chapter focuses on data from interview participants. Where we refer to individual participants, we have used pseudonyms to protect their identity.

While the impact of the closure announcement shocked workers at the site, it also brought into focus a series of pre-existing divisions. Like much of the warehousing industry, the Hume DC's workforce was divided between a core of employees with permanent contracts and many insecurely employed, non-permanent workers. Non-permanent employees at the site were divided between casual workers directly employed by Woolworths and a minority of casual workers employed via a labour-hire agency. Following Erik Olin Wright's framework, the following section outlines how these differences manifested in the articulation of workers' interests at the institutional level before moving into a discussion of differences at the situational level.

Differentiating Precarious Workers at the 'Institutional Level'

Despite being employed under different conditions, workers overwhelmingly undertook a similar type of work at the Hume DC. Some were employed in office-based or cleaning jobs and others worked in a separate section of the worksite as forklift operators; however, 90 per cent of the workforce could be described as store-persons – colloquially known as 'picker-packers' – whose primary job was to physically move products between palettes and shelves in preparation for transportation to retail supermarkets. A further 7 per cent of the workforce described themselves as 'leading hands', who were low-level managers who supervised picker-packers on the warehouse floor and allocated shifts.

Despite the occupational similarity of most workers, the workforce was divided into different formal categories. By August 2015 – two months after the company announced the planned closure and relocation – 59 per cent of workers were on permanent contracts, 32 per cent were employed as casuals and 9 per cent via a labour-hire company.

In institutional terms, 'casual' and 'labour-hire' are embedded features of Australian labour law. Although all employees are formally entitled to minimum 'national employment standards' under the *Fair Work Act 2009*, and many receive additional benefits through industry-wide agreements (known as the awards) or firm-level collective wage agreements (known as Enterprise Agreements, or EAs), there are many basic protections which do not apply to casuals. Casual employment refers to a category of workers who do not have a clear commitment about the duration of their employment or about regular or minimum working hours.

Casuals represent around a quarter of all paid employment in Australia. There is also a category of long-term or 'permanent casuals' who have been employed for 12 months or more with an 'expectation of ongoing employment'. Unusually by global standards, casual workers in Australia receive an hourly wage premium – known as a 'casual loading' – which is meant to compensate for this lack of security or certainty (Campbell et al., 2009). Under the 2013–2017 EA at the Hume DC, casuals received an hourly wage that was 25 per cent higher than other workers. However, casuals had no guaranteed hours of work and were not entitled to any form of paid leave or redundancy pay.

Labour-hire workers represent a sub-category of casual employment which is regarded as 'on-hire employee services': an arrangement in which a 'host employer' hires the labour of workers provided by a third-party agency. Labour-hire is thus commensurate with categories used in other countries such as 'temp' or 'agency' labour. While labour-hire workers are subject to the same basic minimum rights for other casuals in Australia, the wages and working conditions of labour-hire workers are not directly covered by the terms of the host employer's EA.

Long-term casual employment was a major issue at the Hume DC. By August 2016, the average duration of job tenure for casual employees was 11 years, which is higher than the average for all workers at the site (nine years) and only slightly less than the average for permanent full-time workers (13 years). Some casuals had worked for the company for as long as 17 years. Over half (53 per cent) had been employed for more than ten years. While some younger workers preferred casual employment because of its higher hourly wage, casuals had very few rights to convert to permanent employment under the 2013–2017 EA.

Therefore, while the vulnerability of all workers was exposed by the company's closure announcement in mid-2015, the burden fell particularly heavily upon casuals and labour-hire workers – especially those long-term casuals who had accumulated many years of service. Under the 2013–2017 EA, a permanent worker with ten or more years of employment was eligible for a redundancy payment worth approximately three-quarters of their annual salary. This was around 2.5 times better than the national minimum under the *Fair Work Act*. Casuals, by contrast, were to receive nothing under the EA at the time of the company's closure announcement.

Differentiating Precarious Workers at the 'Situational Level'

As outlined above, the institutional disadvantages faced by casual and labour-hire workers at the Hume DC were exposed by Woolworths' closure announcement in 2015. These disadvantages already manifested on an everyday basis – that is, at the 'situational level' – in the workplace. Casual and labour-hire workers were subjected to unequal treatment in the engagement of their working duties and the allocation of their hours.

Workers explained that an informal hierarchy operated at the site, with labour-hire workers at the bottom, followed by directly employed casuals, permanent part-time workers and permanent full-time workers at the top. Labour-hire workers were fully aware of their position at the bottom of this hierarchy:

> When you are [labour-hire] you get thrown around all over the place. It's very, very difficult … [The] difficulty in getting and keeping shifts

when you're on contract [with a labour-hire] agency is horrendous (Phillip, labour-hire worker).

At the other end of the spectrum, permanent workers were aware of the maltreatment of labour-hire workers:

> Exploitation comes to mind. They've put on temporary contracts, and those contracts have come to an end ... [They are] just exploiting them [by] sending them back to the [labour-hire] agency and re-advertising the temporary position at the quieter time of the year (Ryan, permanent worker).

In our interviews, labour-hire workers and casuals complained about the practice of 'favouritism' in shift allocation. A common refrain was that an 'in-crowd' of permanent workers collaborated with leading hands (shift supervisors) in order to occupy the most desirable regular day shifts. Regularity and predictability in weekly shift allocation were highly prized. This in-crowd tended to be comprised of longer-term workers who were related to each other through family or kinship ties or who socialised together inside and outside the workplace. By August 2015, nearly one in five workers had at least one family member or relative who also worked at the Hume DC. In most cases, this was a sibling or a partner/spouse, although some workers' children or parents also worked at the site. These workers overwhelmingly worked in regular day shifts and almost all were permanently employed.

When interviewed, these workers emphasised the existence of a 'tight-knit group' that helped each other on the warehouse floor. Conversely, this sociality was often resented by casuals and labour-hire workers:

> Nepotism ... was thriving there in the place. If you were a brother or a sister or a husband-and-wife team, you would always get the better jobs ... It was just so sickening (Chris, casual worker).

The Articulation of Collective Interests at the Institutional and Situational Levels

While the institutional divisions between permanents, casuals and labour-hire workers were reflected in workplace divisions based on sociality and shift allocation, many workers were also aware that these divisions were a product of management strategies to segment and control the workforce. The key agent in challenging these divisions was the United Workers Union (UWU). In recent years, the UWU has challenged the exploitation of casuals and labour-hire workers in warehouse logistics and has campaigned to change the regulation of labour-hire arrangements. In 2017, the UWU led a new round of negotiations for EAs at key retail DCs in Victoria and New South Wales, including industrial action to push for higher wages, curbs on excessive casualisation, and higher redundancy pay.

Union initiatives at the Hume DC formed an integral part of this interstate campaign. In the lead-up to the new EA negotiations, the UWU's main priority at the Hume DC was to convert casual workers onto permanent contracts so they could access redundancy payments. These efforts were reflected in a shift in the proportion of workers from casual to permanent employment. From August 2015 to August 2016, there was a rise in the proportion of permanent full-time workers from 31 to 41 per cent of the workforce and in the proportion of permanent part-time workers from 25 to 30 per cent. The proportion of casual workers fell from 32 to 18 per cent. The largest number of conversions involved a shift from casual to permanent part-time work.

The campaign for a new EA in 2017 complemented these earlier efforts by improving the terms of redundancy for all workers. The new EA (2017–2020) significantly extended and increased redundancy pay. Casuals could now receive a 'closure payment' of up to $5000. In addition, the calculation used to determine redundancy pay was increased by 25 per cent – from four to five weeks' wages for each year of service – and the payment cap was doubled. Workers could also now 'cash out' leftover paid leave allowances.

These changes, which meant that permanents with ten or more years of service could now receive a payment worth well over a year's salary, were particularly beneficial for long-term casuals who were able to convert to permanent positions prior to the closure. Labour-hire workers who converted, with the union's assistance, to standard casual positions were also able to access casual closure payments as a recognition of their service.

One of the reasons why the union was able to succeed in this process was the high level of engagement with workers across all types of employment. Most casuals and many labour-hire workers were encouraged to join the union, to attend site meetings, and to participate in union campaigning. The proactive role of the union in pursuing the interests of workers across the institutional divide that separated casuals and labour-hire workers from permanents, and in responding to the unequal treatment and experiences of workers on the warehouse floor, meant that most workers were strongly supportive of the union. Despite the persistence of inequality in employment conditions, workers were able to articulate a common interest in union membership and united activity to pursue more favourable outcomes for all workers prior to the closure of the site in 2019.

Discussion and Conclusion

This chapter has focused on the period in the lead-up to the closure, especially in the two years following the initial closure announcement in mid-2015. Although the announcement negatively affected most workers, it also threatened to sharpen prevailing tensions between precarious workers and workers with permanent contracts. The emotional and financial burden of the announcement fell particularly harshly upon long-term casual workers employed at the site due to their exclusion from redundancy pay.

However, the experience at the Hume DC also shows how unions can play a role in positively responding to such workplace divisions. The union did not ignore or seek to marginalise precarious workers; on the contrary, it continuously sought to include casuals and labour-hire workers into union membership, local activities and deliberations and to challenge social and institutional divisions among workers.

At face value, casuals and labour-hire workers exhibited most of the features used by Standing (2011; 2014) to define the precariat. These workers, for example, had little-to-no employment security, labour market security and income security, especially when compared to permanent workers, even though they undertook similar tasks to most permanents in the warehouse labour process and even though all workers had access to union representation.

However, Erik Olin Wright's theoretical re-framing of precarious workers is analytically useful in the light of workers' experiences at the Hume DC. Wright framed precarious workers as both a part of the broader working class but with sets of interests that were articulated in distinctive ways and which, in certain circumstances, conflicted with those of more secure workers. At the institutional level, which involves the formal 'rules of the game' which govern individual rights and entitlements, workers' interests are framed by rules operating at different institutional scales: for example, at the national level for all workers employed in Australia (national employment standards under the *Fair Work Act*), at the industry level (industry-level awards) and at the enterprise level (EAs negotiated between the company and the union).

For the UWU, effectively responding to these institutional divisions within the Hume DC's workforce meant uniting people employed under a range of conditions and with a range of experiences. For instance, it meant responding to the unequal treatment and different experiences of precarious workers as a means of inclusion in local campaigns and as a means of strengthening union organisation in the workplace.

In Wright's terms, precarious workers' interests were also differentiated at the situational level. At the time of the closure announcement, most of these workers were on flexible shifts that changed week to week, often unpredictably, and access to more or better working hours was controlled through an informal hierarchy that discriminated against workers without permanent contracts. The administrative means through which permanent workers were able to dominate preferred working hours and workplace roles reflected the opportunity hoarding behaviour emphasised in Weberian accounts of social class – an approach which, according to Wright, could be partially synthesised with his Marxian approach (see Wright 2009 for an extended discussion). While Standing deployed this Weberian insight to frame precarious workers as an 'ideal type' of class (see Standing, 2011, p. 7), Wright drew upon his earlier idea of workers occupying 'contradictory locations' within social classes (Wright, 1985) to frame intra-class interest differentiation in a more case-sensitive and less static way.

Wright's more flexible approach better positions scholarship to understand how unions can successfully incorporate and advance the positions of precarious workers if they acknowledge and respond proactively to the differentiated articulation of workers' interests at the institutional and situational levels. In the Hume DC case, the union's emphasis on the need to overcome workplace divisions and to unite to achieve the best-possible financial outcome for all workers affected by the closure was important in winning and enforcing conversion rights for casuals and labour-hire workers. This was framed as part of a political and industrial campaign at a national level against exploitative casualisation and labour-hire practices and for improved redundancy entitlements in an industry increasingly affected by labour-saving innovation and job insecurity.

The success of the union in linking this national and industry-wide problem with the specific concerns of precarious workers in the Hume DC was instrumental to the ongoing popularity of unionism at the site. A framework which positions precarious workers as a separate social class whose interests are incompatible with the interests of secure workers cannot explain instances like the Hume DC case when social actors are able to challenge or overcome institutional and situational divisions between workers.

This case study also has implications for analysis in other workplaces where precarious workers are employed alongside more secure or established workers, especially under labour regimes predicated upon the segmentation of workforces in order to lower labour costs and enhance employer control in the workplace. The triadic model outlined in this chapter (permanents, casuals, labour-hire) is common in warehouse logistics workplaces in Australia and internationally. Further afield, workforce segmentation has become a normal employment practice in retail sales, universities, and, increasingly, in construction and manufacturing. These examples suggest that the articulation of conditions and interests at the institutional and situational of power, as theorised by Wright, can potentially be a highly fruitful way of framing the experiences of workers employed under different conditions across variegated labour regimes.

Endnotes

1   This idea is adapted from Alford and Friedland (1985).
2   The transition of work from the Hume DC to the new Melbourne South Region Distribution Centre (MSRDC) is the subject of ongoing research by the authors.
3   Known as the National Union of Workers (NUW) prior to a recent amalgamation.

References

Alberti, G., Bessa, I., Hardy, K., Trappmann, V., & Umney, C. (2018). In, against and beyond precarity: Work in insecure times, *Work, Employment and Society, 32*(3), 447–457.

Alford, R., & Friedland, R. (1985). *The powers of theory: Capitalism, the state, and democracy*. Cambridge: Cambridge University Press.

Anderson, B. (2010). Migration, immigration controls and the fashioning of precarious workers, *Work, Employment and Society, 24*(2), 300–17.

Barnes, T. (2020). Pathways to precarity: Work, financial security and wage dependency among Australia's retrenched auto workers, *Journal of Sociology, 15*(2), 443–463. https://doi.org/10.1177/1440783320925151

Campbell, I., & Price, R. (2016). Precarious work and precarious workers: Towards an improved conceptualisation, *Economic and Labour Relations Review, 27*(3), 314–332.

Campbell, I., Whitehouse, G., & Baxter, J. (2009). Casual employment, part-time employment and the resilience of the male-breadwinner model. In L. Vosko, M. MacDonald, & I. Campbell (Eds.), *Gender and the contours of precarious employment* (pp. 60–75). London: Routledge.

Doogan, K. (2009). *New capitalism? The transformation of work*. Cambridge: Polity.

Millar, K.M. (2017). Towards a critical politics of precarity. *Sociology Compass, 11*(6).

Paret, M. (2017). Working-class fragmentation, party politics, and the complexities of solidarity in South Africa's united front. *The Sociological Review, 65*(2), 267–284.

Rubery, J., Grimshaw, D., Keizer A., & Johnson, M. (2018). Challenges and contradictions in the 'normalising' of precarious work, *Work Employment and Society, 32*(3), 509–27.

Savage, M., Devine, F., Cunningham, N., Friedman, S., Laurison, D., Miles, A., Snee, H., & Taylor, M. (2015). On social class, anno 2014, *Sociology, 49*(6), 1011–1030.

Sheppard, J., & Biddle, N. (2017). Class, capital and identity in Australian society, *Australian Journal of Political Science, 52*(4), 500–16.

Standing, G. (1999). *Global labour flexibility: Seeking distributive justice.* Basingstoke: MacMillan.

Standing, G. (2011). *The precariat: The new dangerous class.* London: Bloomsbury Academic.

Standing, G. (2014). *A precariat charter: From denizens to citizens.* London: Bloomsbury.

Wright, E.O. (1985). *Classes.* London: Verso.

Wright, E.O. (2009). Understanding class: Towards an integrated analytical approach, *New Left Review, 60*, 101–16.

Wright, E.O. (2015). *Understanding class.* London: Verso.

Wright, E.O. (2016). Is the precariat a class? *Global Labour Journal, 7*(2), 123–35.

CHAPTER 7

WORKERS IN WAITING?

Work Ethic, Productive Intensities, Class and Unemployment

Jessica Gerrard and David Farrugia

Introduction

The 'dole bludger' has a particular place in Australian vernacular and culture. Dole bludgers are, figuratively speaking, the dark underbelly of the productive, authentic and hardworking 'worker', that is so central to the articulation of Australian culture. Even in the midst of the rising unemployment in 2020 as a result of COVID-19, after having temporarily raised unemployment benefits for the first time in over 20 years, Prime Minister Scott Morrison lamented that people were choosing not to work as their benefits were too high (on the basis of 'anecdotal feedback' from small and large businesses) (SBS News, 2020). There is a feverish and perennial concern for the idleness of the unemployed, and the potential that they might slip out from the cultural, social and economic ties of paid employment and into a state of permanent – or at least extended – 'unproductivity'. The positioning of the so-called non-worker as abjectly unproductive of course eclipses the foundational importance (and productivity) of the unpaid (largely women's) labour of reproduction (Federici, 2008), and in the Australian context the historical exclusion of Indigenous people as colonial subjects whilst also demanding their forced (and then drastically underpaid) labour power (see ABC News, 2019).

In this chapter, we examine the contemporary conditions of unemployment and suggest that it is best understood not as a site of unproductivity and, therefore, nor as distinct from the formation of class. Whilst 'productivity' is most often traditionally theorised in association with paid employment, we suggest there is a need to understand how productivity is now articulated in the social relations of unemployment in ways that bring classed attachments to 'productivity' into unemployment. In what follows, we theorise the way that the subjectivities of people experiencing unemployment are made productive in the context of post-Fordist incitements to self-realisation through labour. We argue that classed attachments to productivity are articulated within contemporary unemployment through the energetic relationship to potential employment expected of the unemployed. We put forward the concept of 'productive intensities' as a way to theorise how those experiencing unemployment respond to the necessity to become productive and connect this with shifts in the nature of contemporary class and unemployment. Drawing on an individual case study from a larger research project, the chapter shows how productivity becomes part of the affective, embodied and relational capacities cultivated and deployed in and through the activities of unemployment.

A central premise of our argument is that unemployment must be a part of how class is understood and theorised. As noted above, unemployment is a critical site of neoliberal policy intervention. Framed as a dangerous site of idleness ('bludging') and unproductivity, the rise of mutual obligation policies mandate that the unemployed constantly demonstrate their 'work readiness' (see McDonald & Marston, 2005; Considine et al., 2015). Taking up these themes, Lisa Adkins (2012) argues that unemployment must be theorised beyond the notion of 'reserve army of labour'. Adkins describes shifts in the nature of unemployment such that it has become an 'eventful' state characterised by a series of value-creating activities. Indeed, it is important to note that not only are the unemployed productive in their activities for work preparedness, unemployment itself is commodifiable with profitable employment service businesses surrounding it. This has taken place in the context of what Weeks (2011) has called the post-Fordist work ethic, which describes the way that subjectivities are formed through an incitement to create value. Drawing on these ideas, this chapter shows how the subjectivities of the unemployed respond to the post-Fordist work ethic in the context of unemployment as an eventful state, and therefore demonstrates new processes of class formation taking place in relation to unemployment. Here, the concept of 'productive intensities' shows how the work ethic is expressed affectively in ways that extend beyond the accumulation of skills to encompass the basic orientations to the self, the world and the future on the part of the unemployed.

Productive Intensities: The Post-Fordist Work Ethic and the Eventful Character of Unemployment

For political theorist Kathi Weeks (2011), the 'work ethic' provides a critical insight into class formation, enacted in the government and discipline of a productive working class in different eras of capitalist production. The Protestant work ethic offered a spiritual reward (work hard and be saved) while the Fordist work ethic offered a material reward (work hard and consume). In contrast, the reward of the post-Fordist work ethic is ontological: dedicate the self to work and be self-actualised in the broadest possible sense. Weeks suggests that this shift in the work ethic reflects the nature of post-Fordist labour. Critically responding to autonomist Marxist approaches to 'affective labour' (for example, Hardt & Negri 2000; Hardt 1999) and feminist accounts of immaterial and emotional labour (for example, Hochschild 1983) Weeks connects the incitement to self-realisation through work to the emergence of forms of labour that produce affects and social relations, and that thereby produce value from the construction of subjectivity itself (see Weeks 2007; 2011). When the creation of value is also the creation of the self, self-realisation becomes the means by which subjectivities are oriented to the significance of work. In this way, becoming productive is an expansive personal project, going beyond the accumulation of skills or qualifications for a particular task or role, to cultivate the entire self in line with the requirement to produce value. It is in this context that classed subjectivities are formed through different orientations to productivity and value as an aspect of the self (Farrugia, 2021). This relentless 'work-on-the-self' orientation positions self-development and learning as a form of value accrual (Gerrard, 2014). As well as enrolling every aspect of subjectivity into the self as a worker, this process also means that the notion of value comes to encompass every aspect of a worker's life.

It is in this context that unemployment is made into an eventful state, requiring new dispositions and orientations to the world. Considering the ways in which women's labour (paid and unpaid) in particular is positioned in the contemporary economy, Adkins (2012) suggests the need re-conceptualise notions of labour and value in relation to employment and *un*employment. For Adkins (2012), unemployment is being made eventful in part because the unemployed are constituted as a labour force through a series of mutual obligation and workfare regimes that position them as a source of value. It is thereby necessary to become 'productive' even when one is not employed – both demonstrating a commitment to work and performing unpaid labour. 'Productive' and 'productivity' in this sense is not about relationships to the means of production, but rather the kinds of energies, dispositions and activities that are generated and required (Gerrard & Watson, 2021). For instance, there is an expanding range of interventions into the subjectivities of the unemployed which are oriented towards their demeanour, bodily comportment and relational styles. Unemployed people are encouraged to cultivate productivity and employability through the modulation of affect, and interventions into unemployment focus on manners of speech and dress as well as the capacity to interact with others in a pleasing and appropriate manner (Friedli & Stearn, 2015). Moreover, work-for-the-dole and required volunteering schemes muddy the separation of unemployment from commodifiable labour power, particularly when the unemployed perform work that would otherwise require paid employment (Gerrard & Watson, 2021).

Thus, both the post-Fordist work ethic and the eventful character of unemployment describe forms of selfhood oriented towards the necessity to produce value. The relationship between work and the self that is mandated by the post-Fordist work ethic is thereby also manifested in the experience of unemployment, in which the unemployed must make productivity and the creation of value central to their orientation to the world in the most general sense. Interventions into unemployment are therefore aligned with the post-Fordist work ethic. While the unemployed are not 'productive' in the traditional sense of employment (though as noted above, work-for-the-dole and required volunteering does indeed complicate a complete separation of unemployment from the production of surplus value), productivity is nevertheless a mode of affectivity deliberately and constantly cultivated during the experience of unemployment, in which the unemployed demonstrate their preparedness for employment through orienting themselves to its potential arrival. As we go on to explore in the case study below, the perennial engagement in value-accruing activities brings contemporary class subjectivity formation into unemployment.

To address these dynamics, we put forward the notion of 'productive intensities' as a means to theorise how class is articulated into unemployment. The concept describes the way that incitements to productivity and employability are experienced not merely in terms of the accumulation of skills, educational qualifications or financial rewards. Productive intensities refer to how affectivities are cultivated, disciplined and mobilised in order to create and perform the self as a value-producing subject. In referring to intensities, we refer to the embodied self's relationship to the world in an expansive sense, in which the necessity to be productive is expressed through corporeal movements, relational styles, sensuous and emotional experiences and wider aspirations for self-realisation. Working with Berlant's (2011) 'cruel optimism' we view productive intensities to be formed in relation to a normatively constructed seductive notion of the employable/employed (waged and secure) 'good life'. Part of the power of these productive intensities, set against the desired 'good life' (full waged employment), lies in their imagined power to stop a 'fall between the cracks' or, as Berlant evocatively puts it 'hitting the concrete at full speed' (2011, p. 180). Productive intensities are modes of embodiment, relationality and affectivity cultivated in relation to a distant horizon of secure-employment-to-come, but is nonetheless oriented to value-accruing orientations and activities in the present, and in the absence of employment itself (see Gerrard & Watson, 2021).

Thus, the notion of productive intensities is a means to theorise the value-creating capacities that underpin how class is enacted through the experience (and governance) of unemployment. Productive intensities describe the affectivities and social relationships of a subject that relentlessly pursues value-accrual as a normative and performative aspect of unemployment. Whereas elsewhere we have demonstrated the role of affective labour in the formation of class on the margins of employment (Gerrard & Farrugia, 2021), here we demonstrate how the affective labour of productive intensities is connected to the promise of employment in ways that demonstrate the interweaving relationship of contemporary formations of class with the experience of unemployment. In this way, the cultivation of productive intensities offers an insight into the way that class formation takes place in post-Fordist societies through the relationships to employment in the absence of it. Productive intensities are the ways in which the post-Fordist work ethic become realised in the space outside of formal employment, cultivating value-accruing classed subjectivities.

A part of our motivation to do so is to engage in contemporary sociological debates surrounding affective (or immaterial) labour in ways that attend to its classed dynamics (see Gerrard & Farrugia, 2021). Affective labour has brought attention to how contemporary employment in advanced capitalist societies characterised by ballooning service sectors, increasingly involves the production of signs, sensations, relations, vibes and aesthetics. However, as Gill and Pratt (2008) and McRobbie (2010) point to, there is a danger that affective labour is taken to stand in for a presumed middle-class white male (Bolton, 2009) universal experience, rather than as one that is differentially lived and felt, socially and historically situated, with very different classed, gendered and raced articulations (see McDowell, 2008). There is a need to understand how affect and affective labour is articulated through power relations, through for instance, status, wealth, gender, race and class distinctions (see Threadgold, 2020). Thus, here we seek to develop specific understanding of unemployment as providing a context within which the affective labour of job seeking becomes articulated as productive intensities in relation to the contemporary dynamics of class.

Being Busy, Accruing Value: Kara, a Worker in Waiting

To develop the concept of productive intensities, the remainder of this chapter focuses on a case study of a young woman experiencing unemployment in Newcastle, Australia. This example comes from a research project conducted between 2016 and 2018 examining the formation of young people as workers in regions of high youth unemployment (Farrugia, 2021) in relation to classed differences in the contemporary work ethic. This participant – who we will call Kara – was interviewed twice as part of this project, with interviews taking place 18 months apart. The presentation and analysis of this data as a single case is premised on the sociological need and value of in-depth context-bound qualitative exploration of experience (Flyvbjerg, 2006). In doing so, we draw on a sociological tradition that seeks to better understand profound social contradictions through the attentive exploration of subjective experience (for example, Reay, 2002).

In a situation increasingly characteristic of working-class Australians, Kara's parents (who she lived with) were both precariously employed, working multiple jobs as cleaners and taxi drivers. Kara described herself as an 'underdog', positioning herself within an Australian discourse of struggle against adversity as characteristic of Australian working-class life. She had completed year 12 with some difficulty, an achievement she was proud of as her teachers had widely expected that she would fail and had communicated this to herself and her parents. Since finishing school in 2014, Kara had searched for work but was unsuccessful despite progressively accumulating credentials. Nevertheless, whilst the wage labour relation is regarded as the critical exchange through which the working class becomes productive, Kara's interviews focused primarily on her efforts to cultivate productivity whilst unemployed, and to have her productivity recognised by those around her. In this sense, Kara becomes classed not merely through her family background, but also through the way that she draws upon the work ethic in negotiating the experience of unemployment and creating a productive self.

At the time of the first interview, Kara was receiving 'Newstart' payments and was engaged in a series of different TAFE courses. Indeed, Kara was enormously busy. She was engaged in multiple TAFE courses at different levels of qualification and in different areas, as well as a range of other activities with community and voluntary organisations. Kara emphasised how busy she was, and was keen that her constant activity was recognised in the interview and by prominent others around her:

Kara: [I am studying] three main courses and four short ones ... So Certificate III in Hospitality, a Diploma in Community Service ... and then Child Care Cert III online with Open Colleges. Attainments, so WH&S [workplace health and safety], advanced leadership, training essentials and auditing.

Researcher: Why are you doing so many things all at once?

Kara: I am not settled down and it's the opportunity. I did do the childcare last year and just carrying over. I did Cert IV in Community Services last year so I just thought do a diploma because I don't have much experience and they said I won't be able to find a job because of my age and not much experience, go and do a diploma, you've got more of a chance getting a job ... It's kind of like all the underdogs – I surprise people sometimes ... One of the teachers thought I just go home and I do nothing, stay at home ... She was shocked at how busy I am.

Kara was unsure of where any of these certificates would take her. She could perceive no clear pathway to employment, and it appeared to be a remote prospect despite her preoccupation with finding work. Nevertheless, Kara appeared compelled to fill all of her spare time with study and described instances in which others had been surprised or impressed by the breadth of her activities. By cultivating productivity in this way, Kara described efforts to build her self-confidence:

> **Kara**: [on her auditing course] I just wanted just the knowledge. I thought I've got a little bit of time on the Saturday, let's go … you have to do the other units later on to get the full qual. But at the moment I'm thinking some extra units won't hurt me.
>
> **Researcher**: Is this a strategy to eventually get you work or is this just out of interest or …
>
> **Kara**: Both and at the same time give me self-confidence, like I stick to stuff and I know I can do it despite the hard times … Well any time a certificate comes I'm over the moon. It's like yes I really worked for this.

Kara's frantic effort to accumulate credentials was not merely about skills, but about becoming more confident as a person in a broad sense. She said that she was often seen as shy and did not feel that she would be able to engage confidently with others at work. Gaining qualifications gave her a sense of accomplishment which she felt might assist her to be seen as a valuable worker:

> **Kara**: It just gives you confidence because … Especially in the workforce you don't want to be seen as naive and you've got not skills, no knowledge. But shy people are seen as dumb and introvert.
>
> **Researcher**: It seems like a lot of what you're looking for out of your training is more abilities to connect with people and to be able to feel confident just in general in life right?
>
> **Kara**: Yes, accomplished. Yes.

During the interview Kara also mentioned that at times her frantic schedule made her anxious. She said that during quiet moments sometimes she felt that she would 'crack', and that she may have 'too much happening' in her life. When asked what drove her to continue with all of her various activities, Kara described this desire for confidence alongside the hope that she and her family could avoid poverty. She also described wanting to be able to relate to others in an easier and more confident manner, and that this might prove to be a useful capacity if she eventually secured work in the area of community services:

> **Kara**: I'd like to have a bit of financial security … We're sick of being poor.
>
> **Researcher**: If that's not the main thing then what is the main thing that motivates you?
>
> **Kara**: Being happy with myself. I accomplished this and – maybe good workmates. I know they won't always be a happy workplace but just knowing I got this far and I was right to do all these courses and I've – even just doing auditing and WH&S I'm able to find different conversation points with people so ice breakers. So in one way to me as a nervous person I'm happy being able to have conversations with people and that probably helps in community services because everyone comes from different backgrounds. I can maybe relate to them in some way. It's hard to know about the future.

Here, Kara's confidence is both a holistic aspect of herself and her overall approach to the world, and a specific job skill that she hopes might be useful in work that is relationally intensive and involves connecting with a diverse range of people. In this sense, Kara becomes productive not through an exchange relationship taking place with an employer, but rather through her efforts to cultivate productivity amidst unemployment. If, as Weeks (2011) argues, the work ethic is critical to the formation and discipline of the contemporary working class, then Kara becomes positioned as working class precisely through her unemployment.

In cultivating productivity, Kara's overall hope was to avoid poverty, feel accomplished in life, and increase her capacity to connect with others. As part of this, Kara described her involvement in a 'breakfast club' run by a local organisation that provided free breakfasts to whoever desired them. Kara and her father used this breakfast club for its intended purpose (that is, free food and socialising), but she also described her attendance at this club as a form of 'networking' which might assist her to gain work in the community services field in the future. Kara also cultivated relationships with a range of others who she felt might help her with her studies or to secure future employment, and also used the term 'networking' to describe these relationships – a term that typically refers to fluid and strategically negotiated relationships between professionals, but which in this instance was used to describe how Kara's social life informed her efforts to become productive. In her words, she hoped that these relationships would help her 'amp it up a bit more' – enhancing her employability by connecting her to others who would recognise her value. Indeed, her relationships with others were a key preoccupation for Kara and an important aspect of the cultivation of herself as a productive subject, and were part of an expansive range of personal attributes that she hoped to mobilise in order to find work.

As Skeggs (1997) has famously shown, the celebration of the value-accruing individual takes place through the symbolic devalorisation of working-class modes of bodily comportment and relationality, creating forms of both resistance and anxiety amongst working-class women. In this context, Kara felt that her relational abilities and overall bodily comportment were a concern, and she was actively addressing this through a leadership training and public speaking course organised by a local community organisation. Discussing this course, Kara focused on exercises that were designed to refine her self-presentation and capacity to interact with others, which she considered a critical job skill:

Kara: When I did my [leadership training] ... [I] do a lot of public speaking, how to move with purpose, how to ... Use your hands – hands can be distracting as well and your eye gaze as well. I'm really bad at it. Also doing some job skills like being able to not stand too close to a person but far enough away … I had some good praise so I was happy … With the eye gaze we had to stand in front of the group and not smile for a whole minute, just look around and people just nod back. A lot of people broke into laughter. I just stood there and didn't fidget.

Kara's narrative about this leadership training course reveals an expansive definition of 'job skills', which comes to include minute details of her bodily comportment including the movement of her hands, her distance from others, and the length of time she maintains eye contact in conversation. This studied and disciplined approach to her bodily comportment is therefore part of a diverse range of practices including educational qualifications and broader 'networking' practices that are designed to make her productive and employable. Her course in public speaking and the bodily comportment exercises that she practises are preparation for a future in work, where she hopes she will be seen as confident, accomplished and relationally skilled. In this sense, the aspects of herself that contribute to her productivity are limitless, encompassing all aspects of her personal and bodily orientation to the world and to a future defined by the possibility (if not the actuality) of employment.

Interviewed for a second time, Kara remained unsuccessful in finding work. She attended the research interview with printed copies of rejection emails that she had received from multiple prospective employers to demonstrate her ongoing effort to find work. She had applied for a diverse range of jobs, encouraged in part by her own commitment to work and by the increasingly strict mutual obligation requirements placed upon her as part of her welfare payments, which mandated a specific number of job applications per week. As well as submitting these applications, Kara had also been required to attend a series of meetings to discuss her job prospects. She found these meetings intimidating and the process or intended outcomes of these meetings had not been explained to her. She suspected she was being perceived as intransigent as a result of her failure to properly account for herself in these discussions, the rules of which she found opaque.

Nevertheless, despite these discouraging experiences she continued her broader activities to cultivate productivity and enhance her employability. This included a series of volunteer activities and another certification, and her narrative reveals constant efforts to discipline herself and remain motivated:

> **Kara**: People will look and go, 'Why is she still volunteering?' 'What are you going to do with it?' You have to justify why you're doing it. I always say, 'Good referees, I need it' ... I try to give myself a reason. Why I have to make myself go and volunteer. I've been going one Thursday, and then next week I'll go ... I was sick, or I'm trying to avoid it.
>
> [I] might not find that until maybe 30 or 40, what I'm really meant to be doing. I don't know. I just feel like nothing's clear at the moment. Just started a new small qualification ... Bookkeeping. Just for my own interest ... I'm really not a clear-cut case.

Notwithstanding these ongoing and increasingly effortful activities, Kara suspects that she may not find out what she is 'really meant' to be doing for work for another ten or twenty years. Work remains the key temporal horizon around which all of her other activities are organised, but it also appears increasingly distant despite her redoubled efforts to find employment and appear employable. Disciplined and apparently productive, yet unable to find a way forward, Kara describes feeling 'like an outsider':

> **Kara**: I'm not a clear-cut person ... I'm not in the same boat as everyone else. That's what I feel like. I feel like an outsider. I work myself hard, and people notice, but don't always say. I just have to keep going. This is developing a character, now. Like, resilience. If it goes badly, keep going back.

In this, her narrative cites notions of resilience and character that are increasingly part of contemporary notions of employability, in which flexibility and an entrepreneurial mindset are intertwined with 'true grit' in the face of adversity. In public discussions about class in Australia, these characteristics are also associated with the figure of the 'battler' – the white working-class Australian who achieves security and perhaps social mobility through their dedicated commitment to labour. In Kara's case however, these attributes are cultivated through her experience of unemployment, meaning that she both identifies with, and is excluded from, these classed signifiers of moral worth in Australia. Cultivating productivity amidst unemployment is therefore a way that the classed dimensions of the post-Fordist work ethic are articulated in the absence of paid work.

Class, Productivity and Unemployment

In this chapter we have sought to theorise how productivity and class are intertwined in the experience of contemporary unemployment. We have suggested the concept of productive intensities as a way of understanding how the expansive demands of the post-Fordist work ethic frames the relationship of contemporary class to unemployment. The notion of productivity is tied to class inasmuch as productivity is generally assumed to be associated with one's status as a paid worker: it is supposed that it is in becoming a worker that one becomes productive, and in the process becomes classed. Becoming productive in conditions of unemployment therefore represents a new articulation of the relationship between class, productivity and work. Unemployment shifts from the absence of work to the future potential of employment, a future horizon that may be reached through the cultivation of productivity as an aspect of the self. For Kara, being busy, completing certificates, volunteering, and endlessly applying for jobs are all part of the labour she conducts in order to performatively demonstrate her work readiness. This may not be formal labour conducted in exchange for wages, but it is nevertheless a means by which Kara adheres to the post-Fordist work ethic (Weeks, 2011), in that Kara understands these activities are about accruing value of the self. Correspondingly, the value of her labour, and indeed of herself, 'lies not in accumulated embodied skills and experience but in potential capacities' (Adkins, 2012, p. 623). It is in these capacities that we find the relations to class amidst unemployment.

As Kara's case demonstrates, productive intensities are not simply about *doing* the many activities that might lead to employment but are also about the affective relations of these activities. The post-Fordist work ethic makes the aspects of classed subjectivities that are relevant to becoming productive increasingly expansive, encompassing all aspects of bodily comportment, relational style and attitudes towards the future. Kara's narratives of resilience, capacity, discipline, accomplishment, anxiety, bewilderment, frustration all emerge from her relationship with the work ethic and are enacted as classed dimensions of the requirement to become productive amidst unemployment. Productive intensities, thus, becomes a means by which the contemporary articulations of the work ethic are experienced in unemployment, as the unemployed orient themselves to the horizon of employment through engaging in a range of self-valorising activities. Class, in this sense, is articulated through this orientation to potential employment, which goes well beyond 'waiting' for paid work, to enacting and self-directing 'productivity' in unemployment.

References

ABC News. (2019, July 10). Indigenous unpaid wages could be up to $500 million, analysts claim. *ABC News*. Retrieved from https://www.abc.net.au/news/2019-07-10/indigenous-unpaid-wages-real-figure-500-million/11294934

Adkins, L. (2012). Out of work or out of time: Rethinking labor after the financial crisis. *South Atlantic Quarterly, 111*(4), 621–641.

Berlant, L. (2011). Cruel optimism. Durham: Duke University Press.

Bolton, S. (2009). The lady vanishes: Women's work and affective labour. *International Journal of Work Organisation and Emotion, 3*(1), 72–80.

Considine, M., Lewis, J.M., O'Sullivan, S., & Sol, E. (2015). *Getting welfare to work: Street-level governance in Australia, the UK, and the Netherlands*. Oxford: Oxford University Press.

Farrugia, D. (2021). *Youth, work and the post-Fordist self*. Bristol: Bristol University Press.

Federici, S. (2008). *Precarious labour: a feminist viewpoint*. Retrieved from http://inthemiddleofthewhirlwind.wordpress.com/precarious-labor-a-feminist-viewpoint/

Flyvbjerg, B. (2006). Five misunderstandings about case-study research. *Qualitative Inquiry, 12*(2), 219–245.

Friedli, L., & Stearn, R. (2015). Positive affect as coercive strategy: Conditionality, activation and the role of psychology in UK government workfare programmes. *Critical Medical Humanities, 41*(1), 40–47.

Gerrard, J. (2014). All that is solid melts into work: Self-work, the 'learning ethic' and the work ethic. *The Sociological Review, 62*(4), 862–879.

Gerrard, J., & Farrugia, D. (2021). Class, affective labour and exploitation: Unemployment and the creation of work on the margins, *The Sociological Review, 69*(1), 240–255.

Gerrard, J., & Watson, J. (2021). The productivity of unemployment and the temporality of employment-to-come: Older disadvantaged job seekers. *Sociological Research Online*, https://doi.org/10.1177/13607804211009534.

Gill, R., & Pratt, A. (2008). In the social factory? Immaterial labour, precariousnsess and cultural work. *Theory, Culture & Society, 27*(7–8), 1–30.

Hardt, M. (1999). Affective labour. *Boundary 2, 26*(2), 89–100.

Hardt, M., & Negri, A. (2000). *Empire*. Cambridge, MA: Harvard University Press.

Hochschild, A. (1983). *The managed heart: Commercialization of human feeling*. Berkeley: University of Chicago Press.

McDonald, C., & Marston, G. (2005). Workfare as welfare: Governing unemployment in the advanced liberal state. *Critical Social Policy, 25*(3), 374–401.

McDowell, L. (2008). The new economy, class condescension and caring labour: Changing formations of class and gender. *NORA – Nordic Journal of Feminist and Gender Research, 16*(3), 150–165.

McRobbie, A. (2010). Reflections on feminism, immaterial labour and the post-Fordist regime, *New Formations, 70*(4), 60–76.

Reay, D. (2002). Shaun's story: Troubling discourses of white working-class masculinities, *Gender and Education, 14*(3), 221–234.

SBS News. (2020, June 29). Scott Morrison says unemployed Australians are not working because JobSeeker is too generous. *SBS News*. Retrieved from https://www.sbs.com.au/news/scott-morrison-says-unemployed-australians-are-not-working-because-jobseeker-is-too-generous

Skeggs, B. (1997). *Formations of class & gender: Becoming respectable*. London; Thousand Oaks, California: Sage.

Threadgold, S. (2020). *Bourdieu and affect*. Bristol: Bristol University Press.

Weeks, K. (2007). Life within and against work: Affective labour, feminist critique and post-Fordist politics. *Ephemera, 7*, 233–249.

Weeks, K. (2011). *The problem with work: Feminist, Marxist, antiwork politics, and postwork imaginaries*. Durham, NC and London: Duke University Press.

Part 3

Cultural Formations of Class

CHAPTER 8

BOGAN TALK

What It Says (and Can't Say) about Class in Australia

Deborah Warr, Keith Jacobs and Henry Paternoster

What Do We Talk about When We Talk about Class?

In his book *The Bogan Delusion* (2011, p. 34), David Nichols quotes the former Labor federal minister, Lindsay Tanner who, in 2006, wrote: 'It looks like bogan is a new word for working class'. A few years later in a piece for *The Conversation*, the writer and academic, Christopher Scanlon (2014) made a similar observation: 'When we talk about class, we don't use the "c-word". Instead, we use other less threatening terms – "bogan"'. Since the early 2000s it seems we have become comfortable talking about bogans while avoiding the economically and politically charged term 'working class'. This development is problematic because, as Nichols himself insists, 'bogans don't exist' (2011, p. 12). The bogan is not a description of someone who possesses a set of actual characteristics but a figurative concept that, as such, is a muddle of 'stereotypes, cliché, meme, target, scapegoat, folk devil and stigma' (Threadgold, 2019, p. 95). The figure of the bogan is troubling because over the same time that it has enabled us to sidestep issues of class, overt forms of class prejudice have become more socially acceptable. Indeed, referring to people as bogans is a slur that is tolerated in an era when insensitivity to the political and personal implications of social bigotry is otherwise roundly condemned.

There are scattered references to bogans stretching back to the 1980s, but the figure gained prominence in the early years of the 21st century. In his book, *Class in Australia* (1997), Craig McGregor devoted an entire chapter to contentious working-class depictions such as larrikins, 'ockers' and 'hoons', without ever mentioning bogans. By 2007, however, the term had a foothold in everyday parlance. Data from the Google website shows that since 2004 (the first year recorded) search terms including bogan steadily increased until plateauing in 2014. The figure of the bogan coincided with the emergence of the figure of the 'chav' – another euphemism for working class in the UK. Contemporary salience of these figures stems from changes in class conditions and relations associated with the pervasive influence of neoliberalism, and represents an alarming 'new vocabulary' for talking about working-class people (Jones, 2011; Tyler, 2008, p. 17; 2015). For instance, Owen Jones claimed that 'a form of class hatred has become an integral respectable part of modern British culture (2011, p. 6). Commentators such as Nichols detected similar trends in Australia; Nichols (2011, p.72) observed 'the class hatred infused in the rhetoric of bogandom'.

At the same time, there are differences between the two figures that suggest how class is further contoured by national contexts. In this chapter we show how the figure of the bogan reflects both the 'declassing' of inequalities and the socio-historical significance of class in Australia. We also explore how the term is being embedded in everyday language in ways that render working-class people as both visible and invisible with problematic effects. Sociologists have argued that the emergence of figures such as chavs and bogans is related to the conditions of neoliberal capitalism that were ascendant across Western nations in the closing decades of the 20th century. Amid processes of deindustrialisation as manufacturing moved offshore, the casualisation of labour markets, the winding back of the welfare state, and the disintegration of working-class socio-political formations, such as trade unions, the everyday lives of many working-class people, and their communities, were transforming. As economic security declined, neoliberal tenets emphasised personal and local responsibility (Amin, 2005), implying that situations of poverty and relative disadvantage can be attributed to individual failings such as poor choices, imprudent behaviour and ignorance (Lawler, 2005, p. 435; Savage, 2003; Tyler, 2013). The shift from talking about the working class to talking about bogans personifies the neoliberal creed that people are to blame for deteriorating situations.

Referring to people as 'bogans' is tolerated by the political right and left. Many on the right may have long sneered at the working class, and those holding left-wing views also talk shamelessly about bogans. The latter may be explained by divisions among the political left that emerged in the post-war years. The civil rights movement and growing, long-overdue recognition of injustices associated with sexism, homophobia and racism contributed to decentring the significance of class – which identifies the importance of labour relations in structuring socio-economic opportunities and inequalities – within left-wing politics. The rise of the 'New Left', emphasising socially progressive agendas and attracting middle-class supporters, led to tensions with established forms of working-class activism attentive to blue-collar (male) jobs and conditions. Conservatives such as Coalition prime minister John Howard (1996–2007) were able to exploit these tensions recasting disenchanted (frequently male) working-class, blue-collar workers as 'battlers' whose interests align with those of capital.

The combination of social changes that informed new agendas for the political left and rhetorical and policy manoeuvring from the right contributed to complex rearrangements in political affiliations (Paternoster, Warr, & Jacobs, 2018). It was within these contexts that the figure of the bogan came to operate as a signifier for the different kinds of (working-class) unworthiness: bearers of socially regressive views (by the left) and being economically unproductive (by the right). An intriguing aspect of the bogan, however, and particularly compared with the utterly abject figure of the chav (Tyler, 2015), is its ambivalence. For instance, Rossiter

(2013, p. 81) notes that references to bogans can be 'spiked with love', and when confronted with being labelled a bogan, people can react with 'a mix of defensiveness, rejection, subversion, irony, *pride*' (Gibson, 2013, p. 71, emphasis added). People with working-class backgrounds have reflected how portrayals of bogans on television were relatable, funny and uncomfortable (See-Tho, 2014). Despite its largely pejorative connotations, the bogan remains difficult to definitively characterise and decipher. Its floating meanings operate in similar ways to those the cultural theorist, Fredrick Jameson (1979, p. 142), ascribed to the shark in the film, *Jaws* (1975) when he interpreted its significance as 'l[ying] less in any single message or meaning than its very capacity to absorb and organise … quite distinct anxieties'.

It is within this ambivalence that we discern something peculiarly Australian about the term bogan that merits attention. We argue that its floating meanings are attributable to the socio-historical specificities of class relations in Australia. The bogan contains residues of meanings that are related to working-class identities stretching back to the colonial settlement of Australia. To elaborate on this claim, we draw from our research focusing on three notable historical and recent periods of Australian history that involved a resetting of class politics that had enduring popular and political effects (Kirk, 2011; Paternoster et al., 2018). A study of these three periods enables us to chart a genealogy of the figure of the bogan that can help explain its ambivalent refractions of class in contemporary Australia.

The first period is the emergence of the labour movement in the 1890s. This period was the focus of an influential book, *The Australian Legend* (1978 [1958]), by the historian Russell Ward who argued that the Australian labour movement contributed to the formation of a distinctive 'national mystique' that was characterised by egalitarianism, anti-authoritarianism and collectivism, and influenced a nascent (White) Australian identity. The second period is the political ascendancy of Robert Menzies in the mid-20th century when he refashioned egalitarian ideals into a suburban identity for the swelling middle classes at a time when many working-class people were enjoying the prosperity and security of the post-war years

(Brett, 2003). The third period we consider are the *fin de siècle* years of John Howard's prime ministership when he offered another notable reworking of the Australian mystique. This involved reimagining working-class people as 'battlers' and locating ordinary people as a point of contrast against cultural elites. It is this third period that marks Howard's consolidation of neoliberal market logics to the arenas of personal and social life and it is here that the bogan enters vernacular discourse.

This periodisation sets the scene for a discussion of a media analysis that considers in more precise ways how the bogan is deployed in language to talk about processes of social distinction and whether the figure offers any potential to talk about class in meaningful ways. In concluding, we argue for bringing class back into the frame and interweaving it with other processes structuring contemporary inequalities.

The Genealogy of the Bogan

Following white settlement in Australia, the colonies offered unprecedented opportunities for (white, male) workers in a burgeoning agricultural economy and a refuge from the rigid socio-cultural status hierarchies of Europe (Connell & Irving, 1992). Convicts sentenced to transportation included high proportions of Irish Catholics, who had endured intense discrimination. Transported political radicals and agitators, such as the Tolpuddle Martyrs and others supporting the Chartist movement for male suffrage, also influenced working-class politics in the colonies (Moore, 2009). By the 1890s, the labour movement was organising to advance its political representation and was effective in securing good wages and conditions for a largely agricultural workforce. Aided by the imaginative works of writers and poets, a nascent sense of Australian identity became strongly associated with the labour movement and particularly a valorised ethos of itinerant bush labourers that emphasised egalitarianism, a disdain for high culture, and the value of 'mateship' (Ward, 1978 [1958]).

This is not to say that Australia was a workers' paradise. The egalitarian, and anti-authoritarian spirit celebrated by writers and poets did not extend to Aboriginal and Torres Strait Islander peoples who were displaced from their lands and subjected to ruthless cruelty and violence. Nor did fraternal spirit extend to women. In *The Real Matilda* (1976, p. 21), Miriam Dixson noted that in colonial Australia the 'overall standing of women … comes close to the lowest among Western industrial democracies'. Nonetheless, the success of the Labor Party in the early years of the Federation further bolstered the significance of egalitarianism in the Australian national identity (Dyrenfurth, 2010; Paternoster, 2017; Ward, 1978 [1958]). It is important to recognise the complex and unique configuration of circumstances of white settlement that shaped experiences of class and class relations in Australia. It contrasts with other comparable nations such as the UK, where the labour movement challenged an extant feudal monarchy and an established mercantile class; and North America whose economic prosperity was enmeshed with the exploitation of slaves and indentured labourers (Isenberg, 2016).

Australia was also distinctive because of the influence of working-class politics in a formative period of its socio-political history and where white working-class men came to embody a quintessential 'Australianness'. And yet this identity did not dispel contemporary tensions and ambivalence towards working-class figures such as larrikins, a term of abuse that, similar to the bogan, also elicited an amused tolerant affection (Bellanta, 2012). Other qualities of the larrikin are also evident in the bogan, including its association with masculinity. There were, however, notable differences, such as the relative socio-demographic significance and political power of the working class that persisted into the early decades of the 20th century and which may have given the larrikin a more mainstream resonance.

The political influence of the labour movement declined in the years following World War II and the newly established Liberal Party, led by Robert Menzies, formed government following the 1949 federal election and held office until 1972 (with Menzies retiring in 1966). As Judith Brett details in her book, *Australian Liberals and the Moral Middle Class* (2003), their dominance in the post-war years can be attributed to the way that Menzies was able to naturalise middle-class values by transferring working-class associations with egalitarianism and hard work onto suburban families. Reconceiving these families as a 'class of individuals' defined by their 'attributes and moral qualities' (Brett, 2003, p. 9), Menzies described them as:

> The forgotten people ... constantly in danger of being ground between the upper and nether millstones of the false class war: the middle class who, properly regarded, represent the backbone of the country (Brett, 2003, p. 8).

This depiction resounded with voters because the long boom of the post-war years provided conditions that enabled working-class people to believe that hard work and discipline bore fruit. Australia was the land of opportunity as suburban families became homeowners, purchased new appliances and enjoyed well-earned leisure time. One outcome of this period, however, was the entrenchment of longstanding distinctions between a hardworking and diligent, 'respectable' (deserving) working class who were rewarded for emulating middle-class virtues, while condoning disapproval towards an 'unrespectable' (undeserving) element who refused, or were unable, to do so. To some extent, the general affluence of the post-war years cloaked the moral significance that was attributed to class differences, where an unrespectable working class was problematised and pathologised in ways that prefigure the bogan (Finch, 1993).

As the century proceeded, left- and right-wing politics continued to be shaped by social and economic changes sweeping the nation. Widening participation in tertiary education, growing demand for knowledge-based professions, and the emergence of socially progressive movements were reworking traditional political affiliations. New kinds of white-collar work increased and radicalised segments of the middle class, contributing to the electoral success of the federal Labor Party in 1972. As political commentator Paul Kelly observed, Labor had become 'a respectable party for the expanding middle classes' (1994, p. 20). Socially progressive concerns pushed by 'New Left' movements, however, frequently clashed with the preoccupations of those associated with the 'Old' Left whose jobs began disappearing as manufacturing industries contracted and moved offshore, and employer demands for 'flexibility' translated into deteriorating and insecure work conditions. When Australia finally officially recognised itself as a 'multicultural' society and overturned the White Australia policy, Russell Ward's idealised vision of colonial masculinity was subjected to ferocious critique from the 'New Left' for being racist, sexist and ignorant. As the socio-cultural legitimacy of the 'Old Left' waned, John Howard identified a political opportunity in his professed support for 'battlers' who were left feeling disillusioned and abandoned by Labor.

Following Menzies, Howard's electoral success as the second longest-serving Liberal leader can be partly explained by his acumen in reformulating class oppositions. This time distinctions were formed to divide 'battlers' or 'ordinary people' from a 'self-appointed, cultural elite' that impose their self-interested values on others (cited in Brett, 2003, p. 196). In this reworking, the elites included bureaucrats, academics and others paid from the public purse. Once again, values of egalitarianism were invoked but this time they were linked to the legacy of the ANZACs. In a 'headland' speech delivered as leader of the opposition in 1995, Howard claimed that, 'National identity develops in an organic way over time. It may be changed dramatically by cataclysmic events like Gallipoli'. Further on, he explained: 'To me, like many, the Australian identity has always meant practical mateship. It has meant a great egalitarian tradition, shunning pretension and pomposity'. While there is much going on here, one point is that Howard was recuperating the Australian mystique for 'ordinary and hardworking Australians', while Labor countered with an appeal to 'working families'. It is around this time that the figure of the bogan gained prominence in everyday language to represent an updated version of the unrespectable working class that held different kinds of unworthiness. For the right, the figure is a container for those unable or unwilling to be workers – 'leaners' not 'lifters' in the crude parlance of a former treasurer, Joe Hockey. For the left, the figure is a container for anti-progressive attitudes and behaviours.

In tracing these characterisations of the working class across these key periods we suggest that the figure of the bogan operates as a container for residues of meaning and contradictions that are accumulating through complex and intersecting processes of social, economic and cultural change. The bogan personifies an experience of being 'working class' that is being hollowed out through the effects of restructured labour markets and the growing significance of other identify formations that are important in explaining how opportunities and disadvantages are socially structured, such as race and gender. Related to this, middle-class aspirations and values are universalised and valorised as 'normal' and proper for all social groups. This cultural form of 'embourgeoisification' is effectively split off from political demands for economic and social reform (Savage, 2003). Owen Jones (2011, p. 137) recognised this when he wrote:

> Everything is to be judged by middle-class standards because, after all, that is what we are expected to aspire to. The working class is therefore portrayed as a useless vestige made up of 'non-aspirational' layabouts, slobs, racists, boozers, thugs – you name it.

Up to this point our discussion has traced the contexts in which the figure of the 'bogan' gained currency. Next, we extend our analysis by considering how references to bogans in newspapers shed further light on popular understanding of working-class identities in contemporary Australia.

Bogan Talk in the Media

While the anonymity and invisibility afforded by social media contribute careless and frequently vituperative expressions of class prejudice through website and Facebook groups such as 'Things Bogans Like', references to bogans in newspapers present insights into how the figure is being used to talk about class in public arenas. To consider this, we draw on an analysis of references to bogans and chavs in a sample of Australian and UK newspapers, although our discussion focuses on the former. The *Factiva* database was used to identify references to bogans and chavs in a sample of ten newspapers (a mix of five tabloid and broadsheet newspapers from each country). A dataset of 200 items for each national sample was considered sufficient to provide theoretical saturation. Commencing on 31 May 2014 and going back in time, the first 200 media items to mention 'bogans' or 'chavs' were included in the analyses. The final item in the British dataset was published on 15 December 2011 (a time span of just over 28 months), while the final item in the Australian dataset was published on 24 April 2013 (a time span of just over 12 months). During this period, references to chavs dropped off over time, while 'bogans' remained consistent.

In both samples references to bogans and chavs appeared in news reporting, analysis and commentary, lifestyle and entertainment pieces, editorial opinions and readers' letters. While 76 per cent of references to chavs appeared in tabloid papers, they accounted for 45 per cent of references to bogans. References broadly reflected the ways in which the figures of bogans and chavs are generally associated with problematic attitudes, including having poor taste, being badly behaved, and being sexist and racist (70 per cent of the UK sample and 54 per cent of the Australian sample). A small number of references cast the figures as victims of circumstances (Australia: 3 per cent, UK: 5.5 per cent) and 9 per cent of references to bogans were positive, compared to less than 1 per cent of references to chavs. Both samples provided examples of usage that could not be precisely coded because their meanings were assumed, and these were particularly evident in the Australian sample (34 per cent of references to bogans, compared to 16.5 per cent of references to chavs). In the UK sample, many of these references concerned public identities (usually on reality TV programs) and characters in television programs, routinely being referred to as chavs (for example a TV guide in the *Daily Mail* unfailingly described a character as 'chav wife Kylie'). With some contrast, these kinds of references in the Australian media concerned two popular television programs with 'bogan' in their titles – *The Bogan Hunters* and *Upper Middle Bogan* – that were widely discussed during the period of data collection. Other examples appeared in reviews of films, books and other forms of cultural production.

Associating bogans with poor taste or bad behaviour included a reference to 'care-o-bogan prisons' (*Herald Sun*, 14/2/2014), a discussion of the scourge of methamphetamine addiction that was described as, 'not just some bogan aberration in the Badlands on the "wrong side of town". It's everywhere' (*Herald Sun*, 15/11/2013), and a news item in *The Age* (8/2/2014) reporting that a 'small-time bogan dope trafficker [had been] sentenced to 20 years' jail in Bali'. The influence of socially progressive environmental and animal rights movements has widened notions of bad behaviour so that sports such as horseracing were viewed by one writer as supported by a 'bogan culture [that] revels in cruelty' (*Herald Sun*, 31/7/2013), while another wrote that a disregard for the environment is a 'bogan attitude [that] would be funny if it wasn't dumb, dangerous and lazy' (*Hobart Mercury*, 26/5/2014).

This extension of the bogan as tacitly working class and socially regressive was most pronounced in the arts and culture pages. Through a frisky, if glib, use of vernacular, references to bogans conceptualised a generalised, negative socio-cultural positioning. For example, a character played by the actress Cate Blanchett is described as a 'battered wife and bogan who finds Jesus in a snow dome' (*Financial Review*, 28/9/2013), and a character in a Wagner opera is a 'bit of a loutish fool bogan' (*The Age*, 25/11/2013). A poetry reviewer decries 'the bogan mindset' (*The Australian*, 8/3/2014), and science fiction is characterised as 'literature's bogan cousin' (*Financial Review*, 26/7/2013).

Numerous references to two television programs, *The Bogan Hunters* and *Upper Middle Bogan*, are notable for a few reasons. Media items discussing the programs attested to their popularity and they showed how the bogan is also used as a sympathetic trope for dramatising and exploring class relations in contemporary Australia. Evoking the respectable and unrespectable working classes, the two programs also offered contrasting renditions of the bogan. *The Bogan Hunters* blended the formats of reality television and 'mockumentary' to revel in exaggerated and crude stereotypes of an unrespectable working class. Real people, presumably selected for the ways in which they displayed and embodied stereotypical traits attributed to bogans, vied for audiences to vote them 'the biggest bogan'. 'Contestants' also interacted with actors performing hyperbolic bogan personas who egged them on to perform bogan excessiveness. As one television critic mused:

The show is presumably a salvo against what [the creator and star] sees as the insidious creeping force of middle-class values. Casting himself as an antidote, he ... celebrates boganism in all its tattooed, toothless, alcohol-guzzling, petrol-headed glory (*The Age*, 22/5/2014).

The other program, *Upper Middle Bogan*, centred on a woman born to working-class parents and adopted by an upper-middle-class family. Reunited with her biological parents, the humour revolves around her efforts to connect her two families across the socio-spatial distance of class. Emphasising cultural matters of taste and social status, it downplays economic differences. The working-class family are portrayed as authentic, warm and quirky 'cashed up bogans', with ostentatious tastes and living in a 'McMansion' in the outer suburbs, while the middle-class characters are over-invested in the need to display good taste. Avoiding unkind caricatures and judgements of class superiority or inferiority, this even-handed spoofing of class foibles has been described as 'equal opportunity satire' (Threadgold, 2018, p. 122), and praised for its deft 'navigation of the loose, relational structures of class in contemporary Australia' (Campbell, 2014, p. 40).

In different ways, these series tap into the ambivalent meanings associated with the figure of the bogan and contribute to a distinctive *oeuvre* of 'bogan comedy' in Australia (Campbell, 2014). *The Bogan Hunters* mines a similar vein as other series from its creator, Paul Fenech, such as *Housos*, which also treads a fine line between exploiting stereotypes of an underclass and offering what the cultural theorist, Jon Stratton (2017) reads as a satirical, carnivalesque skewering of neoliberal logics. Indeed, Stratton argues that Fenech's portrayals of the underclass in *Housos* are distinguished from representations in comparable UK and North America shows because they are 'offered through a prism of Australian myths, of egalitarianism, anti-authoritarianism and larrikinism' (Stratton 2017, p. 542). Nevertheless, residents of an actual public housing estate in Western Sydney unsuccessfully petitioned the New South Wales government to stop the first series of *Housos* going to air for fear that it recycled stereotypes that would reinforce the burdens of stigma they experienced (Arthurson, Darcy, & Rogers, 2014).

References to bogans in the newspapers showed how the figure is used as a way of talking about working-class and disadvantaged people while linking them to a mixed bag of failings and misdeeds ranging from displaying poor fashion sense, indulging in criminal behaviour to holding socially retrograde attitudes. These connotations support Beverley Skeggs' claim that working-class identities have become associated with being 'unmodern, inferior, ignorant and irresponsible' (2004, p. 99). If the category of 'working class' is revalued as irredeemably negative, then it is a short step to replace it with a slur, and then for this slur to be used to describe an expanding array of problematic attitudes and behaviours, such as being cruel to animals and not caring for the environment. In these ways, as Pini and Previte (2013) have shown, bogans are construed as not just lacking economic, social and cultural capital but also forms of 'spiritual' and 'environmental' capital.

Rubbing up against tendencies to void working-class identities of positive value, the genealogy of the bogan reveals how the figure holds residues of meanings that affirm working-class identities. This is most apparent in the discussions of television programs that use the figure to present a sympathetic working-class standpoint. Deploying the bogan in these ways, as a composite of derogatory and lurid stereotypes, clichés and shifting meanings, involves risks of reinforcing negative associations with, rather than recuperating, working-class identities. Further, while it has comedic potential, there is little prospect of using the figure to interrogate complex issues of identity and inequality.

How to Talk about Inequality?

What conclusions can be drawn from the analysis set out in this chapter? First, the meanings attributed to bogans are mostly negative but flecked with ambivalences that evoke the prominence of working-class identities in social and political imaginaries. Within this ambivalence there is potential for some positive identification, although this is constrained by being freighted with largely derogatory meanings and its implicitly gendered and racialised characteristics (Pini & Previte, 2014). Second, the analysis of references to bogans in newspapers shows that talking about bogans impoverishes our language for understanding how access to employment, labour relations and unemployment contribute to structural inequalities at a time when processes generating inequalities are complex and intersecting with other structuring conditions. These include the legacy of Aboriginal dispossession, racism, sexism and other factors contributing to socio-economic inequalities. Talking about bogans instead of class facilitates a sleight of hand that enables a figure deemed (largely) problematic to become a useful container of all kinds of 'bad' letting an opposite, idealised category off the hook.

As it is, the bogan has currency for the political right and left to segment the working classes who, to date, have borne the brunt of neoliberal economic restructuring. The right uses bogans to defuse the politics of class by distinguishing between aspirational 'ordinary and hard-working Australians' and the economically dispossessed, while among the left, the language of bogans reveals struggles to reconcile class and identity politics. It remains critical for the left to bring these politics together to inform political projects 'that create conditions for solidarity and effective resistance' (Kumar et al., 2018, p. 10). The first step is to resist glib references to illusory bogans and recover and revitalise the language of class.

Acknowledgements

We wish to acknowledge the contribution of Camille La Brooy who worked on the media analyses discussed in this chapter.

References

Amin, A. (2005). Local community on trial. *Economy and Society, 34*(4), 612–633.

Arthurson, K., Darcy, M., & Rogers, D. (2014). Televised territorial stigma: How social housing tenants experience the fictional media represtions of estates in Australia. *Environment and Planning A, 46*, 1334–1350.

Bellanta, M. (2012). *Larrikins: A history*. St Lucia: University of Queensland Press.

Brett, J. (2003). *Australian Liberals and the moral middle class: From Alfred Deakin to John Howard*. Cambridge: Cambridge University Press.

Campbell, M. (2014). Opposite ends of the freeway: Upper Middle Bogan and the mobility of class distinction. *Metro Magazine: Media & Education Magazine,* (181), 36–40.

Connell, R.W. & Irving, T.H. (1992). *Class structure in Australian history: Poverty and progress*. Melbourne: Longman Cheshire.

Dixson, M. (1976). *The real Matilda*. Middlesex: Penguin Books.

Dyrenfurth, N. (2010). 'Never hitherto seen outside of a zoo or a menagerie': The language of Australian politics. *Australian Journal of Politics and History, 56*(1), 38–54.

Finch, L. (1993). *The classing gaze: Sexuality, class and surveillance*. St Leonards, NSW: Allen & Unwin.

Gibson, C. (2013). Welcome to Bogan-ville: Reframing class and place through humour. *Journal of Australian Studies, 37*(1), 62–75.

Isenberg, N. (2016). *White trash: The 400-Year Untold History of Class in America*. New York: Penguin.

Jameson, F. (1979). Reification and utopia in mass culture. *Social Text, 1*(Winter), 130–148.

Jones, O. (2011). *Chavs: The demonization of the working class*. London: Verso.

Kelly, P. (1994). *The end of certainty: Power, politics and business in Australia*. St Leonards: Allen and Unwin.

Kirk, N. (2011). *Labour and the politics of empire: Britain and Australia, 1900 to the present*. Manchester: Manchester University Press.

Kumar, A., Elliott-Cooper, A., Iyer, S., & Gebrial, D. (2018). An introduction to the special issues on identity politics. *Historical Materialism, 26*(2), 3–20.

Lawler, S. (2005). Disgusted subjects: The making of middle-class identities. *The Sociological Review, 53*(3), 429–446.

McGregor, C. (1997). *Class in Australia*. Ringwood: Penguin Books Australia.

Moore, T. (2009). *Death or liberty: Rebels and radicals transported to Australia 1788–1868*. Sydney: Murdoch Books.

Nichols, D. (2011). *The bogan delusion*. Mulgrave: Affirm Press.

Paternoster, H. (2017). *Reimagining class in Australia*. Cham, Switzerland: Palgrave Macmillan.

Paternoster, H., Warr, D., & Jacobs, K. (2018). The enigma of the bogan and its significance to class in Australia: A socio-historical analysis. *Journal of Sociology, 54*(3), 429–445.

Pini, B., & Previte, J. (2013). Bourdieu, the boom and cashed-up bogans. *Journal of Sociology, 49*(2–3), 256–271.
Pini, B., & Previte, J. (2014). Gender, class and sexuality in contemporary Australia. *Australian Feminist Studies, 28*(78), 348–363.
Rossiter, P. (2013). Bogans: A sticky subject. *Continuum: Journal of Media & Cultural Studies, 27*(1), 80–92.
Savage, M. (2003). A new class paradigm. *British Journal of Sociology of Education, 24*(4), 535–541.
Scanlon, C. (2014, February 24). Bogans and hipsters: We're talking the living language of class. *The Conversation*. Retrieved from https://theconversation.com/bogans-and-hipsters-were-talking-the-living-language-of-class-23007
See-Tho, M. (2014). On bogans. *Overland*, 11. Retrieved from https://overland.org.au/2014/11/on-bogans/
Skeggs, B. (2004). *Class, self, culture*. London: Routledge.
Stratton, J. (2017). Pizza and *Housos*: Neoliberalism, the discursive construction of the underclass and its representation. *Journal of Intercultural Studies, 38*(5), 530–544.
Threadgold, S. (2018). *Youth, class and everyday struggles*. Milton Park, Oxon: Routledge.
Threadgold, S. (2019). Figures of youth: On the very object of Youth Studies. *Journal of Youth Studies, 23*(6), 686–671.
Tyler, I. (2008). 'Chav mum chav scum': Class disgust in contemporary Britain. *Feminist Media Studies, 8*(1), 17–34.
Tyler, I. (2013). *Revolting subjects*. London: Zed Books.
Tyler, I. (2015). Classificatory struggles: Class, culture and inequality in neoliberal times. *The Sociological Review, 63*(2), 493–511.
Ward, R. (1978 [1958]). *The Australian legend*. Melbourne: Oxford University Press.

CHAPTER 9

STRUGGLE STREET

Poverty Porn?

Penny Rossiter

Introduction

In 2015, the first series of a new program – *Struggle Street* [henceforth, *SS1*] (Radomsky, 2015) – aired on SBS. Even before the first episode went to air, the promo for the program generated considerable flak including a garbage truck blockade of SBS headquarters. It was filmed in Mt Druitt in Sydney's west, and the local mayor, Stephen Bali (Kerin, Ong & staff, 2015), angrily rejected it as yet another stigmatising and distorted representation of the area: 'What I saw wasn't a documentary, it was simply publicly funded poverty porn'. This view was echoed by many others, but when it went to air, the first-night audience reached 935,000, and the final night attracted over a million viewers; the highest ever figures for a locally made show on SBS (Lallo, 2015). *SS1* was made by independent production company KEO 'franchising the format' (De Benedictis, Allen, & Jensen, 2017, p. 351) off the back of their UK production of *Skint* (2013) filmed in Grimsby and then aired on Channel 4. *Skint* attracted very similar criticism (Pidd, 2014,) but apparently KEO gained little insight from this, or nothing that mattered enough when there's money to be made from poverty. While money is made, people and communities are demonised, and class structure and inequality are naturalised. As Jensen (2014) has argued in relation to the UK experience, '… the national abjects of poverty porn serve to transform precarity into moral failure, worklessness into laziness, and social immobility and disconnection into an individual failure to strive and aspire' (p. 4). The political stakes are high, and the ideological sweep of shows deemed 'poverty porn' is broad but, as I shall demonstrate, attention to national and local specificity is important too.

Despite all the controversy surrounding *SS1*, a second series [henceforth *SS2*] (Howes and Brown, 2017) was made in 2017, filmed (against considerable local opposition) in Inala in Queensland, and Broadmeadows and Seddon in Victoria. Numbers reduced considerably for *SS2*, averaging 250,000 to 300,000 viewers per episode (Blackiston, 2019). That's a shame, for *SS2* is a markedly better production and SBS effectively utilised a range of strategies to structurally and politically contextualise participants' stories. A third series was filmed in 2019 in the Riverina, NSW, but this introduces rural issues that are beyond the scope of this paper. The focus here is the claim that *Struggle Street* is little more than 'poverty porn', that damages rather than educates, and I shall explore this through a comparison of *SS1* and *SS2*. I shall demonstrate that the label 'poverty porn' may reasonably apply to *SS1*, but less so to *SS2*, and that there are both textual and extra-textual reasons for this. However, I also argue that if we attend more closely to form as well as content, and to the affective qualities of the televisual spectacle that is 'Factual Welfare Television' (De Benedictus et al., 2017), a more nuanced reading is available to us. The leakiness of the entangled affectivity of people and place can bolster, but also radically subvert, the pornographic gaze.

Struggle Street Series One: Poverty Porn?

According to Lamb (2016, p. 2), the term 'poverty porn' originated in the critical reception of the award-winning film *Slumdog Millionaire*. One of the first to use the term in relation to *SS1* was Blacktown mayor Stephen Bali after the promo for the show aired. The original promo (revised after public protest) can still be found via a link on *The Guardian* online (Tan, 2015). It is truly awful: shockingly sensationalist, contemptuous of its participants. Threadgold's (2015) description is apt: 'poverty porn produces abjectifying images of the poor through a privileged gaze for privileged gratification'. Poverty porn is a genre of reality TV that focuses on subjects who are (variously described as) poor, disadvantaged, marginalised, in a way that sensationalises, objectifies, and creates for 'disgusted (mainly) middle-class' subjects a form of viewing pleasure that de-contextualises and de-politicises the suffering they are invited to view. Further, it does little to invite any meaningful form of empathy and indeed, often – whether explicitly through voice over, the camera angles, shots, or the selection of 'scenes' for display – solicits a critical and judgemental distance. Alcorn (2015) adds a further dimension to the definition in her argument that it's only poverty porn 'if we have a look, kind of enjoy being sad and shocked and then turn away to other things'. There are two ways of further exploring this: through a consideration of responses to *Struggle Street*, and through a closer look at the relationship between form and content in the show. On the latter, it is instructive to begin with SBS's defence of *SS1*.

SBS Responding to Critics: The Raw and the Cooked

The SBS defence of *SS1* was that these are stories that need to be told; they are shedding light on a grave concern. The then SBS chief content officer, Helen Kellie, justified the first series as follows:

> This is not a sugarcoated version of people's lives, these are the real lives of the participants. These are people living with unemployment, long-term illness and serious drug addiction. It's important that instead of putting commentary around them, we have shown in the raw the footage gained from following these people around (Mediaweek, 2015).

Leaving to one side the claims of trickery and manipulation made by some participants, this is an extraordinarily naive claim about television and filming. In the renunciation of the filmmakers' agency in casting, scriptwriting, lighting, editing, and so on, Kellie implies that they didn't actually *make* anything at all; they just gave us raw footage as if it were all done by GoPro and Dash Cams and the files then simply uploaded. In fact, they did provide both verbal and visual commentary, and often in a way that simultaneously trashed both people and place. Sometimes, the problem was generated by a conflict between dispassionate verbal commentary and disparaging visual commentary. For example, in the introduction to the first episode of *SS1*, a script that may seem unobjectionable, read off the page, is utterly transformed by the camera shots that disparage:

> With more than a third of the population in public housing [shot of abandoned shopping trolley] in some areas [zoom in on fibro house graffitied on the outside]. And around 1 in 3 young people unemployed [matched with film of old red car burning rubber], the area is an easy target for a government hell bent on welfare cuts … when life sticks the boot in … it's about *how* you fight back [shot of a young man beating up another].

This, depressingly, sets the tone for what's to come.

Skeggs and Wood (in Wetherell 2009) argue (based on their UK research), that reality television's scopic regime privileges a 'metonymic morality' that spectacularises and stigmatises (working) classed lives:

> Our analysis showed how close-up long-held filming was constantly used rhetorically to illustrate failure – dirt, chipped nail varnish, plates of food and symbolised key problems. This forensic detailing we suggest constitutes a metonymic morality, whereby parts of a body, home or a particular object or practice stand in for the whole person. Again the metonym plays out class on the surface as a spectacular problem removed from its social context (p. 236).

In *SS1*, the metonymic morality (as seen in the quote above) intertwines the placial and the corporeal. The hopelessness of the place and the people fold into each other through the multimodal narration as if the real causes of inequality are neither structural, economic, political or in failed policy, but here in the material cultures and characters of folks from Mt Druitt. A Guardian journalist (Alcorn, 2015) argued that '*Struggle Street* wasn't really about the western Sydney suburb at all. It was about entrenched poverty, generational disadvantage and the desperate fringe'. But it *was* about Mt Druitt, and indeed people in Mt Druitt probably feel it was about Mt Druitt *again*, given the historically diverse forms of classed and 'raced' stigma that residents have endured (Peel, 2009; Watson, 2014). These stigmas stick to places and people, and amongst both local residents and councillors there is a strong perception of 'postcode discrimination' and a fear that *Struggle Street* will only make it worse (Bevan, 2015).

The Importance of Context

SS1 was criticised for its lack of contextualisation of both people and inequality in Australia. As Wood and Skeggs (2011) argue, a lack of historical and policy context means that 'the consequences of social and material forces are played out through the immediacy of the genre. Participants' failures, and sometimes their successes, are coded as psychological traits at the level of individual responsibility' (p. 15). And indeed, this is how many of the participants in SS1 and SS2 narrate their circumstances. William's self-reflection (Episode 1) seesaws between fatalism and the transformative potential of a more rigorously responsibilised self: 'Things are going pretty bad for me now. But they are only going bad because of the way I'm making it go. If I want it to come good, then I have to step up a bit. These days you need fucking money. Life's life'. Chris (Episode 2) is negotiating complex health issues and family relationships, but he doesn't, however, think 'it should entitle me to supplements and benefits'. As the commentator helpfully chips in: 'Chris is on the disability support pension but he'd rather not take the handout' (what Chris actually says is that he'd rather be 'normal'!). Bob (Episode 2) became addicted to heroin whilst at high school, but still, he too blames himself: 'Nothing's gone my way mate. It could of. Just from me own choices. Wish I wasn't like that, it ruined my life'. However, it is exactly in response to such comments in SS1 and SS2 that a well-made documentary can provide context and depth. As Dr Geoffrey Spurling (2017), a GP in Inala, observes:

> Clearly, some responsibility lies with individuals and their poor decisions. However, repeated studies have shown that people experiencing disadvantage, and all the stress that comes with it, are much more likely to make poor decisions, and then make much better decisions when their poverty and its accompanying stress are relieved.

When left to 'hang' without broader context, the (lack of) responsibilised self again features as the main problem. And the commentary for *SS1* is littered with references to 'staying in the game', as if structural disadvantage can be reduced to individual strategy. Jon Owen (2015), resident of Mt Druitt since 2007, argues that even with the best of intentions, 'it would take extraordinary luck and skill' to capture lived reality: 'The truth to be discovered on *Struggle Street* is not easily observed. It is known through participation'. The modes of solidarity and sociality that glue people to place and each other flies under the radar of a drive-in, drive-out crew. 'The truth is that people on *Struggle Street* routinely practise community in a way that most of Sydney knows only as an ideology' (Owen, 2015). As Owen (2015) also observes (about Mt Druitt): 'What's not shown are the cuts in funding to local schools, and great programs such as Eagles Wraps and the Excel Learning program for Indigenous students'. To be fair, the series is not without pointed commentary and contextualisation though this often comes from participants rather than through voice over. Ivanka Pelikan from Graceades (a local community hub), commenting on Bailee who became homeless at 13 after an argument with her step-dad: 'The system fails somewhere along the line. It does fail. It does fail. Yeah, I don't like saying that but it's the truth. You want the honest truth, it fails' (Pelikan, 2015). But these insights are scattered thinly amidst the narrative and televisual techniques that stigmatise or individualise hardship.

The question of context includes not just the background provided in the show, but also post-airing responses as these also contribute to whether *Struggle Street* is fully captured by the description 'poverty porn'. Importantly, as has now been widely documented and discussed, participants themselves felt shamed and angry. Peta, a participant, and dedicated contributor to community life in Mt Druitt, echoed the views of many others when she said, 'We're shocked, gutted and I feel very hurt. I did not agree to go on the show to be made a fool of' (Moulton, 2015). In response to the show, some organisations swung into action to challenge these representations. The Street University, an initiative of the Ted Noffs Foundation, responded with a video campaign – Made in Mt Druitt – to 'help equalise the negative attention Mt Druitt has been receiving', kicking off with a video featuring the internationally successful DJ Zerish Naera (aka 26th Letter) (noffs.org.au, 2015). The Australian Teachers of Media (ATOM) produced study guides for *SS1* (for Years 10 to 12) and, later for *SS2* (for Years 9 to 12):

> This study guide's key objective is to provide a framework for positive discussion about the experiences of the series' participants. The activities challenge students to think about people experiencing disadvantage in a compassionate way and allow students to engage in important conversations about the ways that we respond to disadvantage as a society (Marriner, 2015).

Such counter narratives were complemented by 'hands-on' engagement and care. After Ben Fordham from 2GB visited Graceades cottage, it was inundated with donations from individuals and offers of help from tradespeople and community groups (Pelikan, 2015). Amongst them, was Turbans 4 Australia, a Sikh charitable organisation, that helped to renovate the cottage, donating and installing air-conditioning units valued at $6000 (Turbans 4 Australia, 2015).

In thinking through the responses to *Struggle Street* – the actual and the potential – and despite her different focus on 'cultures of trauma', the work of E. Ann Kaplan (2012) on empathy is useful. Kaplan distinguishes three different kinds of empathy: 'vicarious trauma' when viewers are so overwhelmed, they turn away from the unendurable; 'empty empathy' in which empathy is triggered but only fleetingly; and, 'witnessing' which 'involves feeling so shocked by suffering that one is moved to act'; 'one is motivated to see that justice is done' (p. 3). The crucial ingredient in the provocation to witness, and the movement beyond the fleeting and overwhelmed, is the provision of information about the context to the suffering. The 'witness' responds not only to the individual but to the *'situation'*. The reception of *SS1* crossed the full gamut of possibilities, ranging from contempt to witnessing 'the situation'. But the scope for witnessing was expanded by the post-hoc provision of context by participants, community organisations, and commentators who corrected the paucity of context in *SS1*.

Struggle Street Series 2: More Poverty Porn?

The filming of *SS2* faced considerable opposition before it began (including from the Queensland Premier, Annastacia Palaszczuk: Inala is in her electorate) as residents, politicians and community leaders feared a repeat of *SS1*. Despite the opposition, it went ahead, and it was filmed in Inala (Queensland), and Seddon and Broadmeadows in Victoria. Thankfully, *SS2* is an improvement on the first series. It comes closer to capturing what Lauren Berlant describes as the 'structural position of the overwhelmed life' (2011, p. 117). It does this through better backstories, narrated by the participants themselves, and through foregrounding participants' informed analysis based on lived experience of structural constraints, governmental disregard, and the misery of bureaucratic rigidity in the direst of circumstances. *SS2* utilised a judicious selection of voice over that complemented, far less jarringly than in *SS1*, the personal testimony from characters, other local residents, community organisations, and professionals. Visually, this was bolstered by screen banners and captions with links to sources of information about poverty, homelessness and other issues. SBS also produced a series of short online educational videos – The Truth About: Poverty (Morgan, 2017a); The Truth About: Disadvantage (Morgan, 2017b); The Truth About: Welfare (Morgan, 2017c); and The

Truth About: Addiction (Morgan, 2017d). These were not an unqualified success, though, in overcoming the 'poverty porn' tag or providing context. As Spurling (2017) argues, KEO missed two important dimensions of context; the background 'causes of the causes' and the other side of life – the vibrant, resilient and resourceful communities of residents and organisations that also define 'Struggle Street' (or, in this case, Inala).

On completion of *SS2*, SBS (Fitzgerald, 2017) aired a conversation between a panel of experts, including Tamara, a participant in *SS2*, and an invited audience, hosted by Janice Petersen, with the explicit aim of answering 'what can we do to bring about change?' The diverse contributions were succinct, well-argued, backed up by research, and very effectively undermined the 'poor by choice or laziness' perspective. As John Falzon of St Vincent de Paul argued, 'inequality is not a choice made by these people. And it's not a tragedy either – it's a choice made by us as a society through our government and our government's failure to reduce inequality is a failure to govern'. John Hewson (ex-leader of the Liberal party and of the federal opposition), with insights drawn from his background as both politician and economist, identified what could be an excellent step in tackling that failure: 'every cabinet submission [should] have an inequality impact statement, so they are actually required to focus on the consequences of what they are doing. And I think you'd change the nature of government quite dramatically'. The response from Megan Williams (of UTS Graduate Health) captured the underlying problem: as a society, in large part, we *already know* what we need to do, we know what works, but we lack the political will to implement it. As Williams said of the Aboriginal Family Welfare Program, referring to 25 peer-reviewed articles that demonstrate its efficacy, 'it's been shown to work – it's time for action'.

But there's a lot more going on than the provision of statistical and policy context that differentiates *SS2* from *SS1*. *SS2* also succeeds through the televisual appeal of the participants; all are facing enormous challenges, but most of them negotiate these with incredible resilience, humour and creativity. There is insufficient space here to do justice to their stories, but most have a narrative arc that ends in some form of resolution which works to both satisfy the expectations of reality TV's 'makeover' culture (an ambiguous outcome), and to alert viewers to the possibility of change with the right supports and services in place. Nick lost his job of two decades when Ford closed (he eventually gets a job). Tamara was sucked in by one of the shonky private service providers of vocational training and ended up with a huge debt for a course she never started (she is finally relieved of that with the support of the community legal service). Norma is an Aboriginal woman from Inala evicted from her home when her daughter was fined for possession of marijuana which puts Norma in breach of the tenancy agreement. 'They wanted me to kick my daughter out. Nuh. I can't do *that*. If I was to kick my daughter out, she'll become another number for this government. Another number on the drugs, on the alcohol. Incarceration. No!' (Episode 2). There's a further backstory; Norma has taken in numerous homeless and at-risk Indigenous young people and in the past, and this has entailed police visits. When Norma is evicted, more than 20 police turn up; it seems completely over the top and Norma is a persuasive figure as she points across the street to remark on how many police came to remove a Black woman and her children from their home. She forges on: 'I walked a mile anyway, another mile ain't gonna hurt me'. She is eventually re-housed. She seems happy and it looks like a nice place.

Michael, who was addicted to drugs and homeless, is now trying to get his life together and receives disability support for mental illness. He is funny, smart, a bit of a wordsmith and, as he says, 'devilishly handsome when I have teeth in my head'. Throughout the show, Michael's fortunes go up and down and as they do, his oscillations between despair and hope, peppered with self-deprecating, insightful and often amusing asides, haul the viewers along with him. As the series closes, we are left hanging about his future. Not so, though, the situation of Michelle and Jessica. Michelle had to give up work to care for Jessica who has a profoundly disabling condition (EDS). They started to raise money, using GoFundMe for Jessica to travel to Baltimore (USA) for the specialist medical treatment she needs. After the episode detailing this aired, the GoFundMe contributions increased significantly, eventually raising $126,273 and Jessica was able to travel to Baltimore for medical treatment due, as they put it, to 'the kindness of strangers' (The Feed, SBS, 2018).

Televisual Intimacy and Affective Proximity

Although the public support for Michelle and Jessica might seem obvious – a response to a heart-rending need, the unfairness of unequal access to health care, Michelle and Jessica's sweet relationship – there is still a gap in our understanding of how *Struggle Street* 'works' and its impact on viewers. Here the audience responses are positive, empathetic, giving. At other times, especially in relation to *SS1*, the responses can be shockingly harsh. What is missing, though, is an account of why, and how, negative representations produce both compassionate and dismissive responses, both ethical responsivity and moralising contempt. We too readily assume that the missing link is what the audience brings to the spectacle – their politics, faith, personal experience and quirks of personality, combined with the power of a show's ideological perspective. However, while the particularity of our primed spectatorship, and our pre-existing views, are important, so too is what happens 'in the moment' of viewing that works affectively as well as cognitively. We don't just form opinions; we respond bodily, unconsciously, sensuously, and these reactions amplify or twist how we think it through.

Wood and Skeggs' (2011) research on audience responses to reality TV illustrates some possibilities for a fresh approach. Their research, utilising Wood's 'text-in-action' method, included physically watching reality TV programs with women from different class backgrounds, attending to their responses in the moment, not just conversational reflections on those responses at a later date. They found 'surprising connections that reached beyond the symbolic violence of the programmes' (p. 18) and from the embodied experience of watching together, through the lens of 'affective economies', they learnt something of 'how affect is converted into judgement' (p. 18). Here, then, is one possible approach that could yield quite different insights into how *Struggle Street* contributes not just to public opinion but also, to the affective and moral economies that energise opinion and sometimes, subvert expectations.

Misha Kavka (2008) also explores the ways in which reality television 'evokes affective responses from viewers which are in excess of controlled meaning-production' (p. 7). She argues that 'affective proximity' is the outcome of the 'performance of reality which generates intimacy as its affect' (p. 25). We can add to Kavka's insights through consideration of the significance of the face in the amplification of affective proximity. A leading theorist in this area, Anna Gibbs (2001), drawing on the work of the influential affect theorist, Silvan Tomkins, discusses the role of the face as the 'primary site of affective communication', and observes that it 'is an extremely rapid medium of communication, and the televisual close up, especially when it is extreme, enhances its communicative possibilities by drawing our attention to details (trembling lips, rapid eye movements, twitching muscles, and so on)'. In *SS1* (Episode 2), this is illustrated in a moment of acute poignancy when Chris is talking with his mother, Cheryl. Chris was placed in foster care as a child as his mother could not care for him due to mental illness and he now lives with her twin sister Michelle. Chris tells us that when he turned 18, he was allowed to access files that he hadn't previously been able to read and, 'I was very shocked. And I was very angry as well. And I started realising why my mum couldn't give that love'. While Chris speaks, Cheryl shakes her head, glances out and down, the sorrow palpable. 'I think, since I've moved down. She's trying to make up for that even though I've already forgiven her, that's in the past'. Again, the camera pans in on Cheryl's face as she struggles with the emotion. There's a quiet pause between them. It's very affecting: her sorrow and regret, combined with his open, generous, loving spirit.

It is in these quiet prolongations of intimacy that settle on the face, that we are beckoned in to read the working through of the participants' emotions. To simply be present. The power of this is not simply in the evocation of empathy with people dealing with painful histories and the most difficult of lives, but in how these histories that are simultaneously past, present and future-oriented, unfold non-verbally in tears, intimations of tears, smiles and sideways glances. In the silences, as well as the words between Chris and Cheryl, we are invited into intimacy and also, to the recognition of complexity. The potential for a more ethical relationship of 'witnessing' resides here in the ways that people escape capture and fixture; the affectivity that lies in the faces, gestures and hospitality of people in letting us into their very difficult lives. Time and again, in both series, I noticed the small scenes of generosity, the forgiving – and not – of self and other, and the repetitions of effort and rethinking of relationships. Classed experiences press on lives in particular ways that may generate class-specific forms of generosity and sociability that prompt the kind of rethink (of self as well as other) that must surely precede a properly ethical response. And that offer alternatives to neoliberal modes of subjectivity – 'proper' living. An alternative ethics of care. And I am reminded: these participants' lives are *given*; they are *shared*, not captured.

Although the role of the face is enormously important in the televisual representation and circulation of affects, it is not only through the face that scenes become affectively provocative. Indeed, it is not only the human that moves us; consider the distancing effect of rubbish-strewn streets, or how shots to nature (a noticeable technique in *SS2*) – fluttering leaves, tranquil waters – can soothe and tamp down the quick move to thought or judgement. In *SS2*, Jarrod and Sharon are the parents of two teens and two younger children. They are also addicted to ice, and beset by complex histories of addiction, violence and infidelity. Jarrod is out on bail awaiting court for drug offences. They have to move out of their temporary accommodation due to ice usage and because Sharon has an AVO against Jarrod. You just want them 'to get themselves together for the children' even though the grasp of ice on their lives is so palpable and unbearable. Jarrod and the two eldest will leave to search for somewhere to stay, spending the first night in a friend's ute. Sharon and the youngest go to a women's refuge. Before they leave, they gather in the living space. The children cling and weep at the separation. Young Paton, balancing up fairness and possibility, asks her mum to give up the AVO so they can be together; a gathering and holding of their family as ballast in the unbearable present. As their arms, tears and wrapped-around bodies attach themselves to their parents, they stick – affectively as well as physically – performatively enfolding the audience into the otherwise buried potentiality of living otherwise for Sharon and Jarrod. Here extended through the visual technologies that allow us to hug with them. Even when it is hard to imagine hugging Sharon or Jarrod, we can feel the warmth of being held by a child. We may not see it through their eyes, but perhaps we feel it through their bodies. We cannot abandon Jarrod and Sharon without abandoning the children.

Conclusion

I hope that I have shown that the question of whether *Struggle Street* is 'poverty porn' is not straightforward; multiple responses may be generated by the entanglements of content and form, through the desires of the participants and the embodied experience of viewing. Although, as the differences between *SS1* and *SS2* illustrate, considerable care can and should be taken to avoid the poor decision making and stigmatising consequences displayed in *SS1*. One way to do this would be to rethink the relationship between the filmmakers and the participants. Sharon and Jarrod's daughter, Trinity, was in Year 11 when *SS2* was made. Her school loaned her a video camera for an assignment. She had to make a mini documentary about 'a marginalised subject'. She chose her father as her subject and interviewed Jarrod about life in jail. It's at this point that the blindingly obvious occurred to me. What might a documentary look like in the hands of these participants, in collaboration with professionals, not simply as subjects of professionals? And what if they began with their own lived experience to pose questions to politicians, service providers, and of policies. As Spurling (2017) asks, 'Why weren't people from Centrelink, Housing and the police interviewed?'. Indeed.

As the panel discussion of *Struggle Street* revealed, so many of the answers to these intersecting forms of inequality are already known, but we lack the political will (or interest?) to action them. However, political will is only part of the answer; we need a more diverse parliament and debates that are sharpened by the insights and passionate commitment that come from lived experience. It is no accident that one of the most powerful contributions to parliamentary discussion of welfare funding came from Jacqui Lambie, who drew on her own past experience as a single mother on the disability support pension:

> It is shameful and embarrassing, but we do it not because we want to but because circumstances put us there ... And for you to take more money off those people, you have no idea how bloody tough it is, every little cent counts to those people. If you really realised the damage that you are doing to that part of society, you would stop doing it. I want you know what it is like to be at the bottom of the crap pile through no fault of our own (ABC, 2017).

It is hard, though, to imagine a reversal of class privilege in Australian politics or to imagine the wider Australian community demanding that. It is fitting to finish with Owen (2015) from Mt Druitt's conclusion: 'Is *Struggle Street* good or bad? It depends what happens next'.

References

ABC NEWS. (2017, March 23). Outpouring of support for Jackie Lambie's emotional Senate speech on social media. *ABC*. Retrieved from https://www.abc.net.au/news/2017-03-23/praise-for-lambies-emotional-senate-speech/8381726

Alcorn, G. (2015, May 15). Struggle Street is only poverty porn if we enjoy watching, then turn away. *The Guardian*. Retrieved from https://www.theguardian.com/commentisfree/2015/may/15/struggle-street-is-only-poverty-porn-if-we-enjoy-watching-then-turn-away

Berlant, L. (2011). *Cruel optimism*. Durham, NC: Duke University Press

Bevan, M. (2015, May 6). Western Sydney residents wary of postcode discrimination in light of Struggle Street documentary. *ABC Radio Sydney*. Retrieved from https://www.abc.net.au/news/2015-05-06/postcode-discrimination-felt-in-blacktown-mt-druitt/6449214

Blackiston, H. (2019, September 2). Struggle Street to return to SBS for third season on October 9. *Mumbrella*. Retrieved from https://mumbrella.com.au/struggle-street-to-return-to-sbs-for-third-season-on-october-9-596220

De Benedictis, S., Allen, K., & Jensen, T. (2017). Portraying poverty: The economics and ethics of factual welfare television. *Cultural Sociology, 11*(3), 337–358.

The Feed, SBS. (2018, June 18). *The kindness of strangers: how the Struggle Street TV series changed a life*. SBS. Retrieved from https://www.sbs.com.au/news/the-feed/the-kindness-of-strangers-how-the-struggle-street-tv-series-changed-a-life

Fitzgerald, M. (Director) & Petersen, J. (Host). (2017, December 7). *Struggle Street: The Conversation* [Television series episode]. Artarmon, NSW: SBS

Gibbs, A. (2001). Contagious feelings: Pauline Hanson and the epidemiology of affect. *Australian Humanities Review*, (24). Retrieved from http://australianhumanitiesreview.org/2001/12/01/contagious-feelings-pauline-hanson-and-the-epidemiology-of-affect/

Howes, L., & Brown, A. (Writers), & O'Rourke, S., Green, T.J., Schist, D., Matthews, P., & Parry, M. (Directors). (2017). In D. Galloway (Producer), *Struggle Street Series 2* [Television series]. Sydney: KEO Films Australia.

Jensen, T. (2014). Welfare commonsense, poverty porn and doxosophy. *Sociological Research Online, 19*(3), 277–283. doi: 10.5153/sro.3441.

Kaplan, E.A. (2012). Empathy and trauma culture. In A. Coplan & P.Goldie (Eds.), *Empathy: Philosophical and psychological perspectives* (Chapter 15). Oxford, UK: Oxford Scholarship Online.

Kavka, M. (2008). *Reality television, affect and intimacy: Reality matters*. London: Palgrave Macmillan.

Kerin, B., Ong, T., & staff. (2015, May 6). Struggle Street: Mount Druitt community up in arms over 'poverty porn' documentary series on SBS. *ABC News*. Retrieved from https://www.abc.net.au/news/2015-05-05/sbs-struggle-street-series-poverty-porn-says-mt-druitt-mayor/6446648?nw=0

Lallo, M. (2015, May 7). Struggle Street sets ratings record for an SBS documentary, with 1.31 million viewers. *Sydney Morning Herald*.
Retrieved from https://www.smh.com.au/entertainment/tv-and-radio/struggle-street-sets-ratings-record-for-an-sbs-documentary-with-131-million-viewers-20150507-ggw15r.html

Lamb, B. (2016). Cathy come off benefits: A comparative ideological analysis of *Cathy Come Home* and *Benefits Street*. *Journalism and Discourse Studies*, (2), 2–21.

Marriner, K. (2015). *Struggle Street: A study guide*. Australian Teachers of Media [ATOM] SCREEN EDUCATION. Retrieved from http://www.theeducationshop.com.au

Mediaweek. (2015, May 7). SBS's Helen Kellie defends Struggle Street. Retrieved from https://www.mediaweek.com.au/sbs-helen-kellie-defends-struggle-street/

Morgan, M. (Writer). (2017a). The Truth About: Poverty [Video]. *SBS Life*. Artarmon, NSW: SBS on Demand. Retrieved from https://www.sbs.com.au/topics/voices/culture/article/2017/11/27/truth-about-poverty

Morgan, M. (Writer). (2017b). The Truth About: Disadvantage [Video]. *SBS Life*. Artarmon, NSW: SBS on Demand. Retrieved from https://www.sbs.com.au/topics/voices/culture/article/2017/11/29/truth-about-disadvantage

Morgan, M. (Writer). (2017c). The Truth About: Welfare [Video]. *SBS Life*. Artarmon, NSW: SBS on Demand. Retrieved from https://www.sbs.com.au/topics/voices/culture/article/2017/12/07/why-smartphones-and-cars-arent-luxury-items-truth-about-welfare

Morgan, M. (Writer). (2017d). The Truth About: Addiction [Video]. *SBS Life*. Artarmon, NSW: SBS on Demand. Retrieved from https://www.sbs.com.au/topics/voices/culture/article/2017/11/28/truth-about-addiction

Moulton, E. (2015, May 13). Final episodes of Struggle Street left viewers shocked rather than offended. *news.com.au*. Retrieved from https://www.news.com.au/final-episodes-of-struggle-street-left-viewers-shocked-rather-than-offended/news-story/5f47a73f8dbdd5ff1ef794b384ab971e

noffs.org.au (2015, May 14). #MADEINMTDRUITT 1 – 26TH LETTER. Retrieved from https://noffs.org.au/street-uni/blog/madeinmtdruitt-1-26th-letter/

Owen, J. (2015, May 7). My friends, the 'stars' of Struggle Street shouldn't be made to pay for their trust. *The Guardian*. Retrieved from https://www.theguardian.com/media/commentisfree/2015/may/07/the-stars-of-struggle-street-shouldnt-be-made-to-pay-for-their-trust

Peel, M. (2003). *The lowest rung: Voices of Australian poverty*. Cambridge, UK: Cambridge University Press.

Pelikan, I. (2015). A special thanks from Ivanka. *Graceades Cottage: News*. Retrieved from https://graceadescottage.org.au/Ivanka-pelikan.html

Pidd, H. (2014, April 2). How Grimsby went to war with Channel 4 over Skint. *The Guardian*. Formerly available from theguardian.com/commentsisfree/2014/apr/01/Grimsby-channel-4-skint-documentary-benefits-street

Radomsky, M. (Writer/Producer/Director) & O'Rourke, S., Cone, B., & Green, T. (Directors). (2015). In D. Galloway (Series Producer), *Struggle Street Series 1* [Television series]. KEO Films Australia.

Skeggs, B., & Wood, H. (2009). The transformation of intimacy: Classed identities in the moral economy of reality television. In M. Wetherell (Ed.), *Identity in the 21st century: New trends in changing times* (pp. 231–249). London: Palgrave Macmillan.

Spurling, G. (2017, December 14). Struggle Street: Beyond the camera's narrow frame are stories of resilience and inspiring leadership. *Croakey*. Retrieved from https://www.croakey.org/struggle-street-beyond-the-cameras-narrow-frame-are-stories-of-strength-resilience-and-inspiring-leadership/

Tan, M. (2015, May 6). Struggle Street protest brings garbage truck blockade to SBS Sydney offices. *The Guardian*. Formerly available from theguardian.com/media/2015/may/06/struggle-street-protest-brings-garbage-truck-bloacked-to-sbs-sydney-offices

Threadgold, S. (2015, May 6). Struggle Street is poverty porn with an extra dose of class racism. *The Conversation*. Retrieved from http://theconversation.com/struggle-street-is-poverty-porn-with-an-extra-dose-of-class-racism-41346

Turbans 4 Australia. (2015). *Fundraising: Community causes*. Retrieved from https://www.t4a.org.au/events-and-causes.

Watson, I. (2014). *A disappearing world: Studies in class, gender and memory*. North Melbourne, Victoria: Australian Scholarly Publishing.

Wood, H., & Skeggs, B. (Eds.) (2011). *Reality television and class*. London: British Film Institute.

CHAPTER 10

WHITENESS, NEOLIBERAL FEMINISM AND SOCIAL CLASS IN AUSTRALIAN RU-ROM

Bridie's Choice

Barbara Pini and Laura Rodriguez Castro

Introduction

The start of the new millennium marked the emergence of a new genre of contemporary women's writing in Australia that has been a publishing phenomenon (O'Mahony, 2020). This new genre, labelled rural romance or colloquially 'ru-rom', has a complex genealogy as Mirmohamadi (2015) explains in charting its ascendancy. She notes its connections with the romance novel, the American western, the colonial romance and the adventure story. Its more recent and direct progenitor is the chick-lit novel, as most famously represented by its earliest incarnation, Helen Fielding's (1996) *Bridget Jones's Diary*. While there are numerous intersections between chick-lit and ru-rom such as their ironic and humorous tone and emphasis on women's agentic sexuality, the setting of the latter provides a vastly different environment for romance. As Taylor (2012, n.p.) observes 'imagine chick-lit gone country, with cosmopolitans replaced by shots of rum, Louboutin shoes by muddied boots, and corporate ladders by regular ones that actually reach past the ceiling'.

Despite its incredible popularity over nearly two decades, rural romance has been subject to limited scholarship. In part this is reflective of the retreat from the study of social class in Australian rural studies over the past two decades (Bryant & Pini, 2010) and the continuing hegemony of a settler 'white farming imaginary' in the national psyche (Alkon & McCullen, 2011, p. 945; see also Pini, Rodriguez Castro, & Mayes, 2021). It is perhaps also because ru-rom, like its generic big sister, chick-lit, and the romance genre more broadly, have not been considered worthy subjects of academic inquiry. They have too often been disparaged and trivialised because of their popularity, generic conventions and association with women. However, as feminist scholars of class have demonstrated, the landscape of popular culture is a key site in which 'classificatory struggles' of distancing, distinction and differentiation are enacted (Tyler, 2015, p. 494).

In this chapter we begin to redress the limited attention to ru-rom through a focus on representations of race and class in *Bridie's Choice* (2012) by Karly Lane. Lane is one of the most well-known, prolific and best-selling authors associated with the genre – as her media sobriquet, 'queen of small town romance', suggests (Gibson, 2020, n.p.). The text is particularly apt for analysis as it is representative of a smaller sub-section of a larger sample of over 100 such works that we have read which are framed by a cross-class romance. Across this sub-group of ru-rom novels, tropes and themes pertaining to social class and coloniality in rural space recur, to such an extent that *Bridie's Choice* can be understood as illustrative of a broader phenomenon. As the synopsis of the plot on the back cover of *Bridie's Choice* proclaims: 'Bridie Farrell and Shaun Broderick come from opposite sides of the tracks' with Bridie's family 'perennial strugglers' and the Brodericks the wealthy owners of Jinjulu – one of the most prestigious properties in the district'. As a 'town girl', central protagonist Bridie differs from her counterparts in most other ru-rom novels. Across the genre this is a subject position that is constructed in negative terms and the only suitable romantic interests for farming men is another farming woman or a professional woman who has relocated from an urban, cosmopolitan setting. However, in the portrait on the front cover she is pictured as a normative 'farm girl'. She is white, smiling broadly with blue eyes and honey-brown hair curling out from under a wide-brimmed hat as she leans against a horse, and presides over a scene of cattle and a windmill.

We begin the chapter with an overview of our theoretical framework introducing the interrelationship between whiteness, class and neoliberal feminism and explaining the relationship between neoliberal feminism and the white farming imaginary. Following this, we focus on three key class themes in the novel. The first is Lane's minimising or dismissal of class as irrelevant. The next two sections examine Lane's more ambivalent stance on class. That is, her acknowledgement but then discounting of class via the Australian white farming imaginary and through neoliberal feminist discourses of individualism and choice.

Whiteness, Class and Neoliberal Feminism

In our analysis of the configurations of ru-rom novels we have identified the ongoing praxis of neoliberal feminism, and consequently it is through this lens that we explore class politics in our selected text (Rottenberg, 2014). As an expression of gender politics neoliberal feminism is related to post-feminism. As Gill (2007) noted in early work on the subject, some of the key tenets of post-feminism, such as the pervasiveness of self-surveillance and discipline, the primacy given to notions of choice and individualism, and the rise of a makeover culture, are entangled with neoliberalism. More recently she has argued that there has been an intensification of different post-feminist sensibilities related to neoliberalism such as imperatives for women to self-monitor and self-optimise, and this has resulted in the rise of what she labels 'gendered neoliberalism' (Gill, 2017, p. 606). This mode of feminism is embedded in the logics of capitalism so that while gender inequality is named it is framed by individual choice and agency (McRobbie, 2004).

Structural impediments and collective action are muted, while personal empowerment, entrepreneurialism and independence are championed, along with a specific affective state of positivity and confidence (Gill & Orgad, 2018). Prügl (2015) elaborates that 'neoliberalised feminism may provide arguments for gender equality and the empowerment of women, but it retains ideological commitments to rationalism, heteronormativity, and genderless economic structures' (p. 619). Accordingly, Ulus (2018) asserts that neoliberal feminism is an ideology that benefits women 'privileged in space and time by market ideologies or those with resources to seek out such spaces', rather than one that seeks to improve the 'lives of women across racial groups, across social classes, across migrant status, across many dimensions of human experience' (p. 165).

Numerous studies have explored how neoliberal feminism and post-feminist sensibilities operate in contemporary contexts (for example, McRobbie, 2004). Similarly, in our broader analysis of ru-roms we found that there is a clear connection between the genre and the construction and privileging of the 'white middle-class woman', as the normative subject position of neoliberal feminism. In the Australian context, Moreton-Robinson's (2020 [2000]) important work *Talkin' Up to the White Woman* provides crucial insight to conceptualise this connection. She explains how white feminism, as attached to the colonial/capitalist/neoliberal project, operates through a deracialised discourse in which 'white race privilege and racial oppression are intimately linked through the subject position "white middle-class woman"' (p. viii). As such, Moreton-Robinson (2020 [2000]) contends that white feminists benefit from colonisation and the construction of nationhood through the abstraction of their embodied experiences of racial and class privilege in Australia.

One of the most salient ways in which neoliberal white feminism has been most evident in rural Australia has been in the incorporation of white, middle-class property-owning women into the white farming imaginary (Pini et al., 2021). The white farming imaginary, which is 'a way to articulate settler sovereignty through the hard work of building the nation' is attached to the colonial construction of *terra nullius* that justified violent colonisation (Kirne, 2020, p. 2; Cairns et al., 2015; Alkon & McCullen, 2011; Moreton-Robinson, 2015; 2020 [2000]). This mythology, which establishes moral and ontological claims of white belonging and occupation in rural Australia, has traditionally been constructed as masculine (Moreton-Robinson, 2015; Mayes, 2018). According to the white farming imaginary, male farmers have shown industry and resolve battling the elements in working what was an otherwise empty and unproductive land. Over generations they have been stewards of the country and have an embodied and affective connection to their farming land.

In the opening page of *Bridie's Choice* male protagonist's Shaun Broderick reflections encapsulate a number of the key themes of the masculine 'white farming imaginary' which, by omission, circumvents the politics of sovereignty:

> His family history humbled him; the original Brodericks had carved Jinjulu out from nothing but a vast scrubby wilderness to the impressive business it was today ... He'd always loved this property; it was part of him and he felt a deep kinship with the land. Jinjulu was in his blood (pp. 6–7).

While this quotation references the type of masculinist white farming imaginary that has predominated in Australian culture, ru-rom novels are notable for their re-gendering of this imaginary. A prevalent storyline is farming daughters taking over the family enterprise and gaining legitimacy as farmers. As O'Mahony (2020) notes in surveying the ascendancy of the genre, ru-rom protagonists 'perform roles usually assigned to men, sometimes outperforming them, undertake labour to find their place and eventually find success in owning or, in some cases, running farm and station properties' (p. 89). Through this process they find a sense of community and home. Thus, the ru-roms construct belonging in rural Australia through centring the white middle-class woman as the normative subject position of neoliberal feminism (see Moreton-Robinson, 2020 [2000]). In the texts, the white farming imaginary is feminised while its racialised and classed dynamics are not only left intact, but legitimised and reproduced.

Discounting Social Class

One of the most recurring themes in studies of social class in Australia is that class is often disavowed or muted (Threadgold, 2018). This is a theme given expression in *Bridie's Choice* by positioning class as only of relevance elsewhere, such as in urban Australia. In this type of construction, rural communities are framed by well-known discourses of communitarism, inclusion and egalitarianism (Bryant & Pini, 2010). Notably, for example, we are told that Shaun's mother, Constance Broderick, who is preoccupied with her class standing and full of class hatred for Bridie, spends most of her time in the family's Sydney apartment. Similarly, Alisha, one of Shaun's past girlfriends, who shares his mother's views on class, lives and works in Sydney and had made it clear she would never live at Jinjulu if their relationship progressed to marriage.

Another strategy by which Lane eschews the centrality of social class is to construct it as only of relevance to older generations. In this respect it is relevant that Constance and Douglas Broderick, Shaun's parents, express the most virulent class prejudice in the novel offering Bridie money to leave Shaun and warning her that she would lose if he was forced to choose between her and inheriting the family property. They are representative of Jinjulu's past and of an age cohort whose influence and authority are eroding. We are led to believe that like other antiquated ideas they hold about environmental management and gender equality, their notions of class will also fade as they do.

Shaun, as representative of a new generation, claims social class is immaterial. This is despite the fact that his first interaction with Bridie was embedded in class hatred. Given Bridie's reputation as a 'Farrell', when a teenager Shaun had accepted a dare from his friends to ask her to attend a party in order to see how quickly he could convince her to have sex with him (p. 48). Now in his late twenties, Shaun reflects on his behaviour, not in class terms, but as the actions of a 'testosterone-fuelled, overconfident country boy' (p. 48). Thus, the violence of class hatred is reconstituted as a single episode of youthful indiscretion.

A similar pattern of renaming of social class antagonism occurs in relation to the depiction of Shaun's younger sister, Phoebe. We come to know Phoebe as pretentious and entitled – demanding her father sponsor her to go to Europe to study art and making snide asides about Bridie's family background to Shaun and his parents. However, by the book's conclusion Lane suggests that what we may have read as classed behaviours were the actions of a misunderstood, hurting and confused young woman. As part of the neoliberal narrative she is transformed and redeemed, taking individual action to overcome her complicated family history, and becoming a more sympathetic character as she develops a friendship with Bridie, and falls in love with one of the employees on Jinjulu. As Lane reports 'Bridie had seen past the spoilt little rich girl exterior and caught a glimpse of the sad, lonely woman behind it' (p. 247).

A final way in which social class is rendered unimportant in the novel is to claim commonalities of hardship and disadvantage between the Brodericks and the Farrells. The message is communicated on multiple occasions throughout the text. For example, early in Shaun and Bridie's relationship when she suggests to him that 'it must be nice to carry on a tradition like yours', he tells her 'sometimes it's a lot to live up to, it comes with a price' before going on to talk about his brother's death (p. 88). Elsewhere in the text, at the end of an evening during which Bridie is humiliated and disparaged by the Brodericks, the family's housekeeper counsels her that the family has 'suffered terrible grief' and 'for all their airs and graces, they're still people and they've had their share of heartache just like the rest of us' (p. 211). This notion of equivalence in the life experience of the Farrells and Brodericks is articulated by reviewers on Goodreads:

> Though it's not immediately obvious, Bridie and Shaun have a lot in common including rebellious younger siblings, the tragic loss of a family member and the burdens of their respective family legacies – Shelleyrae at Book'd Out's Reviews (Goodreads, 2012).

There are undoubtedly life experiences that connect Shaun and Bridie, and it is certainly the case that the Brodericks have dealt with enormous trauma in the loss of a son to suicide. However, Lane's efforts to emphasise sameness between the Farrells and the Brodericks obfuscates the class chasm that separates the two families. As the following section will demonstrate, this marked divide is entwined not just with economic capital, but with a set of social evaluations, meanings and symbols.

Acknowledging but Discounting Class via the White Farming Imaginary

At the same time as Lane seeks to deny social class, she also raises class adversity as an issue only to then discount it through reference to the Australian white farming imaginary of resilience, hard work and care of the land. For example, we are made aware of Bridie's financial struggle and long work hours as well as of the difficulty of finding employment in rural Australia. In an extended conversation with Shaun's parents, Bridie counters their arguments that rural poverty is a result of a lack of will, industry and entrepreneurship and expresses frustration at their 'lack of awareness' of their 'wealth and privilege' adding:

> It went against the grain to hear him dismissing everyone who was in a minimum wage job as simply not working hard enough. Did he have any idea how hard most people worked just to keep a roof over their heads? Not everyone in Tooncanny was lining up for a dole payment each fortnight (p. 122).

The type of class-based insights Bridie offers in this moment are rare in rural romance novels. Unlike its forebear chick-lit, ru-rom has been praised as distinctive for highlighting social problems such as mental health, crime and addiction, but these are typically examined through the lens of farming and farmers (Cavanagh, 2015). As a group the novels have little to say about persistent unemployment in rural Australia (Rohan & Burke, 2019) and the punitive 'moral prism' through which the rural unemployed may be constructed by others (Pini, Price & McDonald, 2010, p. 19). These others include the working poor such as Bridie, who seek to resist stigmatisation and claim 'self-worth, integrity and dignity' by distancing themselves from rural welfare recipients (Butler, 2019, p. 119).

It is therefore significant that the question of work-based inequality in rural communities is raised, but its narrative potency is undermined by Lane's constant recourse to the white farming imaginary. For example, early in the novel Shaun is affronted when Bridie explains her working hours to Shaun with the statement: 'Some of us have to work for a living. Not all of us get everything handed to us on a silver platter' (p. 49). Bridie walks away before he can respond, but Lane ensures his white farming classed position is afforded primacy reporting:

> He did seventeen or eighteen hour days on a regular basis. The day didn't finish once the sun went down – there was always machinery that needed fixing, before the next day's work started, or late-night emergencies to be attended to. For all of its history and opulence, Jinjulu was a working farm first and foremost (pp. 49–50).

What is communicated in this quotation is the oft-repeated conflation of 'hard work' and the middle class which renders this group deserving of their status while simultaneously positioning the poor as lacking industry. The neoliberal mantras of self-responsibility and self-discipline fuse with more traditional notions of farmers as morally superior due to their productivity and diligence. Elsewhere in the text, and despite her own disadvantaged position, Bridie affords farmers further moral weight as stoic and resilient rural actors facing constant adversity:

> Bridie knew farmers were doing it tough out here … It broke her heart to see them so despondent. Since the mines out Parkes and Orange way had opened, it was harder for both farmers and local businesses to keep workers. No one could compete with mining wages. Added to that was the high Australian dollar and a hike in costs of fuel and fertiliser – it was not a great time to be a farmer (p. 19).

Similarly, when Bridie relocates to the Gold Coast following conflict with the Brodericks she meets muscly, tanned, 30-something Tye, a former banker who made money on the stock market and now surfs. Bridie is unimpressed with Tye when he tells her he does 'as little as possible' comparing his 'laid-back attitude to that of the hardworking farming community she'd been born and raised in' (p. 283). In summary, class is acknowledged but its complexities and impact dismissed in the text through recourse to the morally legitimising white farmer imaginary.

Neoliberal Feminism: Acknowledging but Discounting Class via Discourses of Choice

One of the most recurring ways in which social class is acknowledged in Lane's text is via reference to the classed politics of reputation in rural communities. She demonstrates that it is not just economic capital but social and cultural capital which are unevenly distributed in rural locales, and that capital accumulation is tied to a complex politics of reputation which give shape to rural biographies (Bryant & Pini, 2010). However, as with discussions of rural employment, the issue is raised only to be discounted. In this case this occurs through the adoption of an overarching neoliberal feminist discourse of choice.

There are numerous instances in the text when Lane demonstrates that Bridie's life in Tooncanny requires constant negotiation of morally infused negative classed ascriptions associated with being 'a Farrell'. The most traumatic is when Bridie is accosted by a group of men outside the pub after finishing work. One remarks, 'You're a Farrell – scum of the district' before adding 'We know what you are. All Farrell women know the score – they put out to anyone, ain't that right?' (p. 29). Shaun saves her from sexual assault, but she refuses to report the incident to the police resigned to the fact that her family name will mean she will be blamed or dismissed. In this respect Lane introduces the idea that there are pernicious intersections between class, rurality and gender in relation to women's sexuality. However, rather than open this up to critique she endorses the containment of working-class women's heterosexuality against middle-class feminine notions of respectability (Skeggs, 1997), assuring us that

Bridie had very few boyfriends before Shaun, and labelling Bridie's cousin, Cheryl, as deserving of her negative reputation as 'she wasn't exactly shy about sharing her assets with any and everyone' (p. 44).

Moreover, as she raises the issue of class and reputation in rural communities, Lane does what she has done throughout the book, deny the problem. In this instance she does so by contending that the problem only exists if Bridie allows it to exist endorsing neoliberal sensibilities of choice, self-regulation, positivity and confidence (Gill & Orgad, 2018). Class is nothing more than individual choice. In short, if we do not wish to be defined by class we can freely decide not to be. As Shaun tells Bridie when she explains her reticence to report the assault, 'If you had half as much faith in yourself as you do in this warped view of your own reputation, there wouldn't be a problem' (p. 137).

Shaun's advice to Bridie encapsulates the overall theme of the novel and the most ubiquitous and pernicious way in which class is discounted. That is, to render class a matter of personal choice. This is an idea that is foregrounded by the book's title and which propels the narrative. Bridie's choice is whether to leave Tooncanny and escape the class discrimination that has defined her life or stay and be with Shaun. She decides to stay, but only after making another choice that reflects the way in which neoliberal feminism has become so dominant it has infiltrated interior worlds. This is the choice to undergo a neoliberal feminist 'makeover' and adopt a positive demeanour (Gill, 2017), rather than be the 'angry, disillusioned teenager' who had grown into 'an angry, disillusioned adult' as a result of having to negotiate being a 'Farrell' (p. 11).

In the new regime of affect demanded by neoliberal feminism, the legitimacy of anger as a response to oppression and inequality, as well as the potentially generative and productive qualities of anger to energise social action, are not recognised. Instead, anger is individualised and pathologised. Negative experiences – such as the fact that Bridie lost her mother to cancer, witnessed her father's imprisonment, had to leave school to care for her brother and works multiple hours to make ends meet need to be 'reframed in upbeat terms' (Gill & Orgad, 2018,

p. 477). Every occurrence in one's life, including being in receipt of class violence, is individualised and constructed as a matter of personal responsibility. Thus, it is up to Bridie to recognise that 'she'd been bitter for so many years that it had coloured her way of thinking' (p. 292) and it was therefore necessary to let go of 'the anger she had been carrying around' (p. 308).

Positivity provides the necessary path for Bridie to leave the Gold Coast and return to Tooncanny, but not before she visits her father in prison for the first time. In further reinforcement of the book's key theme, Bridie's father cautions his daughter about the fact that he regrets that he is in prison because of the choices he made. Context is denied and he is presented as a completely autonomous individual who simply made the 'wrong choices'. In contrast, Bridie has made the 'right choice' with the adoption of the qualities and feelings valued in neoliberal times. She is a model of positivity, resilience and self-assurance. Indeed, on her return to Tooncanny from the Gold Coast, Shaun observes: 'There was something different about her. A confidence, an inner glow that he hadn't seen before' (p. 300). Taking up this reading of the novel, posters on Goodreads (2013) have written that the book is about 'how we come to define ourselves based on our definitions, not those given to us by society' (Jess on 3/1/13), and 'I loved how Shaun made Bridie open to herself to realise she is more than what she believes of herself and her family reputation doesn't dictate her life and choices' (Tash on 4/1/13).

Significantly, material inequalities between the two star-crossed lovers are addressed by the conclusion of the book. When *Bridie's Choice* comes to an end, Shaun is farming land near the family property which, while leased, is nevertheless still an indication of his access to capital. Further, despite his father's claim that he is out of the will, Shaun tells Bridie that 'he will come around in his own good time' (p. 303). Therefore, we are reassured that he will resume his claim to land and wealth, and on marriage, Bridie's poor economic position will change dramatically. Thus, by the end of the text the economic disparities of class are fully resolved through Bridie's 'choices'.

Conclusion

While our focus in this chapter is on a single text, our reading of a much larger corpus of ru-rom novels suggests that the themes we have highlighted are germane to the genre. There are necessary differences in emphasis in relation to specific manifestations of whiteness, class and neoliberal feminism in rural romance books, but across the sample, de-racialisation, settler occupancy, reinvention, choice and individualism and the need to adopt a positive and resilient disposition are recurring motifs. Central female characters typically need to be 'made over', transforming themselves as Bridie does in letting go of her anger and bitterness, forgiving her father and staying in her hometown to marry Shaun. They are, of course, impediments to the characters' transformative state, such as Bridie's responsibility for her younger brother and impoverished financial position. However, these are easily addressed through the characters' individual strength, determination and optimistic attitude. The resources which allow the characters to take up this affective state are rarely acknowledged. Instead, discourses of freedom and autonomy are privileged. Notably, these discourses of freedom, choice and autonomy are entangled in the processes of white feminism and an Australian white farming imaginary. As Moreton-Robinson (2020 [2000]) contends 'white feminist discourse on "difference" continues to be underpinned by a deracialised but gendered universal subject' (p. xviii).

As we have undertaken our research into ru-rom we have been challenged on occasions by those who deride and dismiss the genre as inconsequential, frivolous and lacking any political importance. In this chapter we have shown the limitations of this view revealing the significant ideological work done by rural romance. Like its sister genre chick-lit, ru-rom provides key insights into contemporary anxieties about gender, and the relationship between gender, class and race. The white middle-class women authors of the novels present a view of rural Australia from a position of privilege. Their dispositions and tastes are afforded value, naturalising inclusions and exclusions and reproducing and legitimating rural social inequality and settler occupancy. At the same time social class is constructed as happening elsewhere and/or decoupled from structural disadvantage. It is depoliticised and refracted through the marketised lens of choice and personal responsibility, rather than viewed as synonymous with systemic structural inequality, so that the need for decolonisation and radical social change are obscured or denied.

References

Alkon, A.H., & McCullen, C.G. (2011). Whiteness and farmers markets: Performances, perpetuations…Contestations? *Antipode, 43*(4), 937–959.

Bryant, L., & Pini, B. (2010). *Gender and rurality*. London: Routledge.

Butler, R. (2019). *Class, culture and belonging in rural childhoods*. Singapore: Springer.

Cairns, K., McPhail, D., Chevrier, C., & Bucklashchuk, J. (2015). The family behind the farm: Race and the affective geographies of Manitoba pork production. *Antipode, 47*(5), 1184–1202.

Cavanagh, M. (2015, March 10). Rural romance writing gets the capital all steamed up. *ABC Rural*. Retrieved from https://www.abc.net.au/news/rural/2015-03-10/rural-writing-australian-romance-readers-association/6295262

Gibson, J. (2020). A day in the life of a writer: Karly Lane. Retrieved from https://jfgibson.com.au/a-day-in-the-life-of-a-writer-karly-lane/

Gill, R. (2007). Postfeminist media culture: Elements of a sensibility. *European Journal of Cultural Studies, 10*(2), 147–166.

Gill, R. (2017). The affective, cultural and psychic life of postfeminism: A postfeminist sensibility 10 years on. *European Journal of Cultural Studies, 20*(6), 606–626.

Gill, R., & Orgad, S. (2018). The amazing bounce-backable woman: Resilience and the psychological turn in neoliberalism. *Sociological Research Online, 23*(2), 477–495.

Goodreads. (2012). Shelleyrae at book'd out's reviews *Bridie's Choice*. Retrieved from https://www.goodreads.com/review/show/458777785

Goodreads. (2013). *Bridie's Choice* community reviews. Retrieved from https://www.goodreads.com/book/show/16087483-bridie-s-choice

Kirne, J. (2020). Agricultural catastrophes: Revising settler belonging and the farming novel. *Everyman's Rules for Scientific Living. JASAL: Journal of the Association for the Study of Australian Literature, 20*(1), 1–12.

Lane, K. (2012). *Bridie's Choice*. Sydney: Allen and Unwin.

Mayes, C. (2018). *Unsettling food politics: Agriculture, dispossession and sovereignty in Australia*. London: Rowman and Littlefield.

McRobbie, A. (2004). Post-feminism and popular culture. *Feminist Media Studies, 4*(3), 255–64.

Mirmohamadi, K. (2015). Love on the land: Australian rural romance in place. *English Studies*, *96*(2), 204–224.

Moreton-Robinson, A. (2015). *The white possessive: Property, power and Indigenous sovereignty*. Minneapolis: University of Minnesota Press.

Moreton-Robinson, A. (2020 [2000]). *Talkin' up to the white woman: Indigenous women and feminism*. Brisbane: University of Queensland Press.

O'Mahony, L. (2020). Australian romance fiction. In J. Kamblé, E. Murphy Selinger, & H.M. Teo (Ed.), *The Routledge Research Companion to Popular Romance Fiction* (pp.73–96). London: Routledge.

Pini, B., Price, R., & McDonald, P. (2010). Teachers and the emotional dimensions of class in resource-affected rural Australia. *British Journal of Sociology of Education*, *31*(1), 17–30.

Pini, B., Rodriguez Castro, L., & Mayes, R. (2021). An agenda for Australian rural sociology: Troubling the white middle-class farming woman. *Journal of Sociology*. Doi: 1177/1440783321999830.

Prügl, E. (2015). Neoliberalising feminism. *New Political Economy*, *20*(4), 614–631.

Rohan, B., & Burke, P.J. (2019). Is there regional lock-in of unemployment rates in Australia? *Australian Journal of Labour Economics*, *22*(2), 93–116.

Rottenberg, C. (2014). The rise of neoliberal feminism. *Cultural Studies*, *28*(3), 418–437.

Skeggs, B. (1997). *Formations of class and gender*. London: Sage.

Taylor, N. (2012, October 15). New pastures. *Time Magazine*. Retrieved from http://content.time.com/time/magazine/article/0,9171,2124877,00.html

Threadgold, S. (2018). *Youth, class and everyday struggles*. London: Routledge.

Tyler, I. (2015). Classificatory struggles: Class, culture and inequality in neoliberal times. *The Sociological Review*, *63*(2), 493–511.

Ulus, E. (2018). White fantasy, white betrayals: On neoliberal 'feminism' in the US presidential election process. *Ephemera: Theory and Politics in Organization*, *18*(1), 163–181.

Part 4

Class and Education

CHAPTER 11

SCHOOLING AND CLASS AS A LONGITUDINAL AND PSYCHOSOCIAL PROCESS

Revisiting the 12 to 18 Project

Julie McLeod and Lyn Yates

To name what we attend to as class or to talk about what we find as class or to designate someone as 'working class' or 'middle class' is to inscribe it (and them) in a particular way, to relate what is said and observed to particular types of wider connections and to particular patterns. To use class as a focus and interpretive marker is to attend to issues of social distinction, hierarchy, power in individual identities and in the patterns of social relationships between individuals. It is also to attend to the relationships between individual formation and subjectivity, especially in the context of family and schooling, and to patterns of work, including the form of work and of different jobs; the structure of what types of jobs people from different backgrounds enter; and the dispositions, capital, power, lack of capital and power that pertain to different kinds of jobs. But, today, none of these are simply replicating their historical forms: the challenge is to consider what class means now and as 'new times' are in formation (McLeod & Yates, 2006, p. 161).

In 1993 we began the 12 to 18 Project to research intersections of class, gender and education in Australia in a fresh way. It was a qualitative, longitudinal project, following 26 young people at four schools from their last year of primary school to their post-school life. We tried to grapple with theories and existing research on what class might mean in Australia and in relation to school education, and we were particularly interested in the new questions, insights and complications that feminist research had raised about these issues. One question of the time was whether it even made sense to talk about class in a country and time that was so different from the Marxian Britain of the 19th century. We embarked on the project very aware of ways in which the idea and experience of class were now so difficult to investigate both conceptually and empirically, including whether class was a category young people themselves thought with. Was class about relations of production, exploitation and class conflict, or shorthand for socio-economic disadvantage? Or was it a concept concerned with ways of being in the world, of individual subjectivity, desire, and educational biography? Or one that sees labour and capital as linchpins for understanding individuals and social relations? Or do attempts to categorise people using class inevitably misrecognise modern forms of being. We saw all these questions as pertinent (McLeod & Yates, 2006, pp.1–28).

There are different histories to what people are trying to *work out and work with* when using the term class. In reference to education, we argued that either working with the concept of class or attempting to do without it or replacing it, is fraught with interpretive, ethical and methodological dilemmas. We wanted to explore what it meant to research class and schooling as much as we wanted to better understand the contemporary social patterns and subjectivity processes of class and schooling.

Empirical research on schooling inequalities clearly showed (and continues to show) different trajectories for those at the top and those at the bottom of the socio-economic ladder. A key question, however, is in what sense is this a function of class? Is class analysis relevant in accounting for the experiences of the great bulk of Australian students (those 'in the middle'), whose futures in school are not so clearly over-determined? Do you begin research by selecting people already categorised as 'representing' particular class categories or do you try to read class structures and processes more inductively in the experiences you see? Is class about how people identify or about how the researcher reads their identity and orientations? For us these questions were prominent from the outset – in how we thought about the methodological approach and design of the study and in how we grappled with building an analysis over the course of the study.

In this chapter we aim to recapture the kinds of issues our research was contending with, including why we continued to want to talk about and use class as a heuristic. We discuss the influence of feminist theorising on the project design and its focus on processes of subjectivity – of class and gender – in formation over time and in interaction with schooling. We were equally conscious that a single study, even one conducted over eight years, could not and did not want to tackle *everything* about class and schooling in Australia at that time. For the students we followed, the school results and Year 12 outcomes were broadly in line with the kinds of predictions you would make from the big SES (socio-economic status) survey data, but this was not the central focus of the project. Rather, it was understanding the trajectories that both fed into and extended beyond this point in time, with a focus on processes of formation (biography in interaction with school cultures) in the context of known social patterns. We illustrate the kind of insights this approach offered and consider from our subsequent work what we see as blind spots in the design and conceptual framing of the project, as well as the continued value of the approach we took. We conclude with reflections on researching class more broadly, including the value of distinguishing between 'research' questions and 'action-oriented' solutions and the need to historicise the contexts and approaches in which questions about class and education rise and fall.

Theoretical and Empirical Contexts

Our focus was on class and schooling and, specifically, the processes through which individual lives encounter education in differential ways and with differential effects on their own subjectivities and outcomes, and the ways in which this contributes to a continued kind of social-relational patterning. Traditionally, quantitative class analysis of schooling had mapped students' distributional outcomes against the occupational categories of their fathers (in a descriptive rather than relational and explanatory sense). From the 1970s, studies had also explored various ways in which the school curriculum and pedagogy were based on and reconstructed middle-class or professional values and knowledge and disadvantaged those from working-class backgrounds (Bernstein, 1975; Apple, 1979).

A prominent Australian study of the 1970s (Connell et al., 1982) examined elite and disadvantaged schools in Sydney and Adelaide and argued that elite schools were 'organic' to their community and class interests in ways that disadvantaged schools were not. It provided an account of class as both a material and cultural phenomenon, one that worked relationally, and that, at the extremes at least, did not need a sophisticated analysis to recognise its form and practices in action. That is, the markers of class distinction were widely and broadly recognisable; for example, elite schools and their rowing sheds (Roper, 1971).

We have included this thumbnail sketch of sociological work at the time to underline two points. First, although what might crudely be called socio-economic class-based inequality had long been an ongoing fact of schooling in Australia, by the 1980s and 1990s much more attention (at least at policy level) was being given to sociological categories of gender and ethnicity/race than to these big and persistent patterns of class-based inequality (Yates, 1993). Many of the Australian states had actually discontinued collecting data by SES (Yates & Leder, 1995). This changed again in subsequent decades with a lot of apparent attention to the effects of poverty on school achievement, even though inequalities of resources continued to burgeon and there is no evident policy interest in rolling back class advantage as distinct from producing bandaids for disadvantage. Second, and more recently, policy reforms have been enthralled with the idea of generic templates for curriculum and accountability, positioning 'effective schools' as the answer to school inequalities (Hattie, 2009). The sociological work on class from the 1970s aimed to show that the cultural, ideological and dispositional elements of schooling worked differentially for those of different class backgrounds, elements that would not be resolved by a new 'effective', one size fits all, template for teaching.

Before we began our project, feminist theory and research had disrupted the frameworks for understanding both class and school inequalities. Women's different relationship to labour markets and the impact of mothers' education and work on intergenerational class relations challenged conventional mapping of class patterns based on fathers' occupations. Moreover, the *form* in which education produced longer-term inequalities seemed to be different through the lens of gender, with questions of 'recognition', cultural difference and identities now more in focus, not only the 'distribution' of economic resources (Fraser, 1997; Young, 1990). Through a class lens, schooling directly produced failures and inequalities that fed post-school life through direct restrictions on entry to tertiary study or work; but gender ideologies of femininity and masculinity could produce differential power and opportunities post-school, even where girls had done as well as or better than boys of the same social class in their school results (Yates, 1993; Collins, Kenway, & McLeod, 2000). Focusing on gender dynamics drew attention to the intersectionality of identity categories and the need to see gender *and* class processes at work in lives and institutions, not just try to work out how to describe social structure or to work out in which box to put people. Challenges to treating class as a one-dimensional categorisation not only disrupted (fatally?) the theoretical models underpinning that kind of research, they also pointed to a gap between theoretical constructions of identity and the embodied and located experience of becoming someone over time. New social movements, such as feminism and disability rights activism, had drawn attention to changing power relations and social structures. Whatever class now is and was, it is clearly a dynamic, not static category – forms of occupations, experiences, relationships and power continue to change.

When we first started thinking about the 12 to 18 Project in the mid-1990s, much research on gender and class in schooling had focused on how people with different group identities had been 'reproduced' via the mainstream curriculum and processes of schooling or how students had 'resisted' (Hall & Jefferson, 1976; McRobbie, 1991). These studies took a short-term rather than longitudinal slice, looking at processes at one point in time (for example, over a year or a term). We wanted to look at individual hopes, dreams and identity-making over time. We did not assume this could be read off from an already existing big theory nor extrapolated from single point in time research data (either qualitative or quantitative).

Feminist attention to subjectivity and to the orientations and capacities people took up in the world over time meant that understanding the relationship between class and subjectivity involved more than simply documenting the educational, social and economic differences in pathways and outcomes of individuals and classes of people. It also involved attention to the affective and embodied resonance of class-based differences. One strand of this work theorised gender and class intersections as psychosocial phenomena (Walkerdine, Lucey, & Melody, 2001), attending to unconscious processes and desires in how identities and aspirations were formed over time. Other feminist education scholarship drew upon Bourdieu's conceptual framework of habitus, field and capitals to explore how gender-class identities and orientations were formed in structured yet improvised ways (habitus) and in interaction with various forms of education, conceived as social fields (Reay, 1998; McLeod, 2005). It is important to acknowledge the type of contestations over class and gender during this earlier period and the considerable attention to theorising class from within or infused by feminist sensibilities. This cluster of work – both the psychosocial and Bourdieu-ian – provided a critical point of dialogue as we incrementally developed our analysis. Given this backdrop and what we saw as limitations of attempts to put together class and gender as a set of categories and explanations, how did we design our longitudinal, qualitative study? We wanted to build in opportunities for reflection on these different theories and for comparative analysis (of like with like and like with different) without locking in a pre-categorisation of what class 'looked like'. We made the first decision about who we would study not by the traditional way of asking potential subjects to fill in a questionnaire with their family's occupation, levels of education and so forth. Rather, our first decision was to select the school sites. We decided on an elite private school, a technical school generally classed as 'disadvantaged', and two 'ordinary' high schools, meaning schools that were not selective or streamed, and were not located in suburbs at the extremes of the SES hierarchy, and where we knew the outcomes for students from the school spanned a spectrum from early leaving to university entrance.

Two of the schools were in Melbourne and two in a provincial city in Victoria. We wanted to follow what was happening to *students who might be categorised as somewhat similar but involved in a different school, place and culture*, and we wanted to see what happened to *students from different backgrounds who attended the same school*. Because many previous studies had focused on the most advantaged and disadvantaged, they often conflated the particular school and location and the class experience. We wanted some opportunity to see interactions of class and gender processes with different school configurations.

We now turn to consider some of the ways of seeing 'class' that our project revealed.

What We Noticed

Exposing Some of the Ideology of Class

One of the themes in work on class and schooling has long been the ideological function of schools: to make outcomes in terms of occupation and power appear to be the result of individual efforts and not of class (Bourdieu, 1976; Bowles & Gintis, 1976). A further theme, especially in Australia, is that 'good' educational practice is what elites and elite schools do (for example, their particular cultural capital, modes of abstraction and networks) and that these practices are what all schools should emulate as an index of a good education. These accounts do reveal some truth in how processes of social differentiation work but there are also ways in which they function themselves as ideological. Here, we offer three examples we discussed in earlier papers on the project.

In Victoria, Australia, where rates of private school attendance are comparatively high, the widespread assumption that a good education is at an elite school (or one of the few state selective schools) is supported by data on retention and VCE/senior school outcomes gathered by governments and websites and printed in newspapers. The official statistics at the time of our study showed the elite school in our study as having a 'retention' rate (that is, Year 12 numbers compared with Year 7 commencements) of over 100 per cent,[1] but two of the eight students we were following there were deeply unhappy and left that school midway through the study. Other students transferred into that school for the final year, but the statistics provide a misleading reporting that adds to the 'gloss' of the desirability of this school. Another example is our two 'middle' high schools. One of these self-consciously presented as a quality school in the state sector: it emphasised traditional uniforms, discipline and offered rowing – emulating private schools. The other school had a reputation as progressive but not particularly high quality in its outcomes. Yet, the patterns of overall Year 12 examination results were not so different between the two schools. The high school that emphasised being like a private school had very different Year 12 outcomes from its private school neighbours. These examples show that both students and parents participate in many misrecognitions that elide class features and performances with good education.

At the elite private school, we heard in many interviews that the school was fairly poor in its computer equipment and teaching in that area; but this did not dampen the students' belief in this as an excellent school; that is, its class-based image exceeded or was sustained beyond shortcomings of practice. Conversely, the most socially disadvantaged of our schools was extremely well-equipped in terms of technology. Students liked those subjects but remained convinced that what 'Education' values is traditional subjects, maths and English. The former students learnt to some extent to 'misrecognise' their own social advantages and to take up an unsympathetic stance to those who lacked these. The students in the second school reinforced a stance of progressive fatalism that had them competing less vigorously for school success (Yates, 2000).

We made the decision to do all the interviewing ourselves. Influenced by feminist research methodology, we wanted to interrogate our own role in the building of interpretations and theorising throughout the project. In the first year, we had been struck (but not surprised) by the contrasting ways of 'being in the world' of those who came from extremes of the social spectrum. In the most disadvantaged setting, we noticed the hesitations and inarticulateness of three girls, and their palpable lack of comfort talking to us as adult strangers. Similarly, we had been impressed by the fluency and ease exhibited by the students attending the elite private school. Later, when we reviewed the transcripts, we were surprised to discover that the language of the latter students was not the model of good grammar and eloquence we thought we had heard. What we were seeing initially was our own reactions to the setting (both coming from provincial high schools and feeling unsettled in such a school) and presentations of self of our interviewees. These matters have additional resonance today when identity resources and presentations of self are an increasingly important focus of job selection (Yates & McLeod, 1996). We were picking up on embodied class markers and mistaking them for a more sophisticated level of personal awareness.

Class Formations in Process

Closely following the hopes, values and decisions of the 26 young people made it possible to see the workings and reworkings of the class/gender orientations they brought to school in the context of their schools. Here we saw glimmers of both the familiar story of class distributional reproduction as well as new subjectivity and class formations in process.

In the familiar vein, we could broadly see different themes in young people's narratives that were, in some sense, a product of their class locations that they brought to and persisted with over their schooling. At the private school, students' own experiences and observations of family and friends were that it was easy to get jobs, often via personal connections. At the poorest end, students had learnt to expect very little or nothing, that they could not be confident of things turning out for the best. To some extent, these views were also reinforced by their schooling experiences, though this was more in the case of the former than the latter school, where the teachers battled valiantly against the low expectations and easy discouragement of students. For those of elite background at the elite school, the themes were about being a 'somebody', a distinctive person, successful in some field. At the other end, the mantra was one of 'taking it as it comes'. Although at the beginning of secondary school, students from poorer backgrounds might have aspirations that sounded like new ambitions compared with their parents, including to attend university or move away from familiar territory, over the course of school their expectations, and the energy they put into any new possibilities, were reined back. Underneath, they were not surprised when hopes were thwarted.

However, we argued this was not simply another story of class reproduction in the classic Bourdieu-ian sense. Rather, the longitudinal design and close-up approach of our study allowed us to see both significant and subtle changes afoot. Changes in gender roles and opportunities and in how gender and class intersected were having a visible impact upon how boys and girls were seeing their futures, and this was particularly marked for the girls at either end of the socio-economic spectrum.

A theme of some feminist psychology literature at the time was girls' rebellion in their early teen years (Gilligan, 1982), when they want to differentiate and individuate from their mothers; this was evident particularly among the most privileged girls. However, most of the girls in the non-elite schools had seen and empathised with their mothers' hard work on behalf of their family and had also seen their mothers' work changing and the impact of this upon family dynamics. This affected their own future thinking as the mothers had taken up new opportunities to return to study or to educate themselves further via jobs such as teaching or youth work. For example, Sally, who attend the former technical school in the regional city, came from a single-parent family where her mother worked and studied part-time at TAFE. Money was tight. Sally would tell us about looking after her four siblings and the housework she did, not in a complaining way but as a matter-of-fact description of what she did outside school. Occasionally Sally would express her dreams – a house of my own, a car that worked – but she would usually pull herself up and reflect that she would just 'take things as they come'. Yet this habituated way of seeing herself in the world was at odds with, what we saw in retrospect (the longitudinal view) was, a more strategising and determined approach for herself to finish school and get a qualification. At the start of school, Sally often said that she was finding the schoolwork hard and was often vague about her future work, as if it would be too ambitious to even think about. But over her school years, with evident support of teachers, a valuable work-experience placement, the knowledge that TAFE was accessible and the example of her mother's own pathway, Sally finished school, enrolled in a pre-nursing course and had a clearer immediate pathway than peers at her school.

This is not a simple story of class reproduction and constrained options; working-class pathways for working-class girls. Nor does it point to greater class mobility and boundless vistas for young working-class women. But it does illustrate how gender and class dynamics intersect and can shift over time in light of school cultures: the proactive vocational orientation of the ex-technical school, family dynamics, and a sense of new possibilities cautiously opening up in response to feminism, the further education of women and the labour market (McLeod, 2000).

In the beginning, we were struck by the energy and optimism of girls' dreams of the future (driving fast cars, travel, and so on) and their sense of opening opportunities as they got older. Boys of the same age were more subdued, with a more uncertain sense of how their future would look. This was not simply about choosing or inheriting job directions but about what their family life would look like and imagined gender roles. We could see how boys and girls from what might have deemed the same 'class' or SES background were beginning to see and recast their thinking about their post-school lives. The example of Nicky offers interesting insight as we observed her trying to juggle the pull of familiar tradition and a sense of new times. She was from a wealthy background and attended the elite school, her father was in a profession and mother not involved in paid work but focusing on family and charity work. When asked about her aspirations and dreams, Nicky in the first years of the project admitted that her main aspiration was to be a wife and mother. 'Admitted' is the apt word here because she made clear to us that in this period and at this school, this was seen as an inappropriate aspiration: all students were expected to have careers and to become someone in their own right. By the end of school, she had found a direction, fashion design, that she hoped would work for her. In terms of class consciousness and class status, Nicky's experiences are also revealing. When we were exploring students' family backgrounds mid-way through the project, she mentioned that she was the fourth generation of her family to come to this school. Here she is identifying with her father and his father and grandfather: this is the first generation when it was even possible for girls to attend this particular school.

The project was designed to also understand the experiences of students and schools 'in the middle', including the differences in school cultures and the kind of student subjectivities they emphasised. In snapshot, the regional secondary school prided itself on its strong sense of discipline and hard work, and an old-style focus on competitive educational success. Students consistently expressed confidence in a meritocratic system and usually had clear plans for their future work, seeing their futures unfold against what was perceived by them at that stage to be a relatively stable world. At the other school, a more informal and consciously creative, student-centred atmosphere prevailed. Students were attuned to changes in the world around them, to inequalities and diversity, and had a strong focus on self-development and the importance of having time to understand 'who am I?' Both schools were providing foundations for their students that were creating different kinds of post-school opportunities and traps for young people of similar backgrounds (Yates & McLeod, 2000).

Class Then and Now

In this chapter we have tried to show that it is not only the category or concept of class that needs examining in relation to schooling, but also the question of what particular things we are trying to see or understand at a specific point in time. Our project did not stand alone and never pretended to provide a definitive perspective on class and schooling. It was developed in a period when quantitative data on school outcomes relative to socio-economic background were available, and where a range of non-longitudinal sociological understandings of how schools and school curricula 'reproduced' class were well established. But feminism raised new conceptual questions about what psychosocial processes are involved in class reproductions and outcomes and drew attention to the complex forms of late-20th-century labour structures. We were trying to ask different kinds of questions about class and schooling: *what is being set in train for the future in students* from particular backgrounds and in particular institutions. Unsurprisingly, it emphasised and noticed some things more than others, such as differences in modes of self-presentation and the new kinds of subjectivities valued in the 21st century, which have only become more important to understand in the contemporary era.

When designing the project, we were clear that we were trying to work with two main kinds of inequality and difference, namely class and gender. This was not because we were indifferent to or unaware of the salience of other social categories and relations of inequality. Rather, we wanted to be analytically clear about the specific types of differences we were attending to and not lump all differences and instances of inequality together as if they were all much of the same generic problem. For example, we tried to understand how and when ethnic and racial differences were foregrounded in students' experiences and relation to school, but these were not the predominant concerns of the study, which is as much a methodological decision as it was a matter of the time and place in which the research was undertaken. Most strikingly, from today's perspective, reflection on Australian education and colonialism was not part of our consideration and no Indigenous students were part of the study.

Initiated close to three decades ago, our project took seriously two foci that have since become much more prominent in the sociological literature: attention to temporality (biographical and school time) and to specificity of place, to the physical and institutional school space, their regional or urban location, and the stigmatised, privileged or 'ordinary' histories that attached to them. Class is also fundamentally about subjectivity – how one understands and positions self and other, rationally and emotionally, and one's sense of potency and possibility. In terms of the institutional site of schooling, we see class as being in (re-)formation, as both drawing on past economic and cultural formations and contributing to both persisting and changing ones. This focus has been taken up by McLeod in a subsequent longitudinal project on intergenerational experiences of schooling with more attention to issues of temporality, memory and place (McLeod, 2017). Many studies of class today continue to attend to the extremes and there is a flourishing field of scholarship on elites (Kenway, 2017) but there seems to be less new attention to understanding the experiences in the middle or the role of schools in forming subjects.

The kind of study we did was intended to feed thinking and interpretations about class rather than designed to produce a simple action agenda in relation to schooling. There is an important distinction – often elided – between research (trying to understand what is happening) and action-oriented and policy agendas (fix inequality of outcomes) when looking at class and education. One blind spot of action agendas is assuming you can discount specificities of difference in what students bring to school, for example, by focusing on template solutions as if there were a level playing field. This has informed Yates' later work on knowledge and what schools can do (Yates, Collins, & O'Connor, 2011).

Today, there is considerable debate about whether educational research has neglected the study of class in recent times and calls for renewed attention. In this clamouring, it is as important to situate the changing concerns and questions about class in a stronger historical context. This includes recognising its dominance in the early formation of the field of sociology of educational inequalities, the different forms research on class has taken and continues to take, and the need to historicise the questions we ask and the problems we are trying to understand.

Endnote

1   Government published data on retention was measured by comparing those who finished year 12 against those who entered year 7.

References

Apple, M.W. (1979). *Ideology and curriculum*. London: Routledge & Kegan Paul.
Bernstein, B. (1975). *Class, codes and control, vol. 3: Towards a theory of educational transmissions (primary socialization, language and education)*. London: Routledge & Kegan Paul.
Bourdieu, P. (1976). Systems of education and systems of thought. In R. Dale, G. Esland, & M. MacDonald (Eds.), *Schooling and Capitalism: A Reader* (pp. 192–200). London: Routledge & Kegan Paul.
Bowles, S., & Gintis, H. (1976). *Schooling in capitalist America: Educational reform and the contradictions of economic life*. New York: Basic Books.
Collins, C., Kenway, J., & McLeod, J. (2000). *Factors influencing the educational performance of males and females at school and their initial destinations after leaving school*. Canberra: Department of Education, Training and Youth Affairs, Commonwealth of Australia.
Connell, R.W., Ashenden, D., Kessler, S., & Dowsett, G. (1982). *Making the difference: Schools, families and social division*. Sydney: George Allen & Unwin.
Fraser, N. (1997). *Justice interruptus: Critical reflections on the 'postsocialist' condition*. New York: Routledge.
Gilligan, C. (1982). *In a different voice: Psychological theory and women's development*. Cambridge, MA: Harvard University Press.
Hall, S., & Jefferson, T. (Eds.). (1976). *Resistance through rituals: Youth subcultures in post-war Britain*. London: HarperCollins Academic.
Hattie, J. (2009). *Visible learning: A synthesis of over 800 meta-analyses relating to achievement*. London: Routledge.
Kenway, J. (2017). *Class choreographies: Elite schools and globalization*. London: Palgrave Macmillan.
McLeod, J. (2000). Subjectivity and schooling in a longitudinal study of secondary students. *British Journal of Sociology of Education, 21*(4), 502–521.
McLeod, J. (2005). Feminist re-reading Bourdieu: Old debates and new questions and gender habitus and gender change. *Theory and Research in Education, 3*(1), 11–30.
McLeod, J. (2017). Marking time, making methods: Temporality and untimely dilemmas in the sociology of youth and educational change. *British Journal of Sociology of Education, 38*(1), 13–25.

McLeod, J, & Yates, L. (2006). *Making modern lives: Subjectivity, schooling and social change*. Albany, NY: State University of New York Press.

McRobbie, A. (1991). *Feminism and youth culture: From 'Jackie' to 'Just Seventeen'*. Basingstoke, UK: MacMillan.

Reay, D. (1998). *Class work: Mothers' involvement in children's schooling*. London: University College Press.

Roper, T. (1971). *The myth of equality*. South Yarra: Heinemann Educational Australia.

Walkerdine, V., Lucey, H., & Melody, J. (2001). *Growing up girl: Psychosocial explorations of gender and class*. London: Palgrave.

Yates, L. (1993). *The education of girls: Policy, research and the question of gender*. Hawthorn: Australian Council for Educational Research.

Yates, L. (2000). Representing 'class' in qualitative research. In J. McLeod, & K. Malone (Eds.), *Researching youth*. Hobart: Australian Clearinghouse for Youth Studies.

Yates, L., Collins, C.W., & O'Connor, K. (2011). *Australia's curriculum dilemmas: State cultures and the big issues*. Melbourne: Melbourne University Publishing.

Yates, L., & Leder, G.C. (1995). The Student Pathways Project: A study of large data-bases and gender equity. *Unicorn, 21*(4), 39–47.

Yates, L., & McLeod, J. (1996). 'And how would you describe yourself?' Researchers and researched in a longitudinal study of secondary students. *Australian Journal of Education, 40*(1), 88–103.

Yates, L., & McLeod, J. (2000). Social justice and the middle. *Australian Educational Researcher, 27*(3), 59–77.

Young, I.M. (1990). *Justice and the politics of difference*. Princeton, New Jersey: Princeton University Press.

CHAPTER 12

THE TRANSFORMING MIDDLE

Schooling Markets, Morality and Racialisation within Australia's Middle Class

Rose Butler, Christina Ho and Eve Vincent

The Global Middle Class in Australia

Transformations in the world economy have reconfigured how 'middle-classness' as a status, identity and trajectory is achieved and maintained, both across the mobile transnational middle classes and within national and regional contexts (Heiman, Liechty, & Freeman, 2012). These changes are the effect of two coalescing phenomena. First, the widespread economic reforms of the late 1970s and 1980s resulted in more conditional and tightly targeted post-Fordist welfare states and reduced the collective bargaining power among workers (Harvey, 2005; Greig, Lewins, & White, 2003), leading to wage growth suppression (Humphrys, 2019). Second, the same period witnessed the rising economic and cultural power of East, South-East and South Asian nations, notably China (Rogers, Lee, & Yan, 2015). The first process resulted in many nation-states either withdrawing or privatising resources for social reproduction (child-rearing, education and work). As a result, individuals and families now absorb much more of the responsibility, risk and cost of the labour required to raise future generations and make a living (Katz, 2004).

These economic and social changes enabled and coincided with a broader reconstitution of the middle classes and the development of a host of 'new' middle-class identities across the globe. While there have always been fractions and tensions within the middle class (Bourdieu, 1984), we refer here to a particular middle-class social formation centred around flexible subjectivities, absorption of the risk and costs of social reproduction (that is, less reliance on, and less expectation of state provision), and the capacity to retrain and respond to shifting demands of the market (Heiman et al., 2012). Such new middle classes are anchored in the same market logics of neoliberal governance and the particular subjectivities they enable and encourage. They carry the responsibility of being independent entrepreneurs and consumers. This is particularly seen in a rapid rise of economically mobile migrants from newly prosperous nations in Asia moving to work and live in migrant-receiving nations (Heiman et al., 2012).

In Australia, the last 30 years of economic reforms (Pusey, 2003), the hegemony of neoliberal ideology across government and businesses, and increased privatisation of services once provided by the state (Greig et al., 2003) all underpin a range of transformations that have taken place within the middle class. The 20th century saw the establishment of a middle class dominated by a weightier professional segment tied to state funding, notably through the welfare state, and a weaker managerial sector located mainly in the private sector (Martin, 1998, pp. 144–5). The White Australia policy ensured that this was a largely white middle class, who in turn symbolised and embodied Australian social norms and ideals (Moreton-Robinson, 2000, p. 177).

The White Australia policy was finally abolished in 1973, although historians point to a more incremental dismantling that took place in the decades prior (Tavan, 2005). And from the mid-1980s, several processes started to alter the structure of Australia's middle class. A key feature was a shift in the balance between the public and private sectors (Martin, 1998). During this period, Australia's middle class experienced a broad decline in relative earnings among most professional occupations, which were heavily dependent on state funding (for example, teachers, social workers), an expansion of the private sector, and a strengthening of its professional and managerial segments (Martin, 1998, p. 145; Pusey, 2003). At the same time, government adoption of variations of neoliberal ideologies and a globalising world economy resulted in a stronger and flourishing private sector (Martin, 1998, p. 145).

Australia's middle class was also transforming in response to changes in the nation's immigration policies. Growing numbers of well-educated and well-resourced members of the global middle class from East, South-East and South Asia were able to enter and settle in Australia (Colic-Peisker, 2011; Tsang, 2013). Today Asian residents from various source countries comprise the largest group of migrants from language backgrounds other than English (ABS, 2017). This immigration, inextricably linked with education opportunities and highly financialised real-estate markets (Robertson & Rogers, 2017), the growth of a wealthy global elite, and international investment in Australia's resource sector, education and housing (Rogers et al., 2015) have all contributed to rapid changes within the nation's middle class.

Finally, while we refer here to a segment of Australia's 'middle class', we recognise that the categorisation of class-based membership in relation to varying forms of capital is a contested and transforming terrain in Australia (for example, Shephard & Biddle, 2017; Adkins, Cooper, & Konings, 2021).

Tensions Surrounding Schooling Markets Within the Transforming Middle Class

Significant changes to Australia's education system and labour market have deeply impacted the capacity of the nation's schools to successfully ensure middle-class social reproduction. The decline in the youth labour market and a rise in job uncertainty have made university education, and the exam results needed to enter high-status university courses, increasingly important to economic security (Campbell & Proctor, 2014). Australia's schools have long sought to offer a range of provisions to cater to geographic and population need. However, a growth of market-driven schooling has seen 'provision' become a matter of 'choice' for families, who must now negotiate a school 'market' (Campbell & Proctor, 2014, pp. 259–260).

Central to this emphasis on 'choice' is a rise in standardised measurement, school examinations, private tutoring and the external ranking of schools within league tables (Watkins & Noble, 2013). This has exacerbated differences between well and poorly resourced schools and entrenched a growing divide between 'public' and 'private' institutions. Private (corporate and religious) schools in Australia are regulated by fees, enrolment policies and in some cases entrance exams. By contrast, public schools have been traditionally defined by their geographical location and required to admit any student living within their enrolment zones. Importantly, the geographical remit excludes academically selective public schools, as we discuss below (Campbell, Proctor, & Sherrington, 2009; Ho, 2011).

This has resulted in a strong movement of middle-class families out of public schools and into private ones (Campbell et al., 2009). Public schools are understood as increasingly socially and educationally 'residual': many middle-class parents have withdrawn their resources from the public system (Campbell & Proctor, 2014). A large proportion of people making this transition to private schools have been white, while public schools have become more linguistically and culturally diverse. In metropolitan Sydney, for example, students from a Language Background Other Than English (LBOTE) on average make up more than half (55 per cent) of enrolments in government schools, compared to less than a third (31 per cent) of students in non-government schools (My School, 2016, cited in Ho, 2019).

However, selective schools present a different case again. These are academically selective public high schools: their entry process is highly competitive. Select public primary schools also offer an 'opportunity class' (OC) in Years 5 and 6, selection for which involves sitting an exam. OCs promise to enhance the chance of being offered a selective high school place. These two types of institutions are strongly concentrated in Sydney and have resulted in NSW offering the most hierarchical public education system in Australia (Sriprakash, Proctor, & Hu, 2015).

The growth of a mobile middle class with an East Asian background in Australia has seen increased public scrutiny of high achieving Asian-Australian students within this selective school system (Watkins, Ho, & Butler, 2017; Proctor & Sriprakash, 2017). Media coverage of the issue speaks to white Australian parents' concern about growing education competition, the rise of private tutoring, and ethnic segregation in schools (Wu & Singh, 2004; Sriprakash et al., 2015; Ho, 2017). As Watkins and Noble (2013) discern, these debates 'ethnicise' educational achievement because they commonly represent certain pedagogical and social practices as 'Asian'. This includes authoritarian methods of disciplining and teaching students, rote learning, criticism of parental focus on individual student success rather than concern for wider school communities, private study and tutoring, and the tracking and measuring of student outcomes. All of these practices can in fact be regarded as germane to the global, neoliberal schooling market more broadly (Watkins & Noble, 2013). In these depictions, 'Asian success' is explained in cultural terms and constructed as being about ethnicity and/or race, a form of essentialism that feeds into a historically resonant politics of racial hostility (Archer & Francis, 2007).

The Moral Project of Making up the Middle

Morality has long been recognised as central to the middle class's claims of legitimacy and is a central means through which the middle class distinguishes itself from others (Bourdieu, 1984; Skeggs, 2004; Sayer, 2005). Moral judgements lie at the heart of how we evaluate the cultural characteristics of others, while the ability to define and judge morality on such terms is central to the workings and transmissions of power and how it is reproduced (Skeggs, 2004, p. 214).

In this respect, any moral order acts as a cultural logic – it is a set of moral rules that operate within a system of expectations around social behaviour and etiquette. Yet it is the middle class who determines the cultural logic needed to produce these rules and the contexts within which they operate and to what effects (Skeggs, 2004). Members of the middle class constitute themselves by controlling the system in which particular actions become recognised as symbolically legitimate. In doing so, the middle class determines which acts are worthy and morally 'right' for 'everyone' at the same time as they align themselves morally to a particular cultural order (Bourdieu, 1984; Sayer, 2005). Through this process, the making of moral boundaries and identities becomes a central terrain through which the middle class is constantly negotiated, struggled against and reproduced (Wacquant, 1991).

Producing Middle-class Morality: A Study of Schooling in Sydney

Schooling in Sydney provides a fruitful case study in this production of middle-class morality and the specificities through which 'middle-classness' is now achieved (Heiman et al., 2012, p. 7). The coalescence of market reforms and the growth of an economically secure and mobile elite within Australia's capital cities, notably from East and South Asian nations, is challenging expectations about who can claim middle-class legitimacy in moral terms. In this chapter we explore two sites of tension surrounding this transforming middle class in relation to schooling.

In our first case study, white parents in an increasingly middle-class milieu share their anxieties surrounding public primary school choice. We document the moral self-positioning of this segment of white middle-class parents, whom we call 'community-minded', and show how they work to reproduce the moral legitimacy of their social status in relation to a 'new' middle class in Australia (Butler, Ho, & Vincent, 2017). In the second case study, we discuss the more high-stakes question of selective high school entry. We analyse the deeply racialised concept of 'natural ability' and consider how it is used by white middle-class parents and students to assert their perceived entitlement to good schooling on moral terms.

Across both examples we explore how 'old' and 'new' middle-class milieus condition white parents' hopes and fears for their children's education trajectories and middle-class futures. These are messy, complex, racialised and anxiety-filled spaces in which these classed social worlds encounter and negotiate one another's ideals, experiences and sensibilities. Both examples offer rich insights into the efforts of white, urban middle-class parents to reproduce a particular form of moralised middle-class identity and to secure their children's trajectories within this altered and racialised middle-class terrain.

Throughout this discussion, we use the term 'white' to refer to a dominant mode of self-perception, even if an unconscious one, among our participants (Hage, 1998), and to reveal the way whiteness functions as an invisible norm through which it maintains its dominance in multicultural settler societies like Australia (Moreton-Robinson, 2000).

The Research

The data for this paper is drawn from two qualitative research projects conducted in Sydney between 2014 and 2018. The first was a study (2014–2016) undertaken by all three authors in an inner-city suburb of Sydney we call 'Cooper' (Ho, Vincent, & Butler, 2015). This research drew on semi-structured interviews with 34 parents, predominantly of white backgrounds, in four public primary schools, as well as with four educators, including two school principals. With a history of industry and manufacturing from the 19th century, Cooper rapidly gentrified in the early 2000s and went from being one of the most culturally diverse working-class areas in Australia, to an area dominated by middle-class white Australians. We examined how this gentrification was reshaping understandings of 'diversity' in Cooper's local primary schools.

The second study, undertaken by Ho, was based on interviews with 30 students and parents with experience of selective high schools, streaming and OC classes, primarily in Sydney's northern suburbs (2016–2018). Through semi-structured interviews, Ho examined how families made decisions about school choice, the preparation undertaken to secure a place in a selective school or class, and social experiences within these environments. Approximately half the interviews from Ho's study were with white middle-class families, and the other half with Asian-Australian middle-class families, mostly from Chinese backgrounds. It is important to note this was a very different middle-class world to Cooper, with less emphasis on progressivism and more on educational and career success.

'Community-minded' White Middle-class Parents' Concerns

In our first Sydney case study of Cooper, primarily white middle-class interviewees spoke of being attracted to the area because of its social and cultural diversity. These parents' embrace of 'diversity' was experienced as an asset to their white middle-class, socially progressive identities. Yet, our research also documented the lived polarisation of race and class across four primary schools within this catchment area (Ho et al., 2015). One of our key findings was the lived contradictions of white parents' desires for social contact with particular forms of ethnicised, but not classed, otherness (Vincent, Butler, & Ho, 2017). The moral self-positioning of a segment of white middle-class parents we call 'community-minded' (Butler et al., 2017) also provided insight into these parents' efforts to reproduce the moral legitimacy of their social status in relation to Australia's 'new' middle class.

'Community-minded' parents share features of a moral identity that previous scholars attribute to an older, white 'moral middle class' (Brett, 2003; Campbell et al., 2009). These are parents who have historically spurned private education and have long claimed a moral preference for social democratic principles. They draw similarities with families in Campbell et al.'s (2009) study who 'remain resistant to private institutions and market-organised fields of choice, in so far as they replace perfectly adequate public institutions and services'. Brett (2003, p. 10) elsewhere depicts a similar branch of this Australian middle class as one which is historically understood as individuals who bear particular 'moral qualities'. This is not a class 'opposed to or in conflict with other classes', but rather 'a mode of social classification opposed to the very idea of economically based social identity and economically based social classification'. A class based in moral membership rather than social and economic positioning, Brett continues, is in theory 'open to anyone who tries hard enough to walk the narrow and respectable path of virtue', and this self-ascribed moral virtue has long been the basis of the Australian middle class's self-identity (Brett, 2003, p. 11). Yet there are perhaps stronger parallels in middle-class formations here with the works of Reay et al. (2008), whose research within inner-city London explores the implications of 'communitarian' values among a fraction of middle-class parents for whom social equality remains idealised in an era of market-driven education.

'Community-minded' parents in Cooper spoke frequently of 'values' and advanced a notion of schooling as ideally preparing their children to be civically minded, respectful of cultural difference, and able to identify and respond to social injustice. They emphasised the importance of participating in the life of the school community, and had often taken up volunteering opportunities, for example, in P&C (Parents and Citizens) committees.

These values and practices were used by these parents to symbolically signpost their difference from the competitive practices associated with 'tiger' parenting (Butler et al., 2017). Viewed as an 'Asian' phenomenon, 'tiger parenting' comprises authoritarian strategies that focus almost exclusively on achieving academic success (Watkins & Noble, 2013). Our white middle-class parents expressed moral opposition to 'over-schooling' or additional family-driven schooling before or after school. They opted instead not to prepare their children for the OC exam outside of the classroom.

As an example, Will, a white Australian father, stressed he was 'not a big fan of homework at this stage, I don't think it's really necessary'. When asked, 'do people train primary school kids for OC? Do people do cram studies around here?' Will continued:

> Definitely. Yeah definitely … whereas we didn't do that, we just showed them the exam the weekend before the exam and said 'this is what the exam's gonna be like, just do your best'.

Another white parent, Mary-Jane, explained that her daughter 'didn't want to [do the OC exam] and I didn't push her into it … we didn't ever get a tutor or anything like that'. While taking the selective schools test was seen as a rite of passage for 'most kids', Mary-Jane continued, more important for her was the perceived negative impact of 'tutoring', 'cramming' and educational 'stress' on children, or 'the feeling of failure maybe' (Butler et al., 2017). Mary-Jane continued:

> At the high school level … they have a selective stream and there are quite a few children in that stream who are tutored within an inch of their life and they actually don't know how to cope with anything that's not handed to them, they don't have those divergent thinking strategies to deal with other situations.

Community-minded parents' criticisms of Sydney's highly competitive public schooling system, streamed classes, the OC model, and selective schooling models of learning were consistent themes of our interviews (Butler et al., 2017). These parents cited concerns about the impact of 'rejection' on children's 'self-esteem' and wellbeing. As one white parent, Sophia, from an Eastern European background explained, 'We didn't invest in any tutoring or anything like that, so if she makes it, if she doesn't, oh well'. Another white parent, Stacey, detailed:

> I don't want that pressure cooker, got to be tutored, you know if she gets 95 instead of 99 she'll do what she wants anyway. I'm not worried about that … I want a school where my child is going to be happy and thrive, not one where they're going to be in a sort of academic hothouse.

These concerns also underpinned criticisms of the 'Gifted and Talented' identity that was pursued through the streaming of OCs, and which was depicted by some white parents as being falsely cultivated through tutoring. As Sophia continued:

> [Tutoring] would give them speed, so that would be a benefit, but if they don't have the inbuilt ability to think in such a way, then they

would not be able to finish the maths ... you can't really teach a child to think unless they've got that ability ... not all parents want their kids to be in the OC class despite being bright as well.

Sophia's focus on 'ability', and 'natural ability' featured far more explicitly in our second case study. Here we draw on Ho's Sydney-based research with students and parents with experience of selective schools and classes (Ho, 2020).

'Natural Ability', 'Cheating', and Selective High Schools

In this second study, white middle-class parents spoke explicitly of tutoring (associated with Asian migrants) as 'cheating', in opposition to the 'natural ability' of white middle-class students. From this standpoint, these participants constructed and identified their middle-class identity as morally superior to those of middle-class students who undertook tutoring. Implicit in this reasoning was the ethnicisation of non-white students' academic achievements (Watkins & Noble, 2013; Proctor & Sriprakash, 2017), wherein forms of education practices and pedagogies mobilised by middle-class Asian-Australian parents and students were constructed by white participants as being morally inferior and suspect.

Tutoring in Australia has historically been used by a small minority of students for remedial purposes for a particular subject (to 'catch up'), but is now commonly used for acceleration and advancement, including by strong students (to 'get ahead') (Sriprakash et al., 2015; Ho, 2020). It is often sought to improve exam technique in the lead-up to high-stakes tests such as selective school admission and Year 12 exams. The consensus among Ho's white middle-class parent respondents was that such forms of academic tutoring were almost universal among Asian migrant families in Sydney's selective high schools and much less common among white families. As Liz, a white middle-class parent, remarked, 'It's rare to see a highly coached non-Asian kid'.

Robert, a white middle-class senior student in a high-achieving selective school, likewise spoke explicitly of how the large number of Asian-Australian students within his school reflected the influence of tutoring. In contrast, he discerned, 'naturally bright' white students had missed out on a place because they had not attended tutoring to prepare for the admissions test. Alternatively, some of his Asian-Australian classmates, he believed, were 'thick' and had 'coached' their way in. Several white middle-class interviewees had similar stories of 'bright' students who did not gain admission because they had not been tutored, while 'Asian' students, they insisted, had 'gamed' the system through tutoring. In these interviewees' minds, the meritocratic system of selective schooling was being undermined by the use of tutoring. In their view, students should not have to train for a test – the test should simply capture the student's 'natural ability'.

In this and other responses we see profound forms of racialised morality associated with the concept of 'natural ability'. In making such arguments, these participants insisted that tutoring had enabled students with lower intelligence to gain a place in a selective school, at the expense of 'naturally gifted' non-tutored students. Students who pursued tutoring were constructed as achieving due to excessive diligence rather than 'natural' aptitude, as also seen in parallel research in the UK (Archer & Francis, 2007). Indeed, many white parents were vehemently opposed to tutoring. In Tricia's view, kids needed to get into a program 'on their own merits … I didn't want them in a situation where they were coached to get in the program and then had to be coached up. So we did no preparation for [the selective test]'. Likewise, Gill explained, 'We were very aware that we wanted them to get in on their ability as opposed to having to swot for it. It was just another stepping-stone, nothing more'. More than one interviewee suggested that tutoring should be banned, while all conceded this was unlikely. Ros, a white mother of a selective school student, went so far as to say it would never be banned because, 'They deny it', referring here to the Asian-Australian students at her son's school. 'Finding proof is like dope testing, isn't it?' her husband added, drawing an explicit comparison between tutoring and doping in professional sport.

Most white student respondents in this sample were also keen to stress they had not attended tutoring, particularly not test preparation. Some in turn emphasised how *little* preparation they had undertaken, again implying that their 'natural ability' was sufficient. Robert, for instance, laughed derisively when asked if he prepared for the exam. He confided during the interview that while he was struggling with some of his subjects, he still refused to join that 'cheating' system of tutoring. Such comments constructed *not* being tutored as a badge of honour among white students and a way of morally distinguishing themselves from Asian-Australian students within this shifting middle-class terrain (Francis, Mau, & Archer, 2017). In this respect, *not* being tutored was a racialised reference to a claim to morality, through which white middle-class families sought to claim a higher moral standard and ethical imperative than their Asian-Australian classmates. In framing this success through such terms, such comments sought to uphold constructions of achievement among white students as 'innate' and 'natural'. Other students were seen to display excessive diligence and hyper-production, a reading of 'Asian' success which reproduced classed and racialised tropes about ability and achievement (Francis et al., 2017).

In contrast, the Asian-Australian parents who participated in Ho's study, and who felt they conformed to such stereotypes in some respects, explained that they found no option but to push their children to excel in school for the family's future security and social mobility. As newcomers and members of ethnic minorities in Australia, educational credentials were their only insurance policy against discrimination and lack of social networks (see also Francis et al., 2017; Archer & Francis, 2007). Monica, a Vietnamese-Australian mother, explained, migrants 'can't afford to be relaxed parents'. The Asian-Australian student respondents in this study were more vocal in answering back to accusations that they used tutoring in order to 'cheat' or 'game' the system. Many argued that tutoring could not be seen as cheating because it required such hard work from students, and hard work should be rewarded with success. Students spoke of hundreds of hours spent in tutoring over many years, and that they deserved to gain a place in a top school as a result. They refuted the argument that 'natural ability' ought to be more highly valued than hard work. In the words of Wei, a senior selective high school student:

> I work really hard, so I think, you might be more talented, but in order to succeed you need to put in the effort ... someone else has put in more effort than you, obviously they will get a better result. You can't complain.

Ultimately, Wei stated, 'I think it's more important to have that drive, rather than be born with a brilliant mind'. Other Asian-Australian student respondents defended their position by emphasising that they had worked in the system and had not broken any rules. Carlo, a selective school graduate, said that he and his classmates were highly offended by public discussions blaming Asian-Australians for distorting selective school cohorts: 'we feel like we've earned our position ... we feel like we've worked in the system. We've done nothing wrong to get to where we are'. Carlo surmised that criticising the 'education practices' of Asian-Australians was just another form of racism in Australian society: 'the tendency is to blame Asians for their success'.

Conclusion

Australia's urban middle class is today a complex, contradictory, tense and deeply racialised space in which classed social worlds confront and grapple with one another's ideals, experiences and sensibilities. The growth of middle-class migrants from Asia over recent decades has propelled particular competitive practices around schooling that white middle-class members often feel threaten their own social position. In this chapter we have shown how such white parents may seek to reproduce a distinctive moral identity around education as part of their effort to secure their children's trajectories within this altered middle-class terrain. In contrast to what they described as a narrow focus on academic success among Asian migrants, achieved in part through strategies such as private tutoring, the white middle-class parents in our research presented themselves as 'community-minded' and more liberal in their parenting. They positioned themselves as the rightful occupants of desirable schools and classes, as opposed to what they described as the instrumental or even 'cheating' strategies of Asian migrant families. Their appeal to a moral positioning in this domain underscores how deeply contemporary class tensions are felt within this complex social milieu. Morality is a central lens through which to interrogate these tensions and to better understand their origins and racialising effects within Australia's transforming middle class.

References

ABS [Australian Bureau of Statistics]. (2017). Migration, Australia, 2015–16 (Cat. No. 3412.0). Retrieved from http://www.abs.gov.au/ausstats/abs@.nsf/mf/3412.0

Adkins, L., Cooper, M., & Konings, M. (2021). Class in the 21st century: Asset inflation and the new logic of inequality. *Environment and Planning A, 53*(3), 548–572.

Archer, L., & Francis, B. (2007). *Understanding minority ethnic achievement: Race, gender, class and 'success'*. London: Routledge.

Bourdieu, P. (1984). *Distinction: A social critique of the judgement of taste*. London and New York: Routledge.

Brett, J. (2003). *Australian liberals and the moral middle class*. Cambridge: Cambridge University Press.

Butler, R., Ho, C., & Vincent, E. (2017). 'Tutored within an inch of their life': Morality and 'old' and 'new' middle class identities in Australian schools. *Journal of Ethnic and Migration Studies, 43*(14), 2408–2422.

Campbell, C., & Proctor, H. (2014). *A history of Australian schooling*. Crows Nest: Allen & Unwin.

Campbell, C., Proctor, H., & Sherrington, G. (2009). *School choice: How parents negotiate the new school market in Australia*. Crows Nest: Allen & Unwin.

Colic-Peisker, V. (2011). A new era in Australian multiculturalism? From working-class 'ethnics' to a 'multicultural middle class'. *International Migration Review, 45*(3), 562–587.

Francis, B., Mau, A., & Archer, L. (2017). The construction of British Chinese educational success: Exploring the shifting discourses in educational debate, and their effects. *Journal of Ethnic and Migration Studies, 43*(14), 2331–2345.

Greig, A., Lewins, F., & White, K. (2003). *Inequality in Australia*. Cambridge: Cambridge University Press.

Hage, G. (1998). *White nation: Fantasies of White supremacy in a multicultural nation*. Sydney: Pluto Press.

Harvey, D. (2005). *A brief history of neoliberalism*. New York: Oxford University Press.

Heiman, R., Liechty, M., & Freeman, C. (2012). Introduction: Charting an anthropology of the middle classes. In R. Heiman, C. Freeman, & M. Liechty (Eds.), *The global middle classes: Theorizing through ethnography* (pp. 3–29). Santa Fe, NM: School for Advanced Research Press.

Ho, C. (2011). Respecting the presence of others: School micropublics and everyday multiculturalism. *Journal of Intercultural Studies, 32*(6), 605–621.

Ho, C. (2017). The new meritocracy or over-schooled robots? Public attitudes on Asian-Australian education cultures. *Journal of Ethnic and Migration Studies, 43*(14), 2346–2362.

Ho, C. (2019). *Ethnic Divides in Schooling*. Retrieved from Centre for Policy Development website: https://cpd.org.au/2019/05/ethnic-divides-schooling-discussion-paper-may-2019/

Ho, C. (2020). *Aspiration and anxiety: Asian migrants and Australian schooling.* Melbourne: Melbourne University Publishing.

Ho, C., Vincent, E., & Butler, R. (2015). Everyday and cosmo-multiculturalisms: Doing diversity in gentrifying school communities. *Journal of Intercultural Studies, 36*(6), 658–675.

Humphrys, E. (2019). *How labour built neoliberalism. Australia's accord, the labour movement and the neoliberal project.* Chicago: Haymarket Books.

Katz, C. (2004). *Growing up global: Economic restructuring and children's everyday lives.* Minneapolis: University of Minnesota Press.

Martin, B. (1998). The Australian middle class, 1986–1995: Stable, declining or restructuring? *Journal of Sociology, 34*(2), 135–151.

Moreton-Robinson, A. (2000). *Talkin' up to the white woman: Indigenous women and feminism.* St Lucia: University of Queensland Press.

Proctor, H., & Sriprakash, A. (2017). Race and legitimacy: Historical formations of academically selective schooling in Australia. *Journal of Ethnic and Migration Studies, 43*(14), 2378–2392.

Pusey, M. (2003). *The Experience of middle Australia: The dark side of economic reform.* New York: Cambridge University Press.

Reay, D., Crozier, G., James, D., Hollingworth, S., Williams, K., Jamieson, F., & Beedell, P. (2008). Reinvigorating democracy? White middle-class identities and comprehensive schooling. *The Sociological Review, 56*(2), 238–255.

Robertson, S., & Rogers, D. (2017). Education, real estate, immigration: Brokerage assemblages and Asian mobilities. *Journal of Ethnic and Migration Studies, 43*(14), 2393–2407.

Rogers, D., Lee, C. L., & Yan, D. (2015). The politics of foreign investment in Australian housing: Chinese investors, translocal sales agents and local resistance. *Housing Studies, 30*(5), 730–748.

Sayer, A. (2005). *The moral significance of class.* Cambridge: Cambridge University Press.

Sheppard, J., & Biddle, N. (2017). Class, capital, and identity in Australian society. *Australian Journal of Political Science, 52*(4), 500–516.

Skeggs, B. (2004). *Class, self, culture.* London: Routledge.

Sriprakash, A., Proctor, H., & Hu, B. (2015). Visible pedagogic work: Parenting, private tutoring and educational advantage in Australia. *Discourse: Studies in the Cultural Politics of Education, 37*(3), 426–441.

Tavan, G. (2005). *The long, slow death of white Australia*. Melbourne: Scribe.

Tsang, E.Y. (2013). The quest for higher education by the Chinese middle class: Retrenching social mobility? *Higher Education, 66*(6), 653–668.

Vincent, E., Butler, R., & Ho, C. (2017). 'They try to avoid': How do parents' feelings about race and class difference shape school communities in a gentrifying area of inner Sydney, Australia? *Emotion, Space and Society, 25*, 29–46.

Wacquant, L. (1991). 'Making class: The middle class(es) in social theory and social structure'. In S.G. McNall, R. Levine, & R. Fantasia (Eds.), *Bringing class back in contemporary and historical perspectives* (pp. 39–64). Boulder, CO: Westview Press.

Watkins, M., Ho, C., & Butler, R. (2017). Asian migration and education cultures in the Anglo-sphere. *Journal of Ethnic and Migration Studies, 43*(14), 2283–2299.

Watkins, M., & Noble, G. (2013). *Disposed to learn: Schooling, ethnicity and the scholarly habitus*. London: Bloomsbury.

Wu, J., & Singh, M. (2004). 'Wishing for dragon children': Ironies and contradictions in China's education reform and the Chinese diaspora's disappointments with Australian education. *The Australian Educational Researcher, 31*(2), 29–44.

Part 5

Interviews

CHAPTER 13

AN INTERVIEW WITH LARISSA BEHRENDT

Reflections on Class in Australia

Larissa Behrendt, Jessica Gerrard and Steven Threadgold

Distinguished Professor Larissa Behrendt OA is a Eualeyai/Kamilaroi academic with a legal background, as well as an award-winning author, filmmaker and host of *Speaking Out* on ABC Radio. Behrendt won the 2002 David Unaipon Award and a 2005 Commonwealth Writers' Prize for her novel *Home*. Her second novel, *Legacy*, won a Victorian Premier's Literary Award. Her most recent book is *After Story* (2021, UQP). Behrendt wrote and directed the Walkley nominated feature documentary *Innocence Betrayed* and has written and produced several short films. She is a board member of Sydney Festival, a director of the Jimmy Little Foundation and a member of the Australia Council's Major Performing Arts Panel. Behrendt was awarded the 2009 NAIDOC Person of the Year award and 2011 NSW Australian of the Year. In 2021, together with Professor Lindon Coombs, she authored the 'Do Better' report into racism at the Collingwood Football Club.

Jessica: We thought we would start with a broad question about the connections between analyses of settler colonialism and analyses of class in Australia. Why is it important for analyses of settler colonialism and analyses of class to be in conversation, to understand each other in Australia?

Larissa: I look at this question from a First Nations' point of view. To that extent, I feel like I look at it from the outside because I think 'class' means something very different for First Nations people in Australia. I think it is important to be looking at intersectionalities wherever they occur, and the more we reflect on diversity of experience and diversity of voice, the richer we are in understanding our past and understanding who we are today, and therefore, being able to think about what we want to be going forward. Without looking at those intersectionalities, people fall through the gaps and get silenced. All of these elements of gender, class, sexuality, culture, all these identities create layering and they're often hierarchical and that can mean that some voices get pushed to the margins while others remain central and dominant. We need to always be questioning that and bringing out those voices.

The other thing that's important is that sometimes, it is in those intersectionalities that we can find our similarities and our connections. I don't think we do that enough. I think we tend to deconstruct and break things down and then not think about how there are connections between different groups. For example, sometimes when we're looking at issues of feminism and really need to be critiquing essentialist approaches, you can then sometimes not see where the connections are. These are really important things to do, but there's a caution around it as well. There can be a tendency in looking at some of those nuances, hierarchies and structures within settler colonialism that can sometimes be used to take away privilege, or deny one's own privilege by saying, 'We came here as convicts, therefore, we're more like the Aboriginal people because we were in the lower classes. We were Irish, and so therefore we were marginalised, and so we're much more like the Aboriginal people'. I think that the interrogation of class is really important, but it can't be used to minimise any sense of privilege in relation to where the settler-colonial state sits in relation to Indigenous Australia.

Jessica: One of the things that you just said is how class looks really different for Indigenous peoples, and I think you've really hit the nail on the head then when you were talking about class as something that convicts and invaders brought with them, and existing structures that got reinterpreted and rearticulated in Australia, whereas the First Nations people were dealing with an invasion and an imposition of this structure. So how can we understand class in relationship to First Nations people?

Larissa: It's the same as patriarchy and misogyny: these have to be looked at as imported ideas. It's a really important point that there were no class structures within our First Nations societies, and there still isn't. You can attain a status because of your knowledge or your wisdom, your skill, but there's no stratification of that. So that's the first thing, there's such a cultural clash between the idea of class and the idea of a First Nation society.

The other thing about class in our contemporary communities is, just as the patriarchal society that was imposed took away Aboriginal women's economic power, their status, their agency, their voice, there was a way in which by being forced into a dominant colonising society, we're placed at that lowest rung, and not even a working-class rung; although there's a tendency to equate First Nations people with that. That is a falsehood that overestimates substantially how much power, influence, and economic power First Nations people were able to attain. You couldn't work for wages. When they were successful, farmers had their reserve land taken from them for the Soldier Settlement scheme, parents lived with the risk of having their children removed, our people lived segregated lives, who weren't given the same opportunities.

Even 'underclass' isn't right for that either. 'Underclass' implies you've slipped through the cracks. That's a different ostracising from that structure. The myth of social mobility was particularly held out to Aboriginal people but was unattainable. You had to work to be white to have the same status as a working-class person, but really, you'd never get there because your race is always a barrier, and in country towns, Aboriginal people weren't employed even when there were jobs.

Then there's another more contemporary phenomenon – what is effectively called an 'emerging Black middle class' from the 1990s if not earlier. Though there were plenty of trailblazers before then, from the 1990s, there was an increasingly significant cohort of people finishing high school, getting qualifications and becoming university educated, particularly entering the teaching, nursing and the public service. So, you saw that socio-economic mobility within Aboriginal families that you'd not seen before. Yet, in a way, it oversimplifies it to just consider this a 'Black middle class'. When people talk about that, it's often said suspiciously or mockingly as though the more middle class you are, the less Aboriginal you are. The more you are able to be socially mobile, and move away from poverty and cyclical poverty, the less Indigenous you are. I think that's a really dangerous way in which class dynamics are used to describe Aboriginal people. Of course, what it means is you are attacking or undermining the identity of Aboriginal people who've successfully navigated a colonial system, but in no way is that ever proof that they've left behind their identity or their heritage or their cultural connections.

The analysis of class in that context, where you could make observations about social mobility from people from other cultural backgrounds, become incredibly problematic within a settler-colonial state, because in a way, you're ignoring the larger framework, the larger dynamics of the societal structures to be able to say, 'Well, given enough opportunity, Aboriginal people can do well too', and that's evidenced by an emerging middle class, and this is a coded way of saying that these are people who've been assimilated and therefore, they're successful in that way, that they've been able to drag themselves out of poverty. The thing that really rankles me about that is the equation of poverty with Aboriginality.

Jessica: That alignment of Aboriginality with poverty is such an obviously dangerous discourse and practice within Australia, and certainly this idea of the professional Indigenous middle class has become really taken up in popular and scholarly discourse. What do you see as the impact and legacy of that generation of Indigenous professionals? How can we understand this emerging cohort, if you like, within Australian politics and Australian cultural life?

Larissa: The thing to understand about it is actually not what the legacy of what this generation is – and I am part of that generation – but that my generation is the legacy of the 1960s and 1970s Aboriginal Rights movement. All of my friends who are also university educated and in what would be called the professional emerging Black middle class, are all people who had parents who were heavily involved in breaking down barriers and opening up opportunities so that we could walk from high school into university. This needs to be looked at as the legacy of the rights movement of the 1970s, in particular, more so than the '60s with the referendum. It was less about changing that constitution, though symbolically, that was very important. The consequences of that in terms of rights, protections and opportunities weren't the same, weren't what people had hoped for, and it was really then as a reaction to that that you see that '70s movement and its politics emerge.

Why that's central is it embraced the concept of self-determination in a really practical way. It's no coincidence that that's when you see the first Aboriginal medical service, the first Aboriginal legal service, the first Indigenous-run kindergarten, the first Indigenous aged care centre; and a lot of this happening in Redfern, where a lot of us grew up. I think that's a really important element because the failure to see that connection, misunderstands the motivation of my generation in terms of our ability to enter a profession and have opportunities that would be equated to a middle-class opportunity in life. It means that we saw ourselves as not aspiring to improve ourselves through socio-economic transcendence; we saw what we were doing as part of a bigger project of changing the way that institutions had to deal with First Nations people. If my father's generation opened the doors so that we could go through, we would've failed them if all we wanted was to emulate middle-class white people.

We've entered professions and taken on careers where we've sought to change those institutions from the inside. Our work is highly transformative in terms of wanting to change laws, wanting to change institutions. My work focuses a lot on law reform, and it focuses a lot on changing content within the university in terms of curriculum, approaches to Indigenous knowledges. I don't think it's a coincidence that I felt unable to have a professional life within a law school because I hated it so much, but I could find a space within the academy in an Indigenous unit, and do the same work. There's a thing about the Aboriginal and Torres Strait Islander professionals of my generation that was very much about an agenda of transformation, and about ensuring that we weren't the only ones there. One of the hallmarks of my generation was that we were often the first with things, because nobody had been through those doors before. It wasn't necessarily because of personal attributes – and I'm not downplaying the hard work that goes into it – but if my dad had had the chances I had, he could've well been the first person to go to Harvard Law School, not me.

There were always lots of 'firsts' in relation to my generation. But the responsibility that I was always taught to have in relation to that was that there had to be many more come behind us. So, when I look at UTS (University of Technology, Sydney) now and we have over 50 Indigenous Higher Degree Research students. That's some of the most important work that I am there to do. Indigenous culture is communal. It understands you don't survive as a community unless you all work together, and the core principles are around reciprocity and sustainability. That is already fundamentally different to Western notions. Class is very individually focused. It's about how you improve yourself individually to have any possibility of class mobility, and if you are unable to do that, that's pretty much your fault because you have not worked hard enough or taken the opportunities or moved yourself out of where you are, haven't pulled yourself up by the bootstraps. So, when we talk about the fact that even though we're labelled 'middle class', we don't have a middle-class sensibility because of our cultural background, I think a lot of it is linked to our sense of community and our cultural teachings around reciprocity, and this idea that we are to continue that work that our parents have done, work we grew up witnessing firsthand. Many of us spent most of our weekends on marches for land rights. So that was something that shapes you when you go forward and reminds you that there are still battles to be won.

Steven: Coming back to what you were talking there about intersectionality. One of the themes that's been in your own work is around gendered emotionalised tropes contained within narratives of the colonial encounter. What do you think these narratives can tell us about the imaginary or the Australia settler state in relation to class?

Larissa: One of the reasons why Eliza Fraser is such a great narrative to look at is because she does clearly show how the idealised feminine form is a middle-class white woman.[1] Her story would not have had the resonance if she had not been of her class. Patrick White's imagining of Eliza in his novel *A Fringe of Leaves* (1976) is really interesting because he does try to challenge that by making his Eliza Fraser figure an ex-convict woman who had a very difficult life, as many people did back in the 1800s. I think what's interesting about that is that even when White challenges the assumption about the middle-class idealism of femininity he's still unable to conceptualise Indigenous women in any way other than as the two-dimensional characters. I think it says something about the Australian psyche that really, in many of those narratives, even if writers do try and deconstruct the stratum of the settler-colonial state, they can only do so against the background of Indigenous people as something to be psychologically reflected against.

Even when Patrick White tries to show a communion between his white woman character, and her more spiritual, natural self, it's in a way that's culturally offensive. It's through a ceremony where there's cannibalism, which didn't exist – that's another fantasy projected onto Aboriginal people – and it's in the context of a woman shedding her middle-class pretensions and becoming her true natural self. Only when she does that, can she commune with the Aboriginals. So, it puts us in this 'noble savage' construct where once again, we're only defined by how white people see us and interact with us, whether they connect to us or not. It's all about their own psychological state. I think that shows that how within those narratives, we still have really a deeply divided society between the colonisers and the colonised. In very subtle ways, most of that literature and our dominant culture storytelling seeks to explore the psyche of those of the settler state, not those of the Indigenous people. We're always outside of it and projected upon it.

There are obvious exceptions to that which are more recent books that show a greater understanding of those dynamics, books such as Liam Davison's *The White Woman* and Kate Grenville's *The Secret River*. These are two examples where the authors accept they can't authentically project the Aboriginal point of view and are really upfront about it as opposed to trying to tell me as a reader that they're going to tell me something about it. They know that their stories only tell me something about their white protagonist, not about the Aboriginal people that are there. So that, I think, is an important revelation and insight into how those narratives should work. What it says is that there is no settler-colonial telling of Aboriginal stories. Room has to be made for those stories to be told on their own terms.

Jessica: This positioning of Indigenous people as most often abjectly outside Australian social relations, also relates to Indigenous labourers, many of them forced labourers – farmers, drovers, domestic workers. These people were forced into work, and were refused not only rights, but any recognition of actually existing, because of course, there was a parallel or attendant practice of genocide happening at the same time. How do we make sense of how settler colonialism and the capital it generated, being dependent on the labour of these peoples who are so often positioned as being outside, eclipsed from view?

Larissa: The only way to have that happen is to continue to tell those stories, and when we talk about an emerging professional class, one of the areas where we have an enormous amount of activity in terms of new generations coming through is actually through storytelling. I had to recently update my *Indigenous Australia for Dummies* book, and the two chapters that took me the longest were the ones on literature and film and television, because so much had been produced in the last ten years, and I think more and more, there is an understanding of the importance of Indigenous people driving Indigenous storytelling, and finding space to tell those stories.

One of the reasons I became a filmmaker was because through my academic and legal work, I started to understand how important it was that I not be just a translator for other people in my community and that I needed to find space for those voices that aren't heard, for the women whose children are still being taken, for people who are still living with the colonisation of nuclear testing. In my own practice, I have developed a self-determination framework and it challenges me to ask whose story am I privileging? It can't be mine.

There's been a greater protection of this driven from our own community. Current ethics guidelines now, the treatment of ICIP (Indigenous Cultural and Intellectual Property), the way in which Indigenous people are engaged with in terms of research has all fundamentally changed just in the last five years, and that has been led by Indigenous people within the Academy and within the performing arts and in the creative arts industries, demanding that Indigenous stories be protected and be told by Indigenous people. That mantra of 'you can't tell our stories without us' is now becoming a really central idea, not just within our community, but with funding organisations. We have to continue to work really hard to privilege, protect and find space for those stories, not just about that history of Indigenous people and work, but its contemporary manifestations. We need to remember the stories of the Stolen Generations, but we need to also be focused on the fact that child removal is still happening now at an increasing rate.

We need to also look at the history of exclusion from the workforce and exploitation of labour, and of child labour, of basic slavery, as part of the economic development of Australia and its industries but we also look at the fact that government reform around welfare often disproportionately impacts negatively on Aboriginal people and the remote employment (Work for the Dole) programs like CDP (Community Development Plan) disproportionately undervalue Indigenous work, which is different to the previous program (the Community Development Employment Program) that ATSIC did, which actually did provide jobs where there were none and created opportunities in a different way. That's not what the current CDP program is.

More appropriate Work for the Dole schemes were abolished to make way for the ones that are now in place which came into force alongside the imposition of the cashless welfare cards. So, there are still really contemporary ways that Indigenous people are denied proper access to wages and employment.

Welfare quarantining is incredibly racist and infantilising, not much different to rations, on the same ideologies. One of the triggers for exponentially increased child removal in the Northern Territory was the Northern Territory Intervention, riddled with narratives around Indigenous people, men, mothers, that reinforced anything that you could have read a hundred years ago that you would look at and think, 'Well, that's pretty racist'. So, I think part of it is not just looking at those narratives of the past, but being really diligent and highlighting how they still manifest today to keep us in a settler-colonial state.

Steven: I'd like to ask a question that relates to this, the professional middle class, and the continuing need to be activists. Do you come across people in our political class and in our policy administrative bureaucracy that have seen your film about the continued forced removal of children, *After the Apology*? Does it have impact in those spaces?

Larissa: People self-select about whether they're going to see it or not, so it has quite an impact when it's shown in schools and universities, because then you might get people who can potentially become change makers. There are real opportunities there, and through Reconciliation Action Plans and their NAIDOC Week events where you hope organisations might show a film like that. I don't make a film like *After the Apology* for Alan Jones or Andrew Bolt because they're quite frankly not interested, and they have their own views, and I'm not going to change what they've got to say. But what a film like that can do is it can speak to people who are genuine about being concerned about the situation of Indigenous people in Australia, and want to see it improved, and don't understand what is going on or what can be done to facilitate real change. It's probably news to them that there's an increased level of child removal. That audience is much more important than the audience that's ideologically opposed to you. I think tapping into that genuinely interested and concerned non-Indigenous audience is hugely important. You want to arm people so that when they're sitting across the table from old racist Uncle Ted, they can argue in their own terms and be able to articulate what they feel is an injustice. I think that's really important.

I think we're misguided if we think that reshaping those narratives is going to change the hard edge of colonialism or people who comfortably embrace those ideologies. But what it can do is create a space for people who are interested in becoming allies, who do have a different view about what Australia should be, have a different sense of the role that Indigenous culture and Indigenous stories should play, who actually feel that if they are living on this country, they want to have some connection and understanding of the culture that's been here for at least 65,000 years before. Those people are important allies and I think that there is an importance in being able to motivate and arm them with ideas and information and stories that go beyond just dismissing that project of speaking to the converted.

The other thing that's critically important in this storytelling has nothing to do with non-Indigenous people. You make a film like *After the Apology* for all of those Aboriginal people who have children taken away from them, unjustly, and are too ashamed to speak out about it. Then they realise that they're not the only ones and that there is something to do and you can stand up and you can find people who will stand beside you. There's a sense of empowerment that comes from those stories – from hearing them and telling them.

Jessica: Really significant Indigenous activism, such as the Gurindji strike, has highlighted the interconnected forms of exploitation and denial that occurs within settler colonialism; the dispossession of land *and* the exploitation of labour. How can this help us understand more about class in the particular context of Australia?

Larissa: What you see when you look at the history of Aboriginal people and the process of colonialism is the dispossession of Aboriginal people of their land which is also a dispossession of livelihood and sustainability, and that results in a position of powerlessness and exploitation of Aboriginal people and their labour. John Maynard's work tracks this really well and highlights instances where Aboriginal people became really successful in terms of farming reserve land, the reserve land was taken away from them and given to non-Indigenous people. There was a deliberate, cyclical way in which people were continually disempowered. We see that again now with the shifts from the CDEP to CDP, where you saw a whole raft of Aboriginal people, particularly men, who lost meaningful work. In addition to that, their wages or their welfare payments were quarantined so they had even less ability to provide for themselves and for their families.

Go back and look at William Cooper's petitions. He was articulate about the connection between land, livelihood, sustainability, and the claims for land were not just about having the land back for its cultural significance. Of course it was that, but it was also about having an ability to be sustaining and to support yourself, and I think that has a particular history for Aboriginal women. You look at the very powerful story of Barangaroo and her reaction to the colonists giving a gift of 4,000 fish to the men across the harbour. She was furious about it and not just because of the waste and this appalling exploitation of resources and a level of greed that's unheard of in Aboriginal culture. She also understood that this activity would undermine the power of Aboriginal women around the harbour, who were the fisherwomen. They would gather the fish. They were providing 80 per cent of the food as most Indigenous women do in hunter-gather societies. Women are primary sources of food. Barangaroo could see how that was going to change and it was prophetic.

There has been a narrative about the fact that changes in the workforce more recently, like with CDP, saw more Aboriginal women employed than men; that women were more able to get the work that was available in some of the places where they were living, often working in the community centres, health centres. But that really masks what the figures show, which is that Aboriginal women make up so much of the casualised workforce, so are often in much more vulnerable economic positions, particularly when compared to their white counterparts. They are in lower socio-economic brackets and more likely to be in casualised work and in the industries where women are historically underpaid, like nursing, teaching, childcare and aged care.

There's a gendered aspect to be looked at in that history as well, that speaks to men's experience in the cattle industry particularly, but also women as well, being forced into domestic work. There are again contemporary manifestations of that, but those histories certainly show the link between land and livelihood, and land and work. You can see that in all these important moments. The '72 Tent Embassy was all about it. They had some, what might seem, very frank claims about land and sovereignty, but those claims went to the heart of challenging the amount of wealth that was being made off the resources coming from Aboriginal land.

The gains that were made around Native Title were often focused on trying to leverage some economic self-sustainability. Land rights in New South Wales is arguably a far superior land tenure compared to Native Title, because at least you can hold it in freehold, so you can build houses on it. You can farm it or you can go into a development arrangement. You can use it in ways that provide an economy for the community. Native Title was first recognised in its very narrow sense and there was no sense here in Australia that it in any way related of any sense of sustainability. Most Australians just thought it was a title to land and probably related to ceremony. But you very quickly got challenges to that around hunting and fishing rights, with people wanting to be able to live sustainably, and the early case law around that really reflected a colonial mentality, which is not dissimilar to what you saw in Yorta Yorta. It was an attitude of 'if you're engaging in commercial activity then that's not traditional, so therefore, it's not covered by native title'. What about all the trade we used to do? You could just see the idea that 'we've given you this little bit of native title, but there's no way we're extending that to ideas of being able to live sustainably or have an economy or an income out of it'.

Steven: How do you see this history of abject exclusion of Aboriginal people alongside intensive surveillance control that's being perpetuated in contemporary policy arrangements?

Larissa: Well, this is a colonial thing, to both exclude and to keep under surveillance and control. The elements of exclusion are still evident in all the policies that get put in where you have to repeal the Racial Discrimination Act. For most Aboriginal people, if you ask them what is the issue that they would most like to do something about, it's racism. We still have structural racism in our society. They're in the pillars of the constitution in terms of its original intent to not create protections against racial discrimination or provide for provisions of equality. Those decisions were made so that we wouldn't have those protections, and they remain. We have a Racial Discrimination Act, but it's not hard to overturn it. You see that in the Closing the Gap figures, that there is proof of exclusion and discrimination.

We see Aboriginal achievement much more because of Aboriginal agency than because of policy. When I see Aboriginal mobility, I see it through education which is done by individuals' assertion of effort, often despite some of the things that have been said and done to them during their schooling. The most successful policy responses to the hard issues in Aboriginal communities in housing, employment and school attendance have been designed by Aboriginal people at a community level, not by policymakers.

Then obviously, surveillance and control take place under two arms of government, through the criminal justice system which has its over-representation, increasing numbers of deaths in custody. There's both structural and systemic racism in that system, and through child protection.

If you go back to the first days of the colony, the massacring of Aboriginal people is a way to control their bodies and then there is the systemic taking of Aboriginal children. It's not hard to draw the lines between what happened at the first stages of colonisation and how those things manifest themselves today. There are deaths in custody and over-representation in the criminal justice system. People seem more reluctant and less willing to put a spotlight on the child removal issue, and partly because I think there's a lot of racism that seems to assume that if child protection is involved, there must be a reason, and that's really hard to convince people otherwise, unless you tell powerful real stories that might get them to change their mind – like we tried to do with the documentary *After the Apology*.

Steven: Before you said you felt really uncomfortable working in a law school. Can you talk a little bit about that in relation to what we're talking about here, and what the legal system is for, but also what it's like to work in it from a working-class Indigenous background?

Larissa: The first thing you notice when you go to law school is that if you come from a public school, you're in the minority. That was the case when I went to law school, and so there's already a sense that you're an outsider, without the same privileges, in a place that's not of your world, and you're there with people who assume that's where they should be. I always sum it up like this: I always hear people say, 'My dad's a judge' or 'I'm the third generation of lawyers'. My brother and I did one of those court visits where you go to court and write a court report. I don't know if they still do them, but you did them back in my day. You go and do a court report, and the defendants were our cousins. So it was quite different!

I was at law school in 1992 when the Mabo case came down, so I did my first couple of years where there was no recognition of Aboriginal rights by Australian law. When I did property law and it was mentioned at the beginning of class there was no legal Aboriginal interest in land, so therefore, we're not studying it and let's move on. Then in criminal law, it's all about statistics. We had a cousin who died in custody who was one of the Royal Commission deaths investigated. Behind the numbers, there are really personal stories but it's all talked about by people who have no understanding about what it's like to be Indigenous, whose own comprehension is nothing but ignorance and racism, and they're making all these judgements.

All those things made the experience of law school challenging, but I was lucky. My brother was there at the same time. Sonja Stewart, Terri Janke and Anita Heiss were at university at the same time as me. And Phillipa McDermott was over at UTS – her dad was the first Aboriginal barrister. So, we had a really great cohort. We were on the cusp of that change. We felt more rebellious.

I found the experience of working in one particular law school to be incredibly toxic. I can remember I was working there when I got my Master's from Harvard and had been accepted to do the PhD program. I was at a staff meeting and there was discussion about the creation of an Indigenous identified position which I worked out was assumed to be for me though I had no interest in it. The discussion that took place around me was that we should not have such a thing because people who don't have merit will be appointed to it. I can tell you that most of those people in that law school did not have a higher degree. Not only that, in this same law school, when I got accepted into Harvard for my Master's degree, someone from that law faculty wrote to the admissions office and complained about me being admitted before two white students because they thought they were more deserving than me. So I was sitting there in a toxic environment thinking, 'Well, what do I care? I've got more education than these idiots'. I just don't see how you feel that's a collegial, safe place. So more power to anyone who's sat through a law school or worked in a law faculty and put up with that, but I decided that was not going to be my life and I went off and did other things, quite happily.

Jessica: Such a powerful example of the surveillance and attempted control of your career; it's those exact same practices replicated.

Larissa: There was no special admissions program for Indigenous people at Harvard. I didn't get in because of anyone feeling sorry for me. I got in on my merits like everyone else did, and still they couldn't do it, and the right-wing press, they loved writing about it. One old white guy commentator has even defamatorily written about how I apparently cheated to get into Harvard on the basis of nothing. You can't even achieve without them trying to take it away from you, for things that they would never be able to do. I mean, honestly, there's nothing that pisses racist old white men off more than Black women achieving. So, I'm just going to keep going out there and winning awards.

The good thing is there are many more fabulous Indigenous women coming through with great powerful voices. I think of people like Chelsea Watego, Amy McQuire, Teela Reid and Alison Whitaker and I just think, 'I'm just going to be an auntie now and watch all these wonderful young women come through'. But that's what we were doing it for, so you'd see these women. I just had the great privilege of reading a copy of Chelsea's new book *Another Day in the Colony*, and I've never read anything that spoke to me so much as an Aboriginal woman. I had a moment in it when I just had a cathartic cry because I've never read anything that spoke to me so much, and I just think, 'This is a great time for voice'.

Steven: You've recently co-authored a very public report into the racism at Collingwood Football Club that has led to significant media attention and eventually the resignation of controversial club president Eddie Maguire. I wanted to ask, not necessarily about the report and what was happening at the club, but about the representation of it and what happened afterwards in the media and the club's reaction. Sport is such an important cultural thing in Australia. How do you see it as crossing over with class and Indigeneity, and what role does the media have in this?

Larissa: The thing that was missed about the report was that Collingwood commissioned it. They asked me and my co-author, Lindon Coombes, to go hard and not sugar-coat it, and that's what I did. I think it was extraordinary that they asked that in the first place. Now, what happened afterwards was out of my control, and certainly when we wrote the report, we didn't anticipate any of that, and we hadn't assumed or recommended any leadership changes.

The reason Collingwood asked for this mirror to be held up in the first place is because there's a First Nations woman on the board, and there's a First Nations woman on the board because within the AFL, they have an Indigenous woman working there who worked really hard to get Collingwood to put a First Nations woman on their board. So, if you want to talk about what the influence of the professional class is, you would not have had a Collingwood report without First Nations people, First Nations women, in those roles. In a way, I did the easy work. The hard work was getting an Indigenous woman on the board of an AFL club, and then the hard work that she did was to get the club to say, 'You've got a problem here and we really need to figure out what to do about it', and bring that whole club with her. So, in a way, to me, there's a part of this story that is really about what happens when you start to get educated, smart people in the right places. They can be real agents of change.

It was a damning report in the sense that Collingwood has a very specific history, but I don't know that there's much about Collingwood that would be different to other institutions. If we talk about the fact that it had systemic racism, that there was structural racism, it's no different to the Australian Constitution. The failure for people to be able to make changes within the club, the absence of policies that effectively dealt with racism, makes it no different to many other workplaces. The real difference was that they had a very high-profile president who probably took bad advice on how to handle the findings of the report, and I would speculate that if he had have handled them differently, he might not have had to resign. But all of that was out of my hands.

One of the things the 'Do Better' report does say is that you can go into any organisation and probably find similar dynamics going on, and the racism that we identified in the report is the product of society, not the product of the Collingwood Football Club. Collingwood didn't have structures to be able to deal with it. I thought one of the things that was really interesting about when the report came out was how many people contacted Lindon and myself to do this similar work in their workplaces, because it's the same. I think the issues come out of sport because sport is such a microcosm of what's happening in the broader community, and there's a thing about sporting teams where there's a different narrative, a sense of comradery and a shared set of values or a shared agenda that's creating a new community, and that sometimes means that it's really difficult for people who are on the margins within the broader community to find a home there. I think what's interesting with sport generally is that we do see it as moments where we can actually be our best selves as well.

I've just been finishing off a film. My next film is on the AFL and I'm just finishing off a film on the NRL. I don't know how I became the queen of sports docos, but it probably goes exactly to the point you're making, which is that it's not about the football. It's actually about culture and it's about racism and it's about excellence and overcoming adversity, and all those very human things. I interviewed Stan Grant for the film that I'm just finishing and he said, 'You think of Lionel Rose coming back and a quarter of a million Australians turned out to see him in the 1960s, before the '67 referendum, when there was segregation in so many parts of the community'. He said, 'Just for a moment, you see a glimpse that we can be a better version of ourselves', and we saw that moment with Cathy Freeman and the 2000 Olympics. But it can be a place where we're incredibly divided as well. People love to talk about the Olympics with Cathy Freeman but they often overlook the terrible press she got when she had the audacity to carry two flags at the time. She did it, she pushed as a nation, and now, two flags is nothing. People would think that it's fanciful to find that so controversial, but you go back and have a look at the coverage. She was called 'un-Australian', a disgrace and it was argued that she shouldn't be allowed to compete under the Australian flag. What the right-wing shrill brigade had to say about her was horrendous. These are brave moments. The same can be said of the moment Nicky Winmar lifted his shirt. There can be moments where they can be polarising and then the rest of the community catches up. They can be really great places to have conversations.

Steven: One of the findings of the report was that in reaction to racist behaviour or incidents in the past, that Collingwood responded with PR, then their initial response to the report was an attempt at PR. Now obviously that's ironic but does the response of that happening again mean that it's more likely that those things will now be taken seriously in the sense that it's almost like a self-fulfilling prophecy?

Larissa: Eddie's decision to step down was related to forces from elsewhere. Not the review. The club had weathered a lot of other behaviours. They did seem to understand that something was shifting. They had observed Rio Tinto and the response to their destruction of ancient rock art. It wasn't what they'd done or that they lost their Reconciliation Action Plan (or RAP) status; it was because people in charge actually lost their jobs. Aboriginal heritage gets demolished every day. Every day, we lose really significant sites. They're really precious to people and nothing happens. People don't even get a rap over the knuckles for it. This time there were consequences.

It was unprecedented and it alerted a segment of the Collingwood Football Club that might have been reluctant otherwise was that this could now be something that has implications for sponsors. You can just look at the United States where Coca-Cola has a view about voting rights. We're living in a time where there's a shift. I don't credit new thinking from the old guard with this. I think what was really evident when we did the review was that the playing group has a different view about what inclusion is because they've gone through a different system, a different school system compared to the old guard. They all know about the Apology to the Stolen Generations and they would say that they don't know everything and there's a lot more to be learnt. When they think of inclusion, they think that there is a place for Aboriginal people. There are some very interesting ideas coming through younger generations, and maybe there's still a long way to go in addressing racism, but if you look at how transformative things have been around sexuality and gender, there's a lot of people from the generations above that are still trying to catch up with what everything means.

I think you look at two places where there was movement within that club; there was someone from the board that reflected a different experience and background, and there was a playing group coming through that represents a different education system, however flawed it still might be, and a different sensibility about the relationship that Australia should have with First Nations people. I think that's a recipe for institutional change – and a cause for optimism.

Endnote

1   See L. Behrendt (2016), *Finding Eliza: Power and Colonial Storytelling*, University of Queensland Press. Eliza Fraser (the namesake of Fraser Island) was shipwrecked, taken in and saved by the Badtjala people. Following her experience she rewrote her story as one of capture peppered with spurious claims of cruelty, in turn tapping into the colonial imagination of Indigenous 'savagery'. As put by Behrendt in *Finding Eliza*, 'Eliza's [fabricated] story is imbued with British fears and insecurities about both the frontier and Aboriginal people' (p. 55). During the writing of this book Fraser Island was renamed as K'Gari, the Buthculla (traditional owners') word for paradise.

CHAPTER 14

AN INTERVIEW WITH RAEWYN CONNELL

Reflections on Class in Australia

Raewyn Connell, Steven Threadgold and Jessica Gerrard

Raewyn is a social scientist who has worked, at various times, in sociology, political science, gender studies and education programs. She has taught mainly in Australian universities but also in three other countries, and has visited universities and activist groups in many more. She retired at 70 and was charmingly made at the same time a Life Member of the National Tertiary Education Union and Professor Emerita at the University of Sydney. Her best-known books are *Ruling Class, Ruling Culture, Class Structure in Australian History* (with Terry Irving), *Making the Difference* (with Dean Ashenden, Sandra Kessler and Gary Dowsett), *Gender and Power, Masculinities, Southern Theory* and, most recently, *The Good University*. Her work has been translated into 23 languages, only four of which she can read. She joined a union of university staff in 1971 and has been a member continuously since. She joined the ALP even earlier, but as a firm believer in tradition, left the party when it gave up the socialist objective.

Steven: First, we'd like to ask, can you tell us about the foundational sociological analysis of class in Australia?

Raewyn: Yes, I can. I can also give you the documentary evidence for it. Back in 1968–69, before I had an academic job, when I was just a PhD student, I was involved in the Free University in Sydney. Which was a kind of experimental, do-it-yourself attempt to model the kind of university that we really wanted, in the student movement of the day. The basic framework of Free University was a series of self-managed research and discussion and learning groups. One of them was about class in Australia, because we thought that was one of the crucial issues about Australian life, one of the key dimensions of struggle that people had to understand. It should have been dealt with solidly in mainstream universities, and by and large it was not.

About the first thing that we did in the group I was involved in, with Terry Irving, was to start gathering the existing writing and debates about class in Australia. Eventually we published the results of that search as a bibliography in what was then called the *Australian and New Zealand Journal of Sociology*, currently the JoS *(Journal of Sociology)*. We found about 1000 publications, and I'm sure that was not a complete search. We were just scrambling around in libraries and looking up back issues of journals and so on and so forth. It was a fairly amateur project with no online search facilities back in the 1960s! But we found a lot of stuff.

Some colleagues in other universities were thinking that they were the first people to explore class – and it simply wasn't the case. There was a long literature, in some ways going back to the 19th century: about class divisions in colonial society, class struggles as the labour movement emerged, relations with the British class structure and whether Australia was the 'working man's paradise' or not. Some of it was empirical research, some of it was what we now call cultural analysis. Some of it was about politics and representation of class systems in politics. You know, there was a hell of a lot of interesting stuff going back something like 70 years. We eventually used a good deal of that search in the book *Class Structure in Australian History* as points of entry to larger documentary sources about

Australian politics, the changing shape of economies, the development of an industrial arbitration system which is a striking feature of Australian class politics, and so on.

So that's what I would regard as the foundational work, that is several generations of grappling, often in a highly engaged way, and by pretty surprising people. Such as, for instance, Robert Menzies who actually used class language when he was organising the Liberal Party in the 1940s. He talked about the middle class as his base and had a clear perception, or at any rate a rhetoric, about what that class position was and how it differed from the organised working class, who were powerful because they had all these terrifying unions. Also different from the rich, who were terrifying because they had all this money and owned the land. So there was this poor little unrepresented middle class which Robert Menzies would come along and represent, and that's how the Liberal-Country Party coalition won in 1949. But he was bankrolled by the rich, and aided by a massive split in the labour movement. Nevertheless, he talked a language of class, and that will go down as part of the history of class consciousness in Australia too.

It was not an academic literature by and large that we found. There was a certain amount of academic research, for instance in some of the education periodicals before the 1960s, and in the 1960s. There was some research about the different rates of entry to university of young people from different class backgrounds. Some psychologists were doing stuff about the relationship between academic success in exams and the class background of the families.

There was a group of social psychologists at the University of Melbourne, led by Oscar Oeser who was the professor of psychology there, who were doing field studies of class relations in factories and rural communities. That was quite remarkable stuff, something you don't see in psychology anymore. So there was a certain academic literature. But class was part of the everyday language of the society too, and there was a great deal of writing about it by cultural analysts, politicians and so on. That's the background that our work came out of.

Jessica: Maybe this is a good place to jump into our second question which is really about how you see your work fitting into that context, and what you were seeing as being the kind of intellectual intervention or political intervention that you wanted to make. So how you see your research sitting in that context, its significance. But then also perhaps thinking back today, reflecting on what would you do differently or how would you approach it if you were to start it afresh.

Raewyn: I think in trying to reconstruct purposes, I'm at risk of mythologising what we were thinking in the 1960s and '70s. But it would be fair to say that the milieu that I came out of was a politically left one. We did think that there was a great cultural and social upheaval beginning to happen in Australia. The New Left was trying to both understand and theorise those changes, and also encourage new forms of expression for marginalised and oppressed groups. So the intention of the work was actually to contribute to the building of a radical culture, even a revolutionary culture.

We were critical of earlier attempts to do that. The New Left had its Marxist wing, but it was also pretty critical of what passed for orthodox Marxism at the time, as represented by the Communist Party of Australia. That was one of the strongly Stalinist parties in the global communist movement, and represented a kind of authoritarian politics which most of the young activists in the New Left regarded with dismay. So we were trying to do something beyond what passed for orthodox Marxism. And also beyond that inchoate discourse about classes that was just part of general cultural analysis in Australia, such as the claims which one often heard that Australia was basically a 'working-class country'. What?!

The background included some quite interesting historical work, on the history of working-class culture by people like Russel Ward and Robin Gollan, these were real contributions. But there was an Old Left tendency to think that all that was interesting and significant in Australian life was the working-class part of it.

It was a little bit shocking in that context to say, 'look, actually Australia is mostly run by the rich, by property owners', and that we need to study up. Ever since the British settlement at the end of the 18th century there have been powerful elites who have had the largest share of state power, who never really let go of the colonial state. Menzies was the latest edition of that. For all his rhetoric of representing the middle class, he was basically an inheritor of an old tradition of ruling class conservative politics. It was tightly integrated (at least up until the 1960s) into the British Imperial structure, and connected culturally and sometimes quite organically with the British Imperial ruling class. You only had to look at the major companies in the country to see that. BHP for instance, the 'Big Australian' as it advertised itself – but it was 80 per cent owned overseas and that was mainly in London. It had been, ever since it became a serious corporation.

So the Australian economy was a capitalist economy, a colonial capitalism, from the start. In the 20th century it became to some extent an industrial capitalist economy. Australia followed the development agenda that was also seen in settler colonialism in South America, Southern Africa, even to some extent in India. In the colonial context you began to get drifts towards industrialisation and a European style of industrial politics.

At the time, we were trying to inject a kind of empirical realism into discussions of class which we thought was lacking. Hence the project that Terry Irving and I launched, which took us ten years to bring to completion. It was a huge data-dredging exercise in Australian history. But we also hoped to inject a more sophisticated kind of theory. Much of the discourse up to the 1960s had been quite innocent of theory. People thought, for god's sake, Stalin was a theorist! So you know we were reading very much more sophisticated stuff, from the French structuralists. We were reading much more sophisticated historiography from people like E.P. Thompson in Britain, or Herbert Gutman in America. We were trying therefore to bring new conceptual tools to bear on class analysis as well as scooping up the massive data that was there.

Jessica: The place of class in public and political academic culture has of course changed significantly. Arguably it had a much more secure presence in scholarly thinking and public life in the 1960s and '70s than today. How do you see this impact your own work, as your early work would presumably have been responding to existing treatments, as opposed to reviving or re-engaging?

Raewyn: It's worth knowing that Australia really had extraordinarily high union density, that is, the percentage of the workforce who were members of unions. I think that continued to increase up to the early 1980s, or at least the 1970s. So a practical understanding of class as industrial struggle at least was still common sense up until the 1980s even into the 1990s. To that extent we weren't swimming against the tide. We were certainly contesting a narrow reading of what class was about. I guess if you look at my personal research trajectory, one of the things I was trying to do was link in issues that had not been central to a class analysis before, such as education, which had been a little bit there, but not a central thing.

I began studying young people and education at the time I was doing my PhD. My PhD was about kids' political consciousness. It drew on European structuralists, particularly on Piaget's theories of cognitive development. Part of that project was not just talking about kids' awareness of queens and prime ministers, but also about their understanding of class. The first piece of individual class analysis that I published was a paper on the development of children's awareness of class and how that changed as kids grew up. Which wasn't a bad piece of research, though I would now have perhaps a different theoretical grounding for it.

But then I became involved in teaching about these things, as soon as I began teaching in 1971. I was teaching first in a political science department and then in a sociology department, and class was a central issue in political sociology. Indeed class was a central issue for the new sociology programs around the country. We were then devising new courses and trying to collect teaching resources. So that got me into working on issues about the Australian ruling class.

As I was mentioning earlier, the idea of a ruling class had not been central to discussions of class in Australia, except in fairly polemical texts, such as pamphlets about the 30 rich families that rule Australia, or was it 50 families? So one of the key bits of analysis that I did in the early '70s was attempting a structural analysis of the Australian ruling class. That is, trying to get a grip on the corporate structure, on patterns of power and conflict in the corporate part of the ruling class, and understanding its relationship with the political wing of the same class. You see the products of that in the book, *Ruling Class Ruling Culture*, which was published in 1977 but was actually finished in 1975. If I remember rightly, I dated the introduction to that book on the day that the Whitlam government was overthrown – class politics in your face.

Steven: How was the book received? Did it get any public kind of analysis in newspapers and the like?

Raewyn: Yes a bit. I can't remember the finer details now, but I think something like 10,000 or 12,000 copies were sold, which was not at all bad for an academic book in Australia. Yes, there was debate about it, and it became a point of reference in some academic literature too.

Steven: So we're kind of moving through time now. Your work has been published and it has been making an impact in sociology in Australia in the '70s and '80s. And then throughout the '90s class becomes this kind of topic of debate of whether it even exists.

Raewyn: Yes.

Steven: It happened in numerous ways I suppose, the Pakulski and Waters book in particular was heavily debated, but there's also at about the same time theories of reflexive modernity – Ulrich Beck and people like that, a little bit later I suppose by the time it is translated into English, that questions the notion of class as well. So could you reflect a little bit about those debates and what they mean to sociology and to the understanding of class.

Raewyn: I remember having a bit of a giggle about that in the 1990s, because it was a kind of a return from the dead. Having had the same kind of discussion in the 1950s and 1960s. The language changed: the later period spoke of the 'end of politics' and so on, the 1950s spoke of the 'end of ideology'. In the 1950s version it was held that there was this grand convergence between the communist regimes and the capitalist regimes. Or there was a grand convergence of rich and poor into an expanding middle class, which had become so gigantic that everyone was now middle class and therefore there were no classes, class really didn't exist anymore. So you know, this is a perennial question and I can't say I got very excited about it in the 1990s.

If you look back, if you've read Piketty's book, you will know that by the time the 'death of class' literature came around in the 1990s, the economic inequality in global-north capitalist societies was already increasing again. The polarisation was growing, not shrinking, at the very time we were being told that class was dead, and that the only things that mattered were identity, or whatever it might be.

I didn't talk about what perhaps was the most important piece of sociological field research that I was involved with in the '70s. That was the work on high schools that became the books *Making the Difference* and *Teacher's Work*, published in the '80s. In this study we deliberately set out to look at the social relationships and kids' educational careers in groups of schools that were contrasted exactly on class grounds. Ruling-class schools on the one hand, mainstream working-class schools on the other.

The most influential idea that came out of that project was the concept of hegemonic masculinity. A concept not in class analysis, but in gender analysis. One of the key points with that study was that we interviewed the families, the parents, in their homes, rather than sending them questionnaires. The gender dimension of social life in those schools and families was in your face, we couldn't avoid it. So were the class dimensions.

So we had to think gender relations and class relations together. That might now be called intersectionality; the word wasn't available at that time and I've never been very comfortable with it for reasons we can talk about. The point is that a pure class analysis was never enough for the empirical realities that we were looking at, when we were thinking about inequalities and social change in Australian life.

Steven: So conceptually I suppose the 'death of class' thing can be interpreted in a couple of ways. I think one of the misnomers of it, there was never an argument about the death of inequality. It was more that many of the arguments were about class as a concept, it wasn't robust or vital enough anymore to understand those complexities. Do you think there were some elements of truth to that because on the other side of things it always seems to be a really good career move to claim the death of something.

Raewyn: Oh yes.

Steven: I always think that in the back of my head when I see those things.

Raewyn: Yes indeed. Have I ever made that move? I'd have to think back!

Steven: And one of the main critiques of class from this time is that it is plagued by methodological nationalism. As in, can it be used as a concept to understand global interaction? How do you think class is still relevant in that sense?

Raewyn: Yes, absolutely, there's force in that. I think the kind of work that I was writing in the '70s is open to that critique. Nevertheless there was a point to it, I would have to say in defence of what we were doing in *Class Structure in Australian History*. That book is about the formation and dynamics of classes in the context of the Australian colonies. It was conceived explicitly as an alternative to the idea that the class patterns in

Australia were simply a reflex of Australia's situation in imperialism. That all you had to understand really was the European class structure and the resulting imperialism, and you had all you needed to know about Australia.

So we were arguing against that. We said in effect, 'look, there is a class dynamic here, there are processes of class formation which have their own distinctive character in this place, and here is our story of them'. I think that was legitimate. Now, I don't think it was enough, and I would do it differently in certain ways. But I think that insight was right. That also applies to other structures too, for instance gender relations. I argue – and have been arguing with boring repetition – that gender structures are different in colonies from what they are in imperial metropoles, and from one colony to another, from settler colonies to colonies of conquest.

The gender patterns are connected, certainly, but they are not the same and one isn't simply a reflex of the other. So getting back to our question of the death of class, I guess by the end of the 1970s, I was well away on a multi-structure sociological path. I was trying to analyse class and gender and sometimes trying to get imperialism or colonialism in there somewhere, although that took me a good while to crystalise out. I was engaged in discussions in the 1980s with colleagues about whether we had to treat sexuality as a structure of relationships and practices that was logically distinct from gender or not. If these are distinguishable, can you analyse sexuality in relation to class, as people like Wilhelm Reich tried to do?

So if I ever thought that class was the one key to understanding social dynamics, by the end of the '70s I'd ceased to think that. I'm not sure that I ever thought that, but class had certainly been the main focus of my work in the early 1970s and that shifted.

Steven: There was at the same time a whole realm of kind of ways of thinking about class that were influenced by Marx and Weber and all the things that came before them. People like Erik Olin Wright and John Goldthorpe and Pierre Bourdieu became really prominent in understandings of class. So not necessarily specifically to their work but just generally, how important are different theoretical perspectives of class? Do you think we need a multiplicity of them, or do we need a more kind of convergence of understanding this to be able to make a real difference to understanding inequalities?

Raewyn: Well we're always going to have multi-faceted perspectives, you can rely on that, just as in gender analysis there are multiple approaches. When we were working on *Class Structure in Australian History* we were trying to bring to bear on Australian realities what we thought was a more sophisticated theoretical toolkit. So we did something which had not been done before, and maybe it's not been done since, which is to preface a history book with a theory chapter. In that chapter we traversed what we thought were the most interesting and relevant theoretical perspectives.

Now, my criticism would be that the range of theories that we found, or looked for, or had easy access to, were essentially European and North American. Mainly European. Not surprisingly they were conceptual frameworks which spoke to the realities of European society and European history and North American society and North American history. I would now argue that was a serious limitation on the toolkit we were working with. It is interesting that at the time we were doing that work, some researchers in Latin America were doing something similar from a perspective much more conscious of the need to theorise coloniality. I'm thinking of people like Aníbal Quijano in Peru, or Cardoso and Faletto, whose great book *Dependencia y Desarrollo en América Latina* came out in 1969. Had we been aware of their work, and able to read it, that might have been immensely illuminating for understanding class relations in Australia.

So this is part of my critique of Australian sociology, for instance in that piece I called 'Setting Sail' about the first ten years of academic sociology in Australia. One of my strongest critiques is its dependence on theoretical frameworks imported from Europe and North America without recognition of the historical situation of settler colonialism here. But that's a critique that applies to my work of the time too, so it's a limitation on the kinds of frameworks that we all had.

Steven: So you see those limitations as well in the likes of Wright and Goldthorpe and Bourdieu?

Raewyn: Erik Wright particularly tried to go global in due course. I have a lot of respect for his work, he was imaginative and he got his fingers dirty in masses of data which is always important for theorists. He did try to build a world perspective. But I don't think it would be unfair to him to say that his theoretical framework was always based in the European Marxist tradition. It's unkind to say it, but I think that basis is now obsolete, I don't think we can do that anymore. I am more critical of Bourdieu; while acknowledging his political positions and critique of the French establishment, his theorising is essentially a kind of left-wing, ironic functionalism. That's true of some latter-day Marxisms as well.

Jessica: Do you think there's anything to be salvaged from Marx and Marxism in terms of understanding both?

Raewyn: Yes. Marx was a wonderfully imaginative intellectual, as well as writing damn good German and having a sense of humour. The capacity to imagine a capitalist order in the way he did is a great model of how one can think big and well. Trying to think rigorously and think from data, from the hard information as well, it's a stunning model of intellectual work, which I have enormous regard for. I don't necessarily think any of his specific claims are still defensible.

If one wanted to spend time doing this, one could show how some of the limitations of Marx's perspective were inherent in the way he set up his theorising of ideas that were actually fairly common to radicals and labour movements in Europe in the 1840s, '50s and '60s. He formalised what were relatively widespread understandings. He did it in a wonderfully influential way, but there were limits to the understandings of the world in the sources he was working from. We can see those limits retrospectively more than they could be seen at the time.

Likewise, I have no doubts that there are things to be learnt from Bourdieu, from Beck, both of them imaginative thinkers. Both of them bold in the kinds of generalisations they attempted. Being closer in time to their work, I can see some of the alternatives they might have taken up. But I would never say don't read these guys. I think people should read them – in an awareness of who they are, where they come from, what they come out of, what they are trying to do in their texts. What are the cultural traditions they're working from, and what other ideas there are in the world that we need to access and work from, which are not present in their frameworks.

Steven: That's a good segue into the next question I think which is specifically about your work on Southern Theory. We'd like you to reflect on how class analysis fits into your Southern Theory critique of global sociology, which I think we've already been talking about, but in relation particularly to Australia. The role of settler colonialism, what role does that play in Australia's class structure?

Raewyn: Yes, let me come to that second because I want to say first that there is actually a good deal of class analysis in the book *Southern Theory*. When I was looking for striking intellectual work, notable pieces of social analysis from the colonised and post-colonial world, what I was finding often were intellectual projects that were either about class or had something to say about class or were about a form of exploitation which interacts with class. So José Rizal produced a stunning analysis of the corruption of late Spanish colonialism in the Philippines, which has a lot to tell us about class relations in a colonial context under colonial rule. The *Subaltern Studies* group in India of course had some Marxist background, and have wonderful analyses of class relations in colonial India, both in the peasant society and in the nascent Indian industrial economy.

Or in the work from Southern Africa that I refer to in *Southern Theory*, especially the work of Solomon Tsekisho Plaatje, *Native Life in South Africa*, which I think should be regarded as one of the great classics of global sociology. Plaatje analyses the displacement of African farmers from the land and the reconstruction of the African population as a landless labour force for white colonising commercial farmers. It's a stunning piece of analysis, about the creation of a specific kind of class structure which is racialised in its origins and its consciousness. Here, class and race are not intersecting structures, they are in effect the same thing in that colonial context.

So, when one says 'southern theory', one says a lot of class analysis – but class analysis which may not look very like European class analysis at all, and for which new paradigms or frameworks may have to be developed. Some of the Latin American thinkers I mentioned, and others in the decolonial school, have offered new understandings that I think are important and exciting intellectual developments.

Having said that, I have to think how to get this understanding across to people who are embedded in a disciplinary culture centred on Europe and North America. Academic life in Australia is governed by the imperatives of university structures which are subject to coloniality, which are preoccupied with league tables that centre on Harvard and Stanford and Oxbridge and so forth. The sources of southern theory are practically invisible to the imagination of university administrators, ministers of higher education, foundations funding research, and so on.

Where there is enormous concentration of attention on the ideas and institutions of the Global North, how do we get across the idea that there is a vast resource of much more relevant thinking out there in the colonised and post-colonial world? How do we install that as central to the social sciences in our universities? There is work being done on that, for instance people are trying to decolonise the curriculum, which is one way of putting the issue, though not necessarily the most powerful because it phrases the approach in a negative way. Nevertheless it's there, it's a project. For instance, the 'Why is My Curriculum White?' movement, which I think is a nice question to ask for any curriculum in any discipline in Australia.

Where does this knowledge come from, where do these frameworks come from, who's going to use them, how relevant is it to the situations where it is most needed? I'm thinking for instance of medical and paramedical faculties and training, which are training the workforce for hospitals and clinics and public health services. Around the world, health services are dealing with populations most of whom are not living in the Global North. Where does their curriculum come from? Mostly from the Global North.

There are huge tasks there and sometimes I'm intimidated by the scale of the intellectual project that we face. But then I'm buoyed up with the resources that we have, with the wealth of knowledge and imagination around the world.

Jessica: I think particularly when you think about it in the Australian context where this question of the racialised inherent character of class which is just so connected to the colonial endeavour and the rooting of capitalism in Australia, it seems like such devastating oversight that this hasn't been central to the way in which class and the theorisation of class has been taken in the Australian context.

Raewyn: There are some specific reasons for that. I think one is the actual pattern of colonisation in Australia, which was very different from the pattern in South Africa for instance. Well not entirely different, but in quite substantial ways different. Except in the pastoral industry and especially in Northern Australia, colonialism in Australia did not subject the Indigenous population as a labour force. It tended rather to drive the Indigenous population out, so it was genocidal rather than inclusive of a racialised subordinate workforce.

That produced a different pattern of racism in Australia which we still have elements of today – exclusionary rather than hierarchical. But the particular pattern of racism that develops in Australia, symbolised in the phrase 'White Australia' and the immigration policy for most of the 20th century, excluding anyone who was not regarded as being of European descent, has a specific connection with the imagination of class and the shape of class politics, that still has to be teased out.

Jessica: We wanted to ask about some contemporary global politics around Black Lives Matter, the rise of far-right ethno-nationalism, feminist debates, Me Too and so on. But also, the comment that you made earlier around your critique of intersectionality, I think it would be interesting to think about. So we are going to ask you about the role of class in the public debates that are occurring around those sorts of movements, the kind of political eruptions in the present moment. How do you see that figuring in analyses and presentations of intersectionality?

Raewyn: I'm not sure that I have much of a grip on the question as you've phrased it. My thinking about these things doesn't really revolve around the concept of intersectionality. But perhaps it revolves a little around the changing structure of class in Australia, the changing structure of economies and the changing rhetoric of class. So if you think back to the story that we told in *Class Structure in Australian History*, which was published right at the end of the '70s, we told a story of the gradual creation of a particular pattern of class relations in the context of a precarious distant settlement that gradually acquired an economic role in terms of pastoralism, mineral resources, gold, silver and so forth.

Then began to follow the path of producing a more autonomous industrial economy, with the growth of steelmaking, manufacturing and so forth through the 20th century. In fact, when we published that book, that story was coming to an end, or at least to a radical new turn. Picking up steam at the end of the '70s and through the '80s, and mingled very much with the advent of neoliberal deregulatory policies, was a reversion to a kind of colonial economy, where the growth point of the Australian economy ceased to be in secondary industry. In fact secondary industry was then winding down, all the State support for secondary industry was dismantled. As we know, the car manufacturing industry has just come to a final end.

The growth point of the economy became primary exports again, coal, iron ore, other minerals and agricultural produce. So a shift in the nature of wealth and power in Australia has occurred, with the economy much more tightly tied into global markets, including financial markets.

The dominant economic powers in Australia were no longer locally based corporations but transnational markets and international consortia. BHP succeeded in turning itself into an international mining conglomerate, not many Australian firms have actually done that.

So the shape of class politics in Australia was reconfigured in a way that made industrial struggle no longer the centre of class relations, but relationships between economically marginalised groups and the new transnational centres of power became the crucial issue. That requires a different way of thinking about the class dynamics, because we absolutely cannot think this simply within national boundaries, it's just not correct any more to do that. Critique of the nation as framework has to be re-thought now to account for this post-colonial re-entry into a kind of colonial status – though a different kind of colonial status.

That means that in Australia, we are more open to interpreting our situations through the lens of what's presented to us by transnational media. It becomes possible to think that terms like 'Black Lives Matter' mean a kind of politics that occurs in Australia. Or the kind of politics that's represented by Alternative für Deutschland, the neo-Nazi politics in Germany, or the Tea Party in the United States, the radical anti-welfare-state movement that opened a path for the Trump campaign.

We can become preoccupied with such concepts and think they also stand for politics in Australia. We've never had the mass slave workforce that the southern parts of the United States had, the Afro-descendant population in the United States that was the principal base of the Black Lives Matter movement, and the kind of racial politics that surrounds the presence of that population in North America. We've never had the kind of political history that Europe has had as the centre of Empire and the rulers of the world. The capacity to construct Islam as the traditional enemy and engage in the synthesis of religious and racial prejudice, that now seems to be very characteristic of the right in Europe.

We have a different history of racism: one which has involved genocidal colonisation rather than a racialised labour force, and an exclusionary White Australia model of understanding the settler community in Australia. This drives the mainstreaming of racism, which is characteristic in Australia not of a far right, not of a fringe right or even of the kind of authoritarian populism that is represented by the Trump movement, but is embedded in our mainstream parties, which once had a consensus for White Australia, and now have a consensus around the 'Pacific Solution', border protection, and so forth, now immovably embedded in the current Coalition federal government.

I mean, we're never going to see from this political order a radical shift in attitudes to Indigenous people. We saw how even that remarkable Uluru Statement was immediately dismissed by the national government. Border politics has now been embedded in the response to the COVID virus and has got new political credibility out of that.

So, this is a long way around to say that we can't read off the problems of analysis and understanding that surround things like the Trump movement, the #MeToo movement or the Black Lives Matter movement as speaking to the social realities of Australia. Of course we can learn from them. Among other things we can learn how dangerous some political movements can be. I started my academic publishing career in the 1960s with a book about the extreme right in Australia, and I've become very much interested in that question again.

Steven: Do you think there's a potential for the development of emancipatory social movements through those kinds of labelistic politics even if they do spring from North America? Or will the original basis of where those things develop always be a problem for some kind of unity or collaboration? Because BLM has been taken up here by some Indigenous activists. Is there no room, for instance, for some kind of growth of emancipatory or progressive politics through those things? Or do you think the kind of relationality of it will always be an issue? It's maybe not either/or …

Raewyn: Well Indigenous groups in the 1960s and '70s drew themes from the Black Power movement in the United States which came out of the African American community, not the North American Indigenous community. It is the case that there are now Indigenous movements in North America and in South America and in other parts of the world. Aboriginal communities in Australia have connections with those movements also. If the Black Lives Matter movement or rhetoric is a resource too, well and good, let's use it. Anything that gives power or impetus to the claims of marginalised and oppressed communities is a good thing.

Yet I think there are risks in translating rhetoric into different situations. I've seen that for instance in a kind of politics that affects me directly, since I'm a transsexual woman. The North American dynamics of identity politics led in the 1990s to the assimilation of various trans groups into an imagined coalition which came to be known as 'LGBT'. That acronym is practically a word now in some languages. It seems to me quite a dangerous export, which spoke to a particular moment in the history of politics in North America, but may be very problematic in other global situations. But because of the enormous cultural authority of North America, and its centrality in global media and aid funding, that phrasing – LGBT or LGBT*, LGBTIQ, etc. – is now almost taken as gospel, as common sense, in politics and in the media all over the place.

So yes, I think that what I'm arguing against here is what I argued against in my critique of globalisation theory in sociology. The globalisation concept usually involved a claim that economic, cultural, media homogenisation on a world scale was happening. All parts of the world were supposed to be coming together in a kind of soup, where we all had the same ideas and the same resources. I've argued vehemently against that as a misrepresentation of what's going on, and I would make the same kind of argument in relation to political categories. We need to think for ourselves! That's what I've been arguing all my career: here we are in a given situation, we're here and now, think about this situation, start from where we are. Gather the relevant resources, intellectually and empirically, but start from where we are, not from a position of intellectual dependency.

Steven: So we have one last question and it's typically sociological in the sense that we're asking you to be reflexive. We've talked to you so far through your intellectual career, particularly regarding your work on class and more recently in terms of the Southern Theory aspects. But we now want you to think about class in terms of your own trajectory and how that affected that trajectory over the past decades. From your entry into sociology, your career through it and maybe you can even say a little bit about what it means to be an intellectual in the world at the moment after that trajectory.

Raewyn: Yes, big question!

Steven: Sorry!

Raewyn: Just thinking of the class situation that I began in, I came from the professional bourgeoisie. My father and mother were intellectual workers, teachers, and my dad became an academic. Their families also included several professions – doctor, lawyer, engineer, minister of religion. In one line of descent the family came from the late-19th-century commercial bourgeoisie in Melbourne. That was the only time any part of my family looked seriously rich! No part of my family in its period in Australia were working class. In the Depression of the 1930s, my mum's family certainly did it tough. But it was not struggle street when I was growing up, at all.

When I went to university in the 1960s, universities were pretty elite institutions. They formed a much smaller system than now, and were strongly class-selective. The people that went into university mainly came from the upper-income brackets and practically all of them expected to be in the upper-income brackets, if they became a doctor or a lawyer or a university academic. So I followed the expected path, I became an academic. The only jobs I've had since I went to university have been in universities.

So, I'm very much a product of the academic world. I have always been a salaried state employee with, for a salaried employee, an unusual freedom of speech and capacity to design my own job. Much more so than is usually the case in universities today! I came in at a time that the university system was expanding fast, new departments were being set up. Teaching and research frameworks were being created and I had a stunning amount of freedom to do things in new ways. It was an amazing moment.

So my class situation has been extremely privileged, in one of the richest countries in the world, one of the best fed. The moment was privileged too: I started working in a boom economy with full employment. It's almost unimaginable now what it was like then. I guess the kind of politics that I and others imagined, in the student movement of the 1960s, assumed that background. We were bitterly critical of the backward-looking right-wing regimes around the country, Menzies and the successors, but we did assume a full employment economy. We had no doubt that we would get jobs, and we could not be intimidated.

Steven: Well that is a big difference in academia today. It's the constant precarious intimidation of the job market that we're all in. It's something that very much introduces a conservatism that we would all like to avoid, but we all seem to take part in, I think.

Raewyn: It's very hard to avoid, given the real situation you're in. So yes, when I think back it's not only class privilege within the local structure, but also the collective privilege of the settler-colonial population in Australia in global class terms. That enabled me to launch the kind of intellectual trajectory that might have been very hard if I'd been subject to more controls or fears, if I'd not had the resources to put together teams of people to work on new and imaginative projects.

I became in a sense an employer, as a head of department, as a chief investigator in research projects that were employing research associates, without strongly feeling that I was an employer. We were in a situation where it was possible to create – perhaps partly it was imaginary, but it felt that it was possible to create cooperative and relatively egalitarian relationships in a progressive university department and in research projects.

Still, there were hard material inequalities even then, and they've got harder. The whole structure of power in universities has shifted from the old professoriate, where I was a kind of dissident member, into the hands of professional corporate-style managers. So it's a very different story now; I write about the shift in *The Good University*.

The other thing I should say is that as a dissident young intellectual in the 1960s, I had a lot of contact with the labour movement, with working-class activists in unions and in Labor Party branches. I was in the Labor Party at the time when that was still basically a working-class mass party. That connection was really important for me, cracking some of the shell of my professional-bourgeois upbringing and the elitism of the high schools that I went to.

So I could have lived in more of a middle-class bubble than I did. The student movement, the anti-war movement, the unions and the Labor Party were a really important part of my life and in various ways have remained so. I have stayed in the union, but I left the Labor Party on the day that Paul Keating was elected leader, which was the last straw for me. I've been saddened as the Labor Party has marched towards a neoliberal future. Of course the party still has a connection with the unions; but the unions have been terribly battered and their coverage has shrunk. In today's conditions the Australian working class is mostly unorganised and unrepresented.

So the world has changed, what a surprise! Class relations change, class consciousness changes, power structures change, the shape of the world economy changes. New forms of politics have developed; some old threads are woven into new shapes. I think I have a stronger sense now of the sheer criminality of the world's ruling classes, from their genocidal histories to their planetary destructiveness today. Perhaps I am less optimistic that intellectual work, such as we do in sociology, can change the world in the short term. But in time it does have an effect, indeed many effects. With what tools we can find, it's important to keep trying. The struggle continues.

ABOUT THE CONTRIBUTORS

Jasmine Ali graduated from Sydney University in 2008, with Honours in Philosophy, a Juris Doctor (Laws) at Melbourne University in 2018. She has worked as a casual academic in the fields of political economy, law and history. She has worked as a research assistant on the ARC Linkage Grant, 'The impacts of industry restructuring', and on a United Workers Union funded project on the closure and relocation of warehousing in Melbourne. Jasmine is an active participant in protest movements for social and economic justice.

Tom Barnes is an economic sociologist at Australian Catholic University (ACU) in Sydney. His research primarily focuses on the political economy of insecure, precarious and informal work. He is currently researching global warehouse logistics and automotive manufacturing. He has expertise on work and economic development in India, having written two books in this area, *Informal Labour in Urban India: Three Cities, Three Journeys* and *Making Cars in the New India: Industry, Precarity and Informality*, and articles in several journals, including *Urban Studies*, *Journal of Development Studies* and *Critical Sociology*.

Larissa Behrendt OA is a Distinguished Professor and Director of Research at the Jumbunna Indigenous House of Learning at the University of Technology Sydney. She has a LLB and B.Juris from UNSW and a LLM and SJD from Harvard Law School. Larissa has a legal background with a strong track record in the areas of Indigenous law, policy, creative arts, education and research. She has held numerous judicial positions and sat on various community and arts organisation boards. Larissa is a Fellow of the Academy of Social Sciences of Australia and a Foundation Fellow of the Australian Academy of Law.

Rose Butler is a Senior Research Fellow at the Alfred Deakin Institute for Citizenship and Globalisation at Deakin University. She studies class, inequality, intimacy and mobilities in Australia, with a focus on young people and families. Rose's current ARC DECRA research examines young people's rural in-migration, relationships and place-making in a rural city of Victoria. Her recent books include *Class, Culture and Belonging in Rural Childhoods*, and *Asian Migration and Education Cultures in the Anglosphere* (edited with Megan Watkins and Christina Ho).

Raewyn Connell is Professor Emerita, University of Sydney, and Life Member of the National Tertiary Education Union. She has taught in several countries and is a widely cited sociological researcher, the author *of Ruling Class Ruling Culture, Gender and Power, Masculinities*, and *Southern Theory*, and co-author of *Class Structure in Australian History* and *Making the Difference*. Her recent books include *The Good University* and the co-authored *Knowledge and Global Power*. Her work has been translated into 23 languages. Raewyn has been active in the labour movement, and in work for gender equality and peace. Details at www.raewynconnell.net and Twitter @raewynconnell.

David Farrugia is Senior Lecturer in Sociology at the University of Newcastle. His current research focuses on youth, post-Fordism and service labour. He is co-director of the Newcastle Youth Studies Network and his most recent book is titled *Youth, Work and the Post-Fordist Self*.

Hannah Forsyth is Senior Lecturer in History at the Australian Catholic University. Hannah writes in both a scholarly capacity and for the public sphere in the history of capitalism and the history of education in Australia and globally. Her first book, *A History of the Modern Australian University*, was quoted in parliament by Senator Kim Carr in 2014 in opposition to fee reforms that would have deployed higher education to deepen inequalities in Australia. She held a Discovery Early Career Award for 2017–2019 and is currently writing a monograph tentatively entitled *Virtue Capitalists*.

Jessica Gerrard is Associate Professor at the University of Melbourne. She researches the changing formations and lived experiences of social inequalities in relation to education, activism, work and unemployment. Gerrard works across the disciplines of sociology, history and policy studies with an interest in critical methodologies and theories. Her books include *Radical Childhoods: Schooling and the Struggle for Social Change* and *Precarious Enterprise on the Margins: Work, Poverty and Homelessness in the City*.

Christina Ho is Associate Professor of Social and Political Sciences at the University of Technology Sydney. She researches diversity and inequality in education, Chinese diasporas and intercultural urban relations. Her books include *Aspiration and Anxiety: Asian Migrants and Australian Schooling*, *Asian Migration and Education Cultures in the Anglosphere*, and '*For Those Who've Come Across the Seas…': Australian Multicultural Theory, Policy and Practice*.

Keith Jacobs is Professor of Sociology at the University of Tasmania. His work focuses on housing and urban politics. Amongst his most recent publications are *Housing, what do we know and what should we do* co-authored with Rowland Atkinson; *Neoliberal Housing Policy: An International Perspective*; and *Philosophy and the City: Interdisciplinary and Transcultural Perspectives* co-edited with Jeff Malpas.

Julie McLeod is Professor of Curriculum, Equity and Social Change, University of Melbourne and researches in the history and sociology of education, focusing on youth, gender, and educational reform. She has a longstanding interest in qualitative methodologies and genealogies of educational ideas. Current projects include 'Progressive Education and Race: A transnational Australian history, 1920s–50s'; and Making Futures, a longitudinal study of youth identities, generational change and education. Recent publications include *Uneven Space-Times of Education: Historical Sociologies of Concepts, Methods and Practices*; *Rethinking Youth Wellbeing* and; *The Promise of the New and Genealogies of Educational Reform*. See juliemcleod.net

Barry Morris is currently conjoint Senior Lecturer in Sociology and Anthropology, University of Newcastle, Australia. He has published fieldwork on Indigenous history, politics and policy and contributed chapters and articles from issues of Indigenous polity and to the paradoxes of egalitarian ideologies of the Australian State. His current research is on the changing contemporary understandings of settler-colonial relations in Australia. He is the author of *Domesticating Resistance: the Dhan-gadi Aborigines and the Australian State* and *Protest, Land Rights and Riots: Postcolonial Struggles in Australia in the 1980s*. The edited collections include *Race Matters: Indigenous Australians and 'Our' Society*, with Gillian Cowlishaw and *Expert Knowledge: First World Peoples, Consultancy, and Anthropology*, with Rohan Bastin.

Greg Noble is Professor of Cultural Research at the Institute for Culture and Society, Western Sydney University. His research interests centre on the intersections of youth, ethnicity, class and gender; cultural pedagogies and Bourdieusian theory; migration, cultural complexity and inter-ethnic relations; and multicultural education. He has published ten books, the most recent of which are *Doing Diversity Differently*, *Assembling and Governing Habits* and *Fields, Capitals, Habitus*.

Henry Paternoster is a sessional academic based in Melbourne, Australia. He was previously a postdoctoral fellow at the University of Melbourne, as part of a collective research project into class-based stigma. His research focuses on histories of ideas. He is the author of *Reimagining Class in Australia: Marxism, Populism and Social Science*.

Barbara Pini is a Professor in the School of Humanities, Languages and Social Sciences at Griffith University. Her work focuses on questions of belonging and inclusion in rural communities. She has undertaken a wide range of projects exploring the intersections between rural life and gender, class, sexuality, disability and ageing. Her most recent research is exploring how a new generation of socially diverse rural authors, including Indigenous people, are using life narratives to connect people to each other, animals, landscapes and place.

Laura Rodriguez Castro is a postdoctoral research fellow at the Alfred Deakin Institute of Citizenship and Globalisation at Deakin University. Her research focuses on the intersections between decolonial feminisms, anti-racism, memory and rurality. She is also interested in arts, visual and participatory methodologies. Laura's book *Decolonial Feminisms, Power and Place: Sentipensando with Rural Women in Colombia* explores how rural women enact and imagine decolonial feminist worlds.

Penelope Rossiter is Associate Dean (Teaching and Learning) and a Senior Lecturer in Culture and Society in the School of Humanities and Communications Arts at Western Sydney University. Whether writing on class or, more recently, on swimming and municipal pools, her research is shaped by an abiding interest in the affective and emotional texture of embodied relationships with place. In 2020, her essay 'The Municipal Pool in Australia: Emotional Geography and Affective Intensities', was awarded the Phillipa Maddern prize for the best essay published in *Emotions: History, Culture and Society*.

Steven Threadgold is Associate Professor of Sociology at University of Newcastle. His research focuses on youth and class, with particular interests in unequal and alternate work and career trajectories, underground and independent creative scenes, and cultural formations of taste. Steve is Co-Director of the Newcastle Youth Studies Network, an Associate Editor of *Journal of Youth Studies*, and on the editorial boards of *The Sociological Review* and *Journal of Applied Youth Studies*. His latest book is *Bourdieu and Affect: Towards a Theory of Affective Affinities. Youth, Class and Everyday Struggles* won the 2020 Raewyn Connell Prize for best first book in Australian sociology.

Eve Vincent is a Senior Lecturer in the School of Social Sciences at Macquarie University. Her books include *Against Native Title. Conflict and Creativity in Outback Australia* and the co-edited collection *Unstable Relations: Indigenous People and Environmentalism in Contemporary Australia.*

Deborah Warr is a sociologist whose research has explored associations between health and place, the implications of place- and poverty-stigma, the interactive effects of social, economic and cultural exclusion in place-based settings and methodologies facilitating participatory, community-based approaches to research. She has held posts at the University of Melbourne and Charles Sturt University and is currently Principal Research and Policy Fellow at the Brotherhood of St Laurence where her work focuses on community inclusion for people living with disability.

Mark Western is Director of the Institute for Social Science Research at the University of Queensland. His research interests include class analysis and social stratification, social and economic inequality, research methods, social networks, and the institutional conditions for advancing the social sciences. His recent publications include papers on informal employment in Indonesia, intergenerational wealth transfers in Australia, and the relationships between socio-economic status, student engagement and student achievement for Australian secondary school students.

Lyn Yates is Redmond Barry Distinguished Professor Emerita of Education at the University of Melbourne. Her most recent work has been on the impacts and implications in schools and in universities of new forms of governance and curricula agendas.

INDEX

12 to 18 Project, 179–81, 183–5, 186–92

Aboriginal people, 12, 30, 50, 84, 132, 152, 217–20, 221, 224–7, 228–31, 234, 254; classed, 13, 140, 152, 216; *see also* Indigenous
addiction, 137, 145, 151, 155, 168
Adkins, Lisa, 11, 63, 110, 112
administrators, 42, 87, 249
adult, 61, 63, 68, 171, 187
affect/ive, 10, 15–16, 110–15, 123, 144, 153–6, 164–5, 171, 173, 184
agency, 25, 48, 78, 163, 217, 228
agriculture, 43, 47, 53, 82, 131, 251
anxiety, 5, 19, 123, 201
ANZAC, 134
assets, 11, 28, 58–9, 61–3, 65–6, 67, 69–70, 95, 171, 202
ATSIC, 224

Barangaroo, 226–7
battler/s, 3, 4, 122, 129, 131, 134
Beck, Ulrich, 242, 248
Behrendt, Larissa, 13, 16–17, 215–35
Berlant, Lauren, 113–14, 140
Black Middle Class, 13, 218, 219
blue-collar, 129
bogan, 5, 16, 127–40
Bolt, Andrew, 225
Bourdieu, Pierre, 10–11, 25–7, 30, 33, 37, 38 (n3), 59, 67, 84, 89, 184, 188, 245, 247–8
bourgeoisie, 8, 61, 63–4, 83, 255
Brett, Judith, 77, 80, 132, 202–3

capitalism, 4, 6, 8, 14, 15, 55, 59, 61–2, 64, 80, 82, 83, 87, 111, 114, 128, 243, 247, 250

capitalist; class, 12–13, 15, 45, 62–3; elite, 40–1, 69–70, 77, 85, 88, 240; logic, 79, 86, 89, 163–4
Cardoso, Fernando Henrique, 246
career, 17, 95, 190, 202, 220, 230, 243, 244, 253–5
casual employment, 32, 97, 99–107, 128, 227
chartists, 52, 53, 131
chav, 128–9, 135–6
choice, 27, 68, 129, 147, 151, 170–4, 198, 200, 201, 202
citizenship, 16, 52, 95
civil service, 47–9
class analysis, 1, 6–17, 25, 36–7, 58–70, 180, 182, 240–1, 243–4, 248–9
class conflict, 79, 85, 88–9, 180, 202
class consciousness, 5, 8, 10–11, 13, 79, 190, 238, 241, 249, 259
class formation, 11–12, 24–6, 45, 59–63, 68, 111, 114, 187, 203, 245
class interests, 83, 93, 96–7, 98, 182
class politics, 9, 130–2, 163, 238, 242, 250, 252
class position, 5, 25–6, 31, 36, 61, 97, 238
class structure, 26, 29, 48, 59, 61–70, 144, 245–6, 249
Class structure in Australian History, 8, 24, 26, 77–8, 89, 236–7, 241, 245, 251
class war, 4, 133
Collingwood Football Club, 231, 232, 234
colonialism, 6, 9, 12–17, 45, 191, 216, 222, 225–6, 240, 245–6, 248, 250
colonisation, 79, 164–5, 174, 223, 229, 250, 252

community, 116, 118–19, 148–50, 152, 157, 165, 170, 182, 200, 202–4, 209, 220, 223–4, 227, 228, 233–4, 252, 253–4
Connell, Raewyn, 7–8, 12, 17, 23–4, 89, 131, 182, 236–57
consumption, 5, 26, 30, 45, 59
convict, 15, 40, 41–55, 80, 131, 216, 217, 221
Coombes, Lindon, 231, 233
Cooper, William, 226
creative, 190, 223
credentials, 86, 116, 117, 207
criminal, 41, 50, 139, 257; justice system, 228–9
cultural capital, 26, 29–31, 67, 69, 139, 170, 186
cultural turn, 77, 78, 79

Davidson, Liam, 222
democracy, 47, 51–2
deserving poor, 4, 133, 169
disadvantage, 5–6, 12, 123, 147–50, 167, 174
disposition, 5, 112, 173, 179, 183
dispossession, 13, 40, 45, 55, 140, 226
distinction, 4, 10, 27, 29, 31, 47, 62, 81, 115, 131, 133, 134, 162, 179, 182
division of labour, 62
dole, 109, 112–13, 168, 224
dominance, 53–5, 216; class, 52, 192; cultural, 3, 171, 201, 217, 222; political, 48, 132, 252
drugs, 145, 152, 155

economy, 7, 16, 43–4, 46, 51, 55, 80, 81, 82–3, 85, 87, 88–9, 112, 131, 195, 197, 227, 228, 240, 248, 251, 256–7
education, 4, 5, 6, 8, 10, 13, 16–17, 28, 30–1, 32, 46, 47–9, 51, 61, 63, 65, 68, 80, 84, 85, 87, 95, 113, 120, 133, 150, 180–3, 184–5, 187, 189–92, 195, 197, 198–9, 201, 202–3, 204–5, 230, 235, 236, 238, 241, 243, 249

egalitarianism, 5, 51, 53, 130–1, 132–4, 138, 166, 256, 262
elite, 4, 15, 28, 40, 45–50, 53–4, 55, 67, 87–8, 131, 134, 182, 185–90, 192, 197, 200, 240, 255
embodiment, 80–1, 84, 110, 113, 123, 137, 153, 156, 164, 165, 183–4, 187, 196
emotions, 104, 111, 113, 154, 192, 221
employment, 10, 15, 28, 50, 62, 67–9, 89, 104, 114–17, 119, 120, 121, 140, 168, 170, 256; Indigenous, 224, 228; productivity, 109–11, 112–14, 122–3; security of, 94–5, 98, 101, 103; structure of, 59, 64–6; unionised, 104, 105, 107
enterprise, 43, 83–4, 88, 95, 100, 105, 165
entrepreneur, 86–7, 122, 164, 168, 196
environmentalism, 9, 78, 85, 137, 139, 166
ethics, 81, 155, 223
ethnicity, 6, 12, 16, 17, 27, 30, 37, 60, 182, 199
exclusion, 5, 16, 41, 60, 69–70, 104, 110, 173, 223, 228, 250, 252
expertise, 24, 65, 81–2, 259
exploitation, 12, 13, 14, 24, 40, 60, 102–3, 106, 132, 138, 180, 223, 226, 248

Faletto, Enzo, 246
falsity, 79, 81, 133, 204, 217
family, 3, 9, 28, 31, 34, 41, 42, 49, 66, 84–5, 102, 116, 118, 138, 147, 151, 155, 162, 165, 166–7, 170, 172, 179, 185, 188–90, 203, 207
feminism, 9, 163–5, 168, 171, 173, 183, 189, 191, 216
feminist, 11, 111, 162–3, 170, 171, 173, 180–1, 183, 184, 187, 188
figures/figurative, 3, 4, 56, 122, 127–35, 136, 138, 139, 152
First Nations, 216–17, 219, 232, 235

266

Index

flexible employment, 5, 122, 134
folk devil, 127
Freeman, Cathy, 233

gender, 4, 6, 7, 8, 9, 10, 12, 16, 17, 27, 30, 31, 37, 42, 55, 60, 67, 68, 86, 87, 88, 115, 135, 140, 163–5, 166, 170, 173, 180, 181, 183–5, 187, 188, 189, 191, 216, 221, 227, 235, 245–6
generation, 4, 30, 42, 49, 62, 77, 78, 85, 95, 147, 165–6, 190, 192, 195, 219–20, 223, 229, 234, 235, 238
gentry, 46–9, 54
globalisation, 8, 9, 86, 95, 197, 254
Goldthorpe, John Harry, 25, 28, 60, 62, 245, 247
Gollan, Robin, 239
government, 13, 16, 40–2, 44–5, 46–7, 50, 52–3, 80, 83, 87–9, 105, 111, 114, 132, 138, 146, 150–2, 186, 196–8, 223, 228, 242, 249, 253
Grant, Stan, 233
Grenville, Kate, 222
Gutman, Herbert, 240

habitus, 27, 33, 84, 89, 184
happiness, 118, 120, 152, 204
hegemony, 7, 82, 162, 196
Heiss, Anita, 230
heuristic, 37, 181
hierarchy, 25, 49, 62, 101, 105, 179, 185
homelessness, 11, 66, 148, 152
homophobia, 6, 129
housing, 5, 11, 65–7, 69, 138, 146, 156, 197, 228
Howard, John Winston, 3, 129, 131, 134

identity, 9, 10, 48, 60, 67, 68, 77, 99, 136, 179, 181, 183–4, 187, 195, 200, 202; class, 11, 58–9, 130–4, 135, 139–40, 196, 201
ideology, 8, 24, 47, 60, 80, 83, 87, 144, 148, 153, 164, 173, 183, 185–6, 196, 197, 224–5, 243

illness, 79, 145, 152, 154
imaginary, 16, 162, 162, 172, 221, 256
inclusion/ive, 78, 85–6, 87, 105, 166, 234, 250
income, 4, 11, 28, 59, 61–8, 80, 95, 105, 228, 255
Indigenous, 9, 13, 14, 16–17, 24, 27, 30, 31, 33, 40, 41, 42, 45, 49, 54, 55, 78, 110, 148, 152, 191, 217–26, 230–3, 250, 253–4; *see also* Aboriginal people
individualism, 6, 13, 148, 163, 171–3
industrial, 8, 41, 43, 63, 85, 93, 94, 103, 106, 128, 132, 133, 223, 227, 238, 240, 241, 248, 251, 252
inequality, 5–7, 10, 15, 26, 27, 66, 139, 147, 151, 156, 169, 171, 173–4, 191–2, 244; classed, 58–63, 144, 182; economic, 12, 64, 243; gendered, 163, 166; housing, 67; study of, 69–70
injustice, 13, 51, 77, 129, 203, 225
intersection/ality, 16, 36, 37, 78, 89, 170, 180, 183–4, 216, 221, 244, 251
Irving, Terry, 8, 12, 77, 89, 236, 237, 240

Janke, Terri, 230
Jones, Alan, 87, 225
Jones, Owen, 128, 135
justice, 32, 47, 51, 150, 151, 228, 225

Keating, Paul, 257

Labor Party, 9, 132, 133, 257
labour, 6, 9, 13–14, 17, 40, 49, 50, 64–5, 89, 95–6, 98, 99, 109–10, 226; affective, 111–14, 116, 165; as commodity, 11, 41–2, 43, 44–6, 49, 55, 62, 93, 122–3, 180, 195, 197; immaterial, 111, 114, 166; market, 5, 6, 15, 43, 69–70, 78, 81, 100–7, 128, 135, 183, 189, 191, 197, 249–50, 252, 257; movement, 129, 132, 140, 237–8, 247, 257
labour-hire agency, 99–107

larrikin, 128, 132, 138
leisure, 47, 48, 49, 67, 133
Liberal Party, 77, 132, 151, 238
lifestyle, 68, 136
logic, 12, 28, 51, 62, 65–6, 67, 69, 79, 80, 88, 96–7, 199

Mabo, 229
Maguire, Eddie, 234
management, 32, 83, 87, 103
managerial authority, 61–2, 64, 65, 83, 84, 86–8
manufacturing, 43, 107, 128, 133, 201, 251
marginalisation, 6, 69, 78, 95, 104, 145, 156, 216, 239, 252, 254
market, 5, 10, 45, 55, 63, 65, 69–70, 82, 95, 105, 128, 131, 135, 164, 170, 183, 195–6, 197–9, 200, 202, 203, 251, 252
marriage, 8, 41–2, 50, 89, 166
Marx, 10, 23, 25, 58, 62, 78, 79, 80, 89, 96, 106, 111, 180, 239, 245, 247–8
masculinity, 12, 55, 132, 134, 165, 183, 243
mateship, 134, 138
Maynard, John, 226
McDermott, Phillipa, 230
McQuire, Amy, 231
McRobbie, Angela, 114–115
Menzies, Robert Gordon, 130, 132–3, 134, 238, 240, 256
merit, 47, 51, 85–6, 88, 130, 190, 206, 230–1
methods, 16, 17, 27, 30, 31, 33, 35, 37, 41, 68–9, 97, 153, 180–1, 187, 191, 244
middle class, 79–80, 129, 135, 197, 257; identity, 195–7, 202–3, 205–6, 219; and morality, 4, 84–5, 200–2; as object, 85, 114, 145, 207; 'values', 33, 132–3, 138, 219, 220–1
moral economy, 80, 81, 154
morals/ality, 4, 15, 16, 40–2, 46, 51, 54, 77, 79, 80, 81–9, 122, 144, 146, 153, 165, 168–70, 195, 199–209

Morrison, Scott, 3, 109
multiculturalism, 134, 201
mythology, 49, 138, 165, 217, 239

Native Title, 237–8
neoliberalism, 5, 77, 95, 110, 128–9, 131, 138, 140, 155, 163–73, 196–7, 199, 251, 257
network/ing, 40, 49, 55, 67, 69, 82, 84, 119–20, 186, 207
New Left, 8, 129, 133–4, 239
normativity, 55, 85, 113, 114, 163, 164

occupation, 15, 28, 32, 43, 87, 89, 95, 99, 165, 182, 183, 184, 185, 196; structure of, 28–30, 68–9, 79, 80
Oeser, Oscar, 238
ontology, 26, 111, 165
opportunity, 60, 65, 106, 116, 133, 134, 138, 185, 198, 218, 219
oppression, 78, 164, 71, 239, 254
optimism, 173, 189, 235, 257

Pakulski, Jan 9, 242
parent/s, 4, 6, 28, 31, 35, 42, 48, 65, 67–8, 84, 102, 115–6, 138, 155–6, 166, 167, 168, 186, 188–9, 198, 199–209, 217, 219, 221, 243
part-time employment, 101, 103, 189
penal colony, 40, 41–4, 55
pension, 147, 157
Piaget, Jean, 241
picker-packer, 99
Piketty, Thomas, 243
Plaatje, Solomon Tsekisho, 248
police, 49, 50, 152, 156, 170
politics, 3, 9, 14, 47, 51–2, 59, 77–8, 79, 88, 93, 95, 129, 130, 131, 132, 133, 140, 153, 157, 163, 165, 170, 199, 219, 237–8, 239, 240, 243, 250–1, 252–3, 254, 256, 257
popular culture, 31, 136, 162
post-Fordism, 110–11, 113–14, 122, 195

Index

poverty, 5, 6, 7, 8, 10, 13, 16, 44, 118–19, 129, 143–56, 168, 182, 218
precariat, 11, 15, 28, 67, 69–70, 93–7, 101–7
precarity, 5, 94–7, 144
privilege, 40, 47–9, 51, 55, 157, 164, 168, 178, 216–17, 223, 231, 256
professional, 78, 81, 84, 87–8
professional class, 15, 79, 86, 88–9, 222–3

Quijano, Anibal, 246

race, 4, 6, 9, 12, 14, 17, 27, 30, 37, 45, 47, 60, 85–6, 87, 88–9 115, 135, 162, 164, 173, 182, 199, 202, 218, 249
racism, 6, 9, 13, 17, 33, 129, 140, 208, 215, 250, 252–3; AFL culture, 231–5; and politics, 228–9
recognition, 13, 26, 104, 129, 155, 183, 186, 222
reconciliation, 224, 234
reflexive modernity, 9, 11, 242
Reich, William, 245
Reid, Teela, 231
representation, 10, 12, 17, 27, 33, 60, 95, 105, 131, 138, 143, 149, 153, 155, 162, 228, 229, 231, 237, 254
resistance, 119, 140, 202
risk, 6, 139, 152, 195, 196, 217, 239, 254
Rizal, Jose, 248
Rose, Lionel, 233
ruling class, 8, 11, 28, 50, 55, 240, 241, 242, 243, 257
rural, 11, 16, 47, 54, 144, 161–73, 238

Savage, Mike, 59, 63, 67–8
SBS, 16, 143–6
schooling, 83, 179–85, 188, 191–2, 197, 199–200, 203–4, 206, 208, 238
self-employment, 61–2, 64, 66
services, 61, 62, 88, 100, 116, 118–19, 152, 169, 202, 250

settler, 12–14, 15, 16, 17, 27, 36, 40, 44–7, 51, 55–6, 78–9, 81, 86, 89, 162, 164, 173–4, 201, 216–17, 218, 221–2, 224, 226, 240, 245–6, 248, 252, 256
sexuality, 6, 9, 12, 16–17, 86, 87, 88, 161, 170, 216, 235, 245
Sheppard, Jill, 11, 67–9
Skeggs, Beverley, 37, 119, 139, 146–7, 153, 170
skills, 43–4, 61–2, 65, 95, 111–12, 113, 117, 120, 123
social capital, 26, 30, 69, 168, 170
social group, 60, 69, 135
social media, 135
social mobility, 13, 14, 59, 68, 122, 207, 217–18
social movement, 183, 253
social order, 55
social practice, 199
social space, 37
social structure, 78, 183
social welfare, 5, 59–60, 66, 120, 144, 146, 150–1, 157, 223–4, 226
social worker, 81–2, 85, 196
sociological, 7, 11, 17, 25, 114–15, 182–3, 191–2, 237, 243, 245, 254
solidarity, 140, 148
squatter, 45–9, 52–5
Standing, Guy, 15, 69, 93–6, 105–6
status, 6, 8, 10, 13, 16, 17, 46–51, 55, 61, 79, 95–6, 115, 122, 131, 138, 164, 169, 181, 190, 195, 197, 200, 202, 217, 234, 252
Stewart, Sonja, 230
stolen generation, 84, 233, 234
strategy/ies, 88, 90, 103, 117, 119, 144, 148, 168, 189, 203–4, 208–9
struggle, 5, 11, 26, 37, 54, 115, 168, 237, 241, 252, 255, 257
subjectivity/ies, 41, 110, 111–13, 114, 123, 155, 179–81, 182, 184, 187, 190, 192, 196
suburb, 7, 8, 83–4, 98, 130, 133, 138, 147, 185, 201

symbolic, 10, 49, 61, 119, 153, 200, 203, 219

TAFE, 116, 189
taste, 16, 27, 28–9, 31–3, 136, 138
television, 16, 30, 33, 130, 136–7, 139, 144–6, 148, 151, 153–5, 223
temporality, 31, 37, 70, 121, 192
Tent Embassy, 227
terra nullius, 15, 40, 45, 55, 164
Thompson, Edward Palmer, 24, 85, 89, 240
traditional, 9, 10, 28, 31, 55, 67, 85, 94–5, 97, 110, 113, 133, 165, 169, 182, 185–7, 198, 228, 252
training (vocational), 50, 61, 63, 116, 117, 119–20, 152, 250
trajectories, 15, 17, 31, 32–3, 35, 37, 59, 65, 180–1, 195, 200, 201, 208, 241, 255–6
transition, 10, 45, 52, 198
transportation (convict), 41, 43, 50–1, 131
trope, 137, 162, 207, 221

underclass, 138, 217
unemployment, 16, 17, 70, 109–14, 118, 122–3, 140, 145, 168
union/ism, 60, 64, 93–5, 97–8, 103–7, 129, 221, 236, 238, 241, 257
university, 28, 87, 149, 185, 188, 197, 218–20, 230, 236–7, 238, 249, 255–6, 257
upper class *see* elite; ruling class

values, 4, 55, 79–81, 132, 134–5, 138, 182, 187, 203, 233
violence, 51, 54, 55, 132, 153, 155, 165, 166, 172
vocational, 32, 63, 152, 189

wage, 4, 11, 13, 65, 82, 95, 100–1, 103, 113–14, 116, 122, 131, 168, 169, 195, 217, 224, 226

Ward, Russel, 78, 130, 134, 239
warehouse, 15, 94, 97–9, 102, 103–5, 107
Watego, Chelsea, 231
Waters, Malcolm, 9, 242
Weber, 58, 62, 80, 89, 106, 245
welfare state, 63, 82, 83, 128, 198, 196, 252
Whitaker, Alison, 231
White Australia (policy), 134, 196, 199, 250, 252–3
White, Patrick, 221–3
white-collar, 78–9, 87, 89, 133
whiteness, 17, 161, 163–73, 201
Winmar, Nicky, 233
Woolworths, 98–9, 101
work ethic, 4, 109, 111, 113–14, 115–16, 118, 122–3
workfare, 112
workforce, 64, 89, 98–9, 103, 105–7, 117, 131, 223, 227, 241, 250, 252
working class, 8, 11, 15–16, 28, 32–4, 64, 67, 77–8, 84, 95–6, 105, 111, 115–16, 118, 119, 122, 127–9, 131–4, 139, 179, 182, 189, 217–18, 229, 238, 239, 243, 255, 257
working families, 3, 134
Wright, Erik Olin, 15, 36, 59–62, 67, 99, 105–7, 245, 247; class schema, 62–5, 96–7; contrast to Marx, 24–5; critique of Standing, 94–5

youth, 10–11, 115, 166, 189, 197

zombie category, 9